The Sacred Overlap is a winsome push beyond the either/or to the both/and, a disturbing nudge that moves us beyond the tribal, an inspiring prod to the way of God at work in the world in Jesus Christ. I hope you'll read this book, written so well by an engaged mind, and let it challenge your imagination to become the kind of Christian our world is so desperate for.

DR. DAVID FITCH, BR Lindner Chair of Evangelical Theology at Northern Seminary and author of *Faithful Presence*

The Sacred Overlap calls us out of a formulaic faith lacking fruit and vibrancy, and calls us to the experience and practice of a faith that is rooted in truth, intriguingly mysterious, authentically joyful, and abundantly practical. J.R.'s words will be humbly inviting and challenging for believer and seeker alike as he reintroduces the person of Jesus and the life of his followers.

THE REV. CANON DR. DAN ALGER, Canon for Church Planting, Anglican Church in North America

How is it possible that a book specifically designed to acknowledge the tension-filled space of our faith could bring such a sense of affirmation and peace to the struggle we live in every day? J.R.'s work here is a true gift to those of us who have been trying to put our finger on exactly what the kingdom is. He gives language to something that is often so hard to define that we shake it off as untrue. He says, "No, look again. That is real."

MARTY SOLOMON, creator of the *BEMA Podcast*

Integration. That one word sums this phenomenal work. J.R. refuses to settle for a narrow spirituality. But don't be fooled—because he doesn't advocate the current cliché, syncretistic, abstract heterodoxy either. Instead, he faithfully expands our pursuit of the kingdom—the both/and reign of God. I highly recommend this creative and historically grounded work.

AJ SHERRILL, lead pastor of Mars Hill Bible Church and author of *The Enneagram for Spiritual Formation*

The reality of God will always be greater than our knowledge of God. The inclusivity of Jesus and the narrowness of Jesus both stretch us. Somewhere at the center of it all, the living truth of God is revealed to us in Jesus. J.R. Briggs is a wise guide for us here, helping us find the gift that the both/and kingdom of God in Christ is to us.

ALAN FADLING, president of Unhurried Living, Inc and author of *An Unhurried Life*

If vibrant, transformative faith is going to thrive in our highly polarized and combative time, it will require robust and nuanced voices. J.R. Briggs is such a voice. His book *The Sacred Overlap* comes just in time to show us a better way. J.R. invites us into a deeper faith that holds tension, looks for the both/and, keeps balance. This book represents significant research and thought and in it. J.R. offers us a way of thinking and a set of practices that keep our faith fresh and nimble."

STEVE CUSS, pastor and author of *Managing Leadership Anxiety*

At the very center of our faith is constellation of unfathomable mysteries: Good pastors don't duck or dumb down the mysteries; they don't reduce Christianity to the merely "practical." No, they embrace gospel mystery, honor it, and serve as tour guides through its limitless terrain. J.R. Briggs is one of those guides, and *The Sacred Overlap* is one of those books—challenging, comforting, and inviting in equal measure. Read it and be changed.

ANDREW ARNDT, pastor of New Life East, Colorado Springs, and author of *All Flame: Entering the Life of the Father, Son, and Holy Spirit*

The world and the church are fragmented by either/or extremes. The best leaders I know are border-stalkers who live on the edges, move in and out, and bring reconciliation across the divides. J.R. Briggs is one of those people, and he has given us a manifesto for those leaders who brave the spaces between what is and what can be.

REV. DR. MICHAEL BECK, author, pastor, and director of re-missioning, Fresh Expressions US

In a day where the world, our culture, and the church are marked by a continual default to division and defensiveness, J.R. Briggs offers us a vision of an interconnected, integrated, and incarnated way of being in the world. In the engaging and entertaining "both/and" character of this book, Briggs helps us to see God and reality in ways that are both deeply inspiring and profoundly uncomfortable, completely biblical and distressingly disruptive, breathtakingly spiritual and shockingly down-to-earth. This book should be read by all those who want to be formed into someone who can personally participate in crossing divides and working for a genuinely restorative common good—and are willing to have their assumptions challenged every step of the way.

TOD BOLSINGER, author of *Canoeing the Mountains* and *Tempered Resilience*

In *The Sacred Overlap*, J.R. explores some of the most complex aspects of discipleship by integrating the idea of paradox at the heart of theological truth, experiencing the world through a both/and frame, seeing the sacred in ordinary things. This is not just well-written book, it is also a very convincing one.

ALAN HIRSCH, award-winning author and founder of Forge Missional Training Network, Movement Leaders Collective, and The 5Q Collective.

If we have any hope of discipling the next generation in the way of Jesus, it's vital we release our fear of mystery and make a home in the sacred overlap. J.R. Briggs writes with thoughtful discernment about how the nuance and complexity of life can find resolution in the peace of Christ, even when we don't have all the answers. I am deeply grateful for this book.

EMILY P. FREEMAN, *Wall Street Journal* bestselling author of *The Next Right Thing*

We live in a chaotic world where life is often messy, if not paradoxical. Such paradoxes saturate the Scriptures. In *The Sacred Overlap*, J.R. Briggs helps us to learn to live and thrive in the tension of the paradoxes of the Christian faith.

WINFIELD BEVINS, director of church planting at Asbury Theological Seminary, author of *Ever Ancient, Ever New*

This is a book I wish I could have written. The invitation to paradoxical mystery in the Christian life is not only something we desperately need to hear about, we couldn't hear it from a better teacher. Briggs has crafted something beautiful here worthy of our attention. Here's to entering the glorious mystery.

DR. A.J. SWOBODA, assistant professor of Bible and theology at Bushnell University and author of *After Doubt*

One of J.R.'s great gifts is his ability to ask unique questions in ways that help us all live more fully into kingdom realities. *The Sacred Overlap* is another such example. In a deeply divided world of either/or thinking, J.R. helps to chart a course that not only embraces the tensions of life but allows us to see that this is actually a better way. There is rich wisdom for those who desire to live the "in between" faithfully.

ADAM L. GUSTINE, Center for Social Concerns at the University of Notre Dame and author of *Becoming a Just Church*

In the early days, it was a core Christian capacity to live in tension—in but not of the world. With agility, J.R. Briggs teaches those first-century Eastern Christian skills to twenty-first-century Western Christians. As we are stretched to hold these seemingly incompatible truths in our small minds and bodies, we, as individuals and a movement, may be transformed!

MANDY SMITH, pastor and author of *The Vulnerable Pastor*

In a time when our world, the culture, and the church are polarized like never before, J.R. helps us to explore "Jesus in the both/and." Not a middle-of-the-road faith that lacks conviction, but a bold, fresh way of seeing the brilliance of Jesus displayed in the tension of the opposites. Steeped in Scripture, classic thinkers, and storyful metaphors, *The Sacred Overlap* is a much-needed perspective and spiritual life reboot.

PAUL BALOCHE, songwriter and pastor, LeadWorship.com

Jesus knew that metaphors, stories, symbols, and even language itself guide and shape how we think and act. Thus, he deployed vivid stories, metaphors, and demanding truths about himself and the world set in fascinating, paradoxical tension. This place of yes-and-no, both/and, and already/not yet is where Spirit-attuned Christians have lived—and at all times have been tempted to escape. In this book, J.R. Briggs returns our focus to that kingdom tension, this sacred overlap, recovering, retracing, and rediscovering anew ancient paths that remain freshly true for us today.

LAURA M. FABRYCKY, author of *Keys to Bonhoeffer's Haus: Exploring the World and Wisdom of Dietrich Bonhoeffer*

J.R. has won back an important piece of ecclesial history for the church. This writing should be a foundational understanding for any leader desiring to be more effective on the frontlines of the gospel.

VERLON FOSNER, pastor, author, and director of Dinner Church Collective

Filled with surprising metaphors, thoughtful synthesis, and compassionate challenges, *The Sacred Overlap* exposes the dead end of either/or mindsets and invites us all to join Jesus in living in the beautiful tension of the both/and. J.R. draws from a deep theological well but writes in language accessible enough for everyone to read. J.R. offers several practices to embody the invitations to live into the overlap. Read this book for yourself and then read it with others who seek to be kingdom people faithfully living Jesus' call to unity in a world filled with divisions.

CYD HOLSCLAW, pastor of discipleship at Vineyard North, coach, spiritual director, and coauthor of *Does God Really Like Me?*

Life is messy, but then, you already know that. Simple black-and-white categories of thought are elusive in the cut and thrust of real life. *The Sacred Overlap* is a timely reminder that even in the gray, there is hope. As St. Augustine might say, take and read.

FRANK A. JAMES III, president of Missio Seminary, Philadelphia

Our world insists we pick sides, but Jesus insists we hold paradoxes and balance tensions. Instead of picking sides, *The Sacred Overlap* invites readers to pick the way of Jesus.

CHRIS HORST, chief advancement officer at HOPE International

We need wise guides to help us discern how best to honor God in our attempt to experience true life. In *The Sacred Overlap*, J.R. Briggs proves he is one of those guides.

REV. JON CAVANAGH, campus pastor, Taylor University

Over the four centuries of the modern age, the fragmentation of either/or thinking has done much violence to humanity, to creation, and to our very souls. J.R. Briggs, in *The Sacred Overlap*, challenges us to stop this violence. Briggs offers a profound vision of healing these deep wounds by recognizing the many ways we exist as both/and creatures, and by inviting us to allow our minds to be transformed.

C. CHRISTOPHER SMITH, founding editor of
The Englewood Review of Books and author of
How the Body of Christ Talks and *Slow Church*

Justice or grace? Belief or practice? Sinners or saints? Our world seeks compartmentalization. J.R. Briggs looks for common spaces in these paradoxes, and in Jesus, who embodies the sacred overlap in his incarnation. Following this example, the place of tension is where peculiar practices can enable authentic faith to thrive.

DR. MICHAEL HAMMOND, provost/EVP, Taylor University

THE
SACRED
OVERLAP

THE SACRED OVERLAP

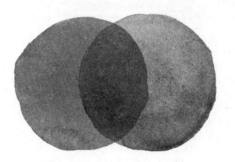
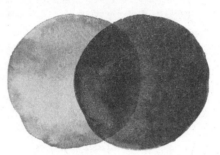

LEARNING to LIVE FAITHFULLY
in the SPACE BETWEEN

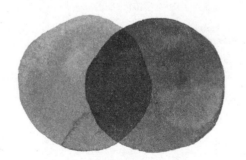

J. R. BRIGGS

To Carter and Bennett.
May you grow to live in the Sacred Overlap.

CONTENTS

Foreword by Skye Jethani..............................xv

Introduction: A Simple Shape, an Italian Word, a Way of Life xix

PART 1: JESUS IN THE BOTH/AND

1. Overlapping Worlds: When God Moved into the Neighborhood 1
2. Scandalous Misfit: Hanging with Saints and Sinners 20
3. Double-Major Jesus: Embracing Justice and Embracing Grace 32

PART 2: WHEN JESUS BLOWS UP YOUR EITHER/OR LIFE

4. Orthoparadoxy: Right Believing and Right Living ...53
5. Resident Aliens: Too Christian, Too Pagan 60
6. Being Peculiar: Inhabiting the Space between Normal and Weird.....................74
7. Faithful Witness: Living the Right Preposition 86
8. The Prayer of Sacred Overlap: How Jesus Teaches Us to Pray...................107

PART 3: JOINING GOD IN THE SACRED OVERLAP

9. Dual Engagement: Evangelism and
   Discipleship at the Same Time...................129
10. Practicing Resurrection Together:
    Peculiar Practices of the Overlapped Life.........150
11. Sacred Celebration: Embracing Joy
    amidst a World Riddled with Pain................177
12. Mandorla Mission: Living Out Fresh
    Expressions of Church.........................188
13. Faithful Posture: Convicted Civility..............217

A Final Word: The Ampersand God......................231
A Note from the Author..............................233
Acknowledgments 234
Notes 236

FOREWORD

I remember when ordering coffee was easy. There were really only two decisions—regular or decaf, and black or cream and sugar. Today, ordering coffee feels like applying for a bank loan. There are literally thousands of options available. Some celebrate this as progress—the market providing more choices to fit each consumer's taste. Others lament it for contributing to the tyranny of choice which complicates modern life.

However one sees coffee today, the shift from simplicity to complexity represents larger social trends. By any measure, today's world is far more complicated than the one we were born into. Consumer capitalism, digital technology, social media, ethnic diversity, and religious pluralism have made virtually every aspect of modern life less intuitive. For example, when I was a high school student in the early 1990s, the question, "What is marriage?" never entered my mind. Today, my three teenage children—along with everyone else—must wrestle with and answer that question for themselves. A single definition of marriage is no longer assumed or shared by the culture.

Whether the issue is coffee or matrimony, ever-increasing complexity is the nature of all modern consumer societies. This also helps explain, at least in part, the rise of anxiety disorders among modern people. With the need to make more choices, about more things, more of the time, and with fewer shared assumptions, among fewer people, in fewer communities, the individual can soon feel overwhelmed. This is when, according to sociologists, authoritarian leaders and fundamentalist belief systems become appealing, and right now we're witnessing the rise of both across the globe.

Fundamentalism promises to bring back simplicity by offering an absolute answer to every possible question. It offers us the blessing of not thinking, of not worrying, of not making so many decisions about everything. Imagine being paralyzed by 30,000 possible coffee choices. Fundamentalism provides an escape by saying, "True coffee is only regular and black. All others are fake, and those who drink them are an abomination." In this way, fundamentalism provides freedom from anxiety by taking away our freedom of choice. As the world becomes more complicated and life becomes more stressful, that's a trade more people appear willing to make.

Unfortunately, the byproduct of this return to simplicity is conflict. Competing fundamentalisms arise on both the Left and Right with absolutist visions of how the world ought to operate, who is legitimate, what words are allowed, and who must be "cancelled." People are assigned a single, immutable identity as one of "us" or "them" rather than seen as complex persons with many layers of identity and belonging. And every election, cultural issue, or church policy becomes an "either/or" apocalyptic battle for the fate of the world. In the end, no diverse community can survive, let alone thrive, where members are viewed primarily as enemies rather than as neighbors. Simplicity comes with a heavy price.

This is why J.R. Briggs' book is so critical for those of us seeking to follow Jesus today. While sympathetic to the stresses and anxieties of modern life, he exposes the false comfort of every kind of fundamentalism. Instead, he invites us to find rest and direction through the enduring wisdom of Jesus and his kingdom which is not of this world.

Unlike the absolutist, either/or clarity offered by competing fundamentalisms, Jesus' kingdom welcomes us with a both/and vision of life and faith. As Briggs draws from history and theology, he reminds us that mystery and paradox are not Christian aberrations but are central to our most essential and cherished doctrines. Jesus is both fully human and fully divine. God is one and exists eternally as three persons. Likewise, we can follow Jesus Christ and bless our neighbors who do not. We can affirm the importance of personal salvation and the call for social transformation. We can recognize the pervasiveness of evil and the reality of God's image in every person.

Sadly, our culture is being torn apart by leaders—both political and pastoral—who seize upon our anxiety and exploit the conflicts that result from simplistic, either/or declarations. This has only been exasperated by social media, which rewards ham-handed hashtags rather than nuanced thinking. Moving beyond this destructive conflict will only be possible when more Christians stop listening to these divisive voices and choose a different path—the one revealed in this book.

Thankfully, we are not without hope. J.R. Briggs represents the faithful leadership and vision the church requires right now. Briggs, and those like him, are showing us that Christian faith can thrive in a complicated, pluralistic society if we release our need for control and its false comforts to rediscover the ancient vision of God's kingdom. In order for the way of Jesus to shine once again, we do not need fearful voices calling us back to the simple past. Instead, we need faithful voices applying the wisdom of Jesus today. That is exactly what you will discover as you read the pages that follow. So engage them carefully, reflect deeply, and process them in conversation with your friends over whatever kind of coffee you prefer.

Skye Jethani
June 2020

INTRODUCTION

A Simple Shape, an Italian Word, a Way of Life

My father and I ate lunch in Europe, enjoyed dinner in Asia, and then returned to our hotel in Europe later that evening—and we never left the city.

We had embarked on a two-week study trip to Turkey and Greece, which began with three days in Istanbul, a city full of rich history, beautiful architecture, delicious food, hospitable people and breathtaking views. Istanbul is the linchpin which holds Europe and Asia together, a city split by the waters of the Bosporus Strait, which connects the Black Sea with the Sea of Marmara. That afternoon, we left our tour group, grabbed a taxi, and caught a twenty-minute ferry ride to the eastern side of the city. We left Europe and entered Asia. There was no need to clear customs, show identification, or pass through extensive security on our transcontinental adventure. We didn't need our passports. Nobody asked us our names. We were within the city limits the entire time.

As we sat on the top deck of the ferry and watched the sun slip over one of the city's seven hills, creating a silhouetted postcard view of the spires of the Blue Mosque on one side and Hagia Sophia on the other, I marveled at how a transcontinental adventure could seem so relatively routine. For many people, this is their daily commute to and from work. At about the halfway point between the two ports,

I swiveled my head back and forth—glancing at Asia, then Europe, and then back again at Asia—trying to comprehend my reality. At that moment, we were, in a sense, on *both* continents. I imagined what it must be like for our ferry captain to travel back and forth between continents about a dozen times *every single day*.

I'm realizing that the life Jesus led was like our experience in Istanbul. He straddled different continents—not lands mapped out by geopolitical demarcations, but different spiritual realities. And in that straddling and overlapping, he invites us into both the spiritual and the physical worlds. This invitation is both fascinating and scary. I am beginning to see with unsettling clarity how frequently Jesus held two seemingly opposing ideas at the same time.

Jesus was committed to crossing cultural, social, political, and religious *either/or* waters, engaging in many *and also* activities. He said his mission was for the Jews *and also* honored the faith he saw in a Roman centurion (Luke 7:1–10) and a woman from Syro-Phoenicia (Mark 7:24–30). He spent time in Israel *and also* in the hostile territory of Samaria. He comforted the disturbed *and also* disturbed the comfortable. He was too religious for the pagans *and also* too pagan for the religious elites. He was invited to eat at the home of a Pharisee (Luke 7:36–50) *and also* invited himself to eat at the home of a tax collector (Luke 19:1–9). He hung out with filthy lepers *and also* dined with the filthy rich. He encouraged common sense, like loving your friends, *and also* confusing stuff, like loving your enemies. He encouraged rejoicing in times of celebration *and also* rejoicing in the midst of persecution. He followed the Jewish Law *and also* knowingly broke many of the religious rules and customs of the day. He rebuked people *and also* rebuked people for rebuking people. He was alarming *and also* disarming at the same time. He was constantly traversing continents by submerging himself in the river—and he invites us to join him.

In my younger years, in a tiny Southern Baptist church, I was taught to think that as a Christian I could not, or even should not, swim in the swirling waters that straddle and overlap continents. Navigating the Bosporus was clearly off limits; you picked one continent or the other. Between sword drills and AWANA, I was taught to be sold out for Christ with no compromise: Jesus is the way, the truth, and the life. My church emphasized that we should retreat from the sinful ways of the world and remain holy. And while that was not wrong, it communicated only part of the kingdom life, thus creating a religious *us/them* dynamic in my thinking, a skewed and domesticated version of the good news.

We've all heard about the need to be lifelong learners, but I've had to participate in some massive unlearning, some significant reworking of my mental circuit board. In my younger years, this would have sounded dangerous to me. In my growing up years, those in my relational circles might have labeled me as strange, cowardly, or something worse: liberal. Yet now, I'm learning that if I want to live like Jesus, I'm going to have to learn to navigate the middle.

I still believe Jesus is who he said he is—more so than ever. In fact, all throughout the Bible, we see clear elements of delineation and separateness. The whole idea of holiness is about being separate. The essence of day two of creation is about separation (Gen. 1:6–8). God divided the clean from the unclean, the earthly from the heavenly, the carnal from the spiritual (Luke 12:51; John 7:43). Jesus clearly calls people to either choose him or reject him. As author Leonard Sweet wrote, the invitation of Jesus is one big *either/or.*[1]

In the Old and New Testaments, we read about clear choices presented to God's people. Moses challenged the Israelites to choose life or choose death (Deut. 30:19). The Lord commanded the people of Israel to stand on two mountains, Ebal and Gerizim, and shout blessings on one and curses on the other (Deut. 11, 27; Josh. 8; Judg. 9). Joshua told the nation of Israel to choose this day whom they will serve (Josh. 24:15). Elijah, in his dramatic act atop

Mount Carmel, asked how long the people would waver between two opinions: "If the Lord is God," he challenged them, "follow him; but if Baal is God, follow him" (1 Kings 18:21).

In the New Testament, Jesus claims he is the only path to God (John 14:6). Paul writes to the church in Corinth that Christians should not be unequally yoked (2 Cor. 6:14). First John deals with the separation between light and darkness. Paul wrote about the war being waged between the desires of the flesh and the desires of the Spirit (Gal. 5:16–17). Jesus said, "No one can serve two masters" (Matt. 6:24). The cross was God's way of announcing separation. In essence, separation from the world is what it means to be a Christian.[2] In Revelation, Jesus spoke directly to the Laodiceans about this very thing: "I know your deeds, that you are neither cold nor hot. I wish you were either one or the other! So, because you are lukewarm—neither hot nor cold—I am about to spit you out of my mouth" (Rev. 3:15–16). Coffee, hot or iced, is fine, but God forbid, not room temperature.

And yet, while there are *either/or* scenarios throughout Scripture, the Christian life is also an invitation to a *both/and* existence. Think of the statements Jesus made in the Gospels (emphases mine):

My yoke is easy *and* my burden is light. (Matt. 11:30)

Be as innocent as doves *and* wise as serpents. (Matthew 10:16)

Love your neighbor *as you love yourself.* (Mark 12:31)

The kingdom of God is near *and also* here. (Mark 1:15)

Exalt yourself *and* you'll be humbled, humble yourself *and* you will be exalted. (Matt. 23:12)

It was the philosopher Hegel who said that truth is found neither in the thesis nor the antithesis, but in the synthesis. Life isn't always separated into tidy boxes of black and white; neither is faith.

There are binary themes in Scripture such as light and darkness (1 John), wisdom and foolishness (Prov. 9; Ps. 1; Deut. 30:15). But in the arc of Scripture, once we've committed to follow the great *either/or*, we are called into faith-filled *both/and* living with startling regularity. This synthesis is not dissonance but harmony. I came to this conclusion not by looking to the trends of current culture or the opinion of friends or from a trendy book I pulled off the shelf while perusing the aisles of the spirituality section of a bookstore. I arrived at it by studying the life of Jesus in the Scriptures. In doing so, I've learned that *either/or* faith can be two-dimensional, but *both/and* trust offers a three-dimensional faith in Christ. This, I found, was really good news.

Long ago, I devoted my life to exploring and discovering the things that matter most—and Jesus is that thing. The more I study Jesus, the more I realize he is inviting us to life off the paved road of tamed religiosity and into something greater, more adventurous, and more uncertain than I had previously imagined. Jesus lived outside of—and apart from— the nice, snug, and clear-cut categories in which I so desperately wanted him to remain. He is "the man who fits no formula," as Eduard Schweizer so aptly described him.[3] I needed to train my mind—my whole life, really—to not grow anxious or afraid when Jesus doesn't fit perfectly into the neatly organized *either/or* categories I, or others, have devised. I didn't need to invite Jesus into my heart; I needed to invite him into every area of my life. I needed him to be front and center—not just on Sunday, but Monday through Saturday as well.

For the sake of clarity, because it is so crucial to the scope of this book, I need to press the pause button for a moment: I am not proposing a mindless, spineless embrace of moral gray areas or a popular religious syncretism that combines bits of truth, wisdom, and perspective from various world religions, personal preferences, and ideologies and throws them into a giant cosmic blender to concoct a tasty theological smoothie. There certainly are significant issues that place us on one side of the spiritual fence or the other. But it continues to jar me how often Jesus spoke of and lived his life in a protruding manner, free from tidy, dichotomized categories. In fact, it was one of the primary reasons the religious leaders of the day were so angry with him: he didn't fit into their prescribed, tidy theological bento box. To paraphrase St. John Chrysostom, a comprehended God is no God at all.

This topic is not just important to me personally. It's essential for the church in North America, especially in our current moment in history. Why? Because we are living in a world that is increasingly global *and also* tribal. Around the world, the rich are getting richer, and the poor are getting poorer. In North America, we see the reality of a shrinking middle class. The cultural, religious, political, relational, and familial divides are growing stronger; the arguments are becoming more explosive; and the defending of our opinions is growing more and more intense. Even a global pandemic, which had the potential to unite us and draw us together, has driven us further apart. If there is ever a time for the church to see a crucial opportunity to bring hope to our current context, this is it. The widening of extremes provides the church a fertile opportunity to live in the midst of the tension, to live in radical love and faithfulness between the extremes.

Yet sadly, over the past few decades, the church has largely (though certainly not entirely) joined in on the entrenchment mentality, with a clipboard and moral checklist in one hand and a megaphone in the other. Theologian David Fitch, in his aptly titled book *The Church of Us vs. Them,* offered that such a divisive posture in the church has been "disastrous for our witness to Christ and his lordship and salvation in North America."[4] Later he stated that we live in a world where "others" are the people we disagree with. The world, Fitch writes, runs on antagonisms, what he calls an "enemy-making machine—a social dynamic in which we are always forced to take sides."[5]

Without attempting to overstate the matter, the sacred overlap—lived out faithfully, both personally *and also* communally—is the way forward. It is one of the greatest opportunities for the church today for faithful witness and engagement in God's mission in the world. It most certainly won't be easy, but it does offer us real, tangible hope for the future. It is becoming more and more evident: the divisions between us are growing wider and more intense. As my friend Rich Villodas, a pastor in New York City, said, "The Church is not to be found at the 'center' of a left/right political world. The Church is to be a species of its own kind, confounding both left and right, and finding its identity from the center of God's life."[6] If we can grow to see Christ, who is present and active in that messy middle, if we can notice the one who is inviting us to join him in that hope-filled mess, then the church can actually become the kind of church Jesus intended it to be.

The native language of Christianity is *and also*. God is one *and also* God is three. If we were to overemphasize one or the other, it becomes heresy. Modalism is an unorthodox belief that overemphasizes God's oneness by stating that God is one but shows up in three different modes. Subordinationism is an unorthodox belief that swings the pendulum too far in the other direction, overemphasizing God's three-ness and diluting his oneness. To see Jesus accurately is to grasp that he is both holy divine *and also* wholly human at the same time.[7]

This *and also* way of thinking makes it possible to talk about the sweet spot of Christianity. It brings mystery back into the equation, something the church lost through Enlightenment thinking. Seeing life as overlapping, rather than in separate categories, is much more of an Eastern way of thinking, a mindset which shaped Jesus' thought and imagination.[8] This way of thinking can make you nervous at times, but that shouldn't be surprising. The late pastor and author A.W. Tozer wrote that our real idea of God lies buried under a pile of religious notions, and only after times of painful self-probing do we really discover what we *actually* believe about God.[9] Jesus' invitation to this way of life is found most often in the *both/and* rather than the *either/or*. It's uncomfortable, *and also* true.

American writer F. Scott Fitzgerald wrote that, "the test of a first-rate intelligence is the ability to hold two opposing ideas in the mind at the same time, and still retain the ability to function."[10] Similarly, another American author, Jim Collins, wrote in his popular business book, *Built to Last*, that great leaders reject the tyranny of the "Or" and embrace what he called the "genius of the And."[11] Instead of choosing A *or* B, they figure out a way to have both A *and* B. In the fourth century BC, Aristotle wrote that the way to a virtuous life was to find "the golden mean" between two extremes.[12] We feel these extremes in relationships: autonomy and connection; being open and being closed; novelty and predictability; equality and inequality. All of us attempt to mitigate these tensions in our relationships.

The more I studied Jesus, the more he broke my mold. Jesus was—and still is—fascinating and also attractive and also irresistible. I love him, and I'm loved by him, even if he still frightens me. He wrecks my tight and carefully constructed box. I've slapped packaging tape across the top and scribbled "the Divine" on the lid with a Sharpie. And yet somehow, in my attempt to box him up, I'd forgotten that this same Jesus can walk through walls.

When we live like this, it puts us in the middle of weighty, important, and complex issues, Gordian knots of life and faith. These spaces are messy and sacred—sometimes like a delivery room and at other times like a surgery tent in a Civil War film. These messy yet sacred issues include poverty, politics, sexuality, war, race, justice, gun control, gender, immigration, and how to honor and dignify each and every human being from conception until death. I'm not saying there aren't stances to take on the side of truth. There are, most certainly. What I am saying is that it's complex—and when sides are chosen and lines are drawn, one of the most courageous things we can do is straddle *both* worlds rather than retreat to our bunkers.

Even my struggle with sin is *and also*. During high school I memorized Paul's hope-filled words: "Therefore, if anyone is in Christ, the new creation has come: the old has gone, the new is here!" (2 Cor. 5:17). I love this promise—I'm a new person in Christ. And yet I can still get all wrapped around the axle on this, my doubts swirling in my head and heart: *Why then do I still struggle with impatience and anxiety and bouts of lust year after year? Am I doing this Christian thing wrong? Which is it: am I a new creation or am I still my old self?* Maybe it's both. Maybe this is the same struggle Paul felt in his spirit in Romans 7:15–23, where he wrote,

> I do not understand what I do. For what I want to do I do not do, but what I hate I do. And if I do what I do not want to do, I agree that the law is good. As it is, it is no longer I myself who do it, but it is sin living in me. For I know that good itself does not dwell in me, that is, in my sinful nature. For I have the desire to do what is good, but I cannot carry it out. For I do not do the good I want to do, but the evil I do not want to do—this I keep on doing. Now if I do what I do not want to do, it is no longer I who do it, but it is sin living in me that does it.
>
> So I find this law at work: Although I want to do good, evil is right there with me. For in my inner being I delight in God's law; but I see another law at work in me, waging war against the law of my mind and making me a prisoner of the law of sin at work within me.

Like Paul, I'm led to believe that tripping over the threshold of the kingdom of God and into God's big family is both an event *and* a process. Justification *and* sanctification. To bring the cookies down to a lower shelf, I was saved, but I am also still in the process of being saved.

Writing this book has me a bit on edge because I anticipate some people will read this, misunderstand its theme, and misconstrue my words. If you truly understand the essence of the book, I assure you: the lights won't start blinking on your heresy dashboard. But it will burst some wineskins and cause a mess on the floor, which somebody's gotta clean up. It has burst a few of my own wineskins in the process. But writing this book also invigorated me, because readers like you will catch the vision and find it a worthy way of thinking and, most importantly, living.

As I mentioned, this mindset is somewhat difficult for those of us who live in the West. Jesus was born, grew up, and lived in an Eastern context, where life was seen as interconnected, the pieces not merely touching but overlapping. Angel hair pasta, not waffles. To grasp the sacred overlap, we must think with a mindset similar to that of Jesus in his first-century Jewish world. Living the life of overlap is not a new philosophy, trendy theology, or modern ideology; it is a way of life—the Jesus life which comes to us in surround sound. Living out this approach is learning to sing your life in harmony.[13]

The vision of this book is not rooted in fearful reaction of our culture becoming more pagan, nor is it a call to return to the schmaltzy sentimentality of the Christian good ole days. I want to blow the foam off of stale Christianity in order to challenge individuals and entire communities of faith to live as Jesus did, in both worlds—*not out of compromise, but out of love.*

My hope with this book is that the words that follow make you think, make you wonder, and may even do some good. Let me pull over on the side of the road here and turn on my flashers so we can get the lay of the land and let you see where we're heading.

The book has been shaped into three parts.

In part 1 we'll explore Jesus' life and how he lived, loved, and led in the sacred overlap. We'll address the overlap of the incarnation, how the God of the universe became flesh and blood and moved into the neighborhood in order to fully express his love (chapter 1). We'll look at the misfit Jesus who hung out with saints and sinners rather than shielding himself from others (chapter 2). We'll unpack Jesus' dual yet equal emphasis on justice and grace and the damaging effects of prioritizing one over the other (chapter 3).

In part 2 we will delve deeply into the kind of life Jesus calls us into, the Jesus way, which necessitates leaving behind the paved roads of *either/or* predictability and participate in off-roading *both/and* adventures. We'll dive into the essential posture of double-majoring in right believing *and also* right living (chapter 4). And we'll find that when we faithfully follow Jesus, we are too Christian and too pagan at the same time (chapter 5). We'll then look at how we join God in his overlapping world, embracing our calling to be peculiar people, and see how it's quite different from being weird and also quite different from being normal (chapter 6). We'll uncover how one little preposition can have an enormous impact on how we live (chapter 7). We'll look at the Lord's Prayer and how this serves as a guide, not only for praying, but also for living this sacred overlap (chapter 8).

Finally, in part 3 we'll look at how we join God in the overlapped life by providing ridiculously practical ways forward. We'll deconstruct—and then reconstruct—our understanding of evangelism and discipleship, learning how we need to be engaged in both of these at the same time (chapter 9). We'll see what it means to practice resurrection together as we live for eternity, even in the mundane and ordinary peculiar tasks of our days (chapter 10). We will also explore what it means to be joyful in the midst of heart-wrenching pain and suffering in the world (chapter 11). We'll look at ways to engage with God's mission together with those who are intrigued about Jesus but turned off by church (chapter 12). And we'll look at what it means to maintain a posture of convicted civility which emphasizes both grace and also truth (chapter 13).

God has extended an invitation to us: to join him in the *both/ and* life.

PART 1

JESUS IN THE BOTH/AND

We must abandon the polarities of *either* and *or* and embrace instead the dissonance of *and*. They lend themselves to certainty—and also to curiosity. They are foundational to our creeds—and yet fundamental mysteries.

—JEN POLLOCK MICHEL

God became man so that man might become God.

—ST. IRENAEUS OF LYON

CHAPTER 1

OVERLAPPING WORLDS

WHEN GOD MOVED INTO
THE NEIGHBORHOOD

The last thing any of us needs is more information about God. We need the practice of incarnation, by which God saves the lives of those whose intellectual assent has turned them dry as dust, who have run frighteningly low on the bread of life, who are dying to know more God in their bodies. Not more about God. More God.

—BARBARA BROWN TAYLOR

If I am asked, "Do you believe in the divinity of Christ?" I answer, "Yes, otherwise how could he have been so wonderfully human?" And if I am asked, "Do you believe in the humanity of Christ?" I answer, "Yes, otherwise how could he have been so profoundly oriented toward God?"

—DOUGLAS JOHN HALL

I never thought a simple geometrical shape could dramatically change the way I live. Until a few years ago, I wasn't aware it had a name.

In 1880 an English mathematician, logician, philosopher, and lecturer named John Venn wrote a paper for the *Philosophical Magazine and Journal of Science* titled "On the Diagrammatic and Mechanical Representation of Propositions and Reasonings." The paper is about as exciting as it sounds (I know: I read it), but Venn offered a clear way to communicate similarities and differences through simple overlaps and intersections of ideas. He wrote:

> I now first hit upon the diagrammatical device of representing propositions by inclusive and exclusive circles. Of course the device was not new then, but it was so obviously representative of the way in which anyone, who approached the subject from the mathematical side, would attempt to visualize propositions, that it was forced upon me almost at once.[1]

Venn called these overlapping symbols Eulerian circles; but today we know them as Venn diagrams. In the fifteenth century, these corresponding circles were known as Borromean rings, as the Borromeo family from northern Italy incorporated the rings into its family crest. John Venn did not invent the shape, but he was the first to utilize it in a way the general public found useful.[2]

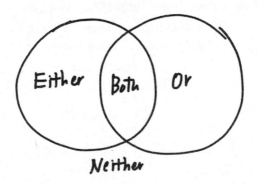

Venn diagrams may look simple but they can be rather complex, especially when brilliant mathematicians get involved. They can include three, four, five, or even more overlapping shapes at once, which look a lot like the Spirograph designs I created as a kid.[3] In June 1948, Winston Churchill famously drew a three-class Venn diagram to explain the mutual relationship between the British Empire, Europe, and the English-speaking world. Venn diagrams aren't always comprised of circles; they can include other shapes such as ellipses and triangles. In addition to giving the world *Alice's Adventures in Wonderland* and *Through the Looking Glass*, Lewis Carroll was also a mathematician who built on Venn's circular diagrams, developing square and rectangular Venn diagrams as well.

Venn diagrams have been used in various fields such as math, logic, philosophy, geometry, computer science, art, design, education, and even reading comprehension and literacy. I'd like to add one more to that list: the Christian life. Interestingly, Venn's father was a minister who played a significant role in the evangelical movement in England through his involvement in international missions. Venn's grandfather helped start the Clapham Sect, an influential group of Christian friends and reformers whose members included Hannah More, John Newton (who wrote the hymn "Amazing Grace"), and William Wilberforce, the influential member of Parliament who was the primary force and leading voice behind the abolition of the slave trade in Great Britain.[4] Though he never wrote about it explicitly, I wonder if John Venn had the Christian life in mind when he developed his diagrams. In addition to being elected as a fellow of the prestigious Royal Society, he was also an ordained priest. John Venn lived his own diagram.

I've always been enamored with Venn diagrams. But whenever I would draw one on a restaurant napkin to explain a point to a friend or on a whiteboard during a training seminar, I'd be at a loss for words when trying to explain that little space in the middle where the circles overlap. I'd simply describe it as the football shape. But a few years ago, the curtains were thrown open, flooding my mind with light, when I learned that the little overlapping space in a Venn diagram actually has a name: *mandorla*, the Italian word for almond, which its shape resembles.

The almond has long been considered a sacred nut. Ancient Greek myths linked almonds and their shape with new life and fertility. In the biblical tradition, God issued specific instructions to the nation of

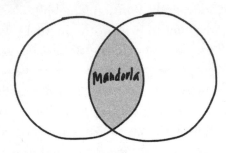

Israel for making sacred objects for the tabernacle, including the branches of the menorah, to resemble almonds (see Ex. 25, 37). Additionally, the Book of Numbers records that when Aaron's rod was placed in the Tent of Meeting before the Ark of the Covenant, its buds produced almonds (Num. 17:1–8). The next time you pop a few in your mouth, remind yourself that you're eating something healthy, tasty, and sacred.

This peculiar-looking football shape has another name: *vesica piscis*, a mathematical term for the shape formed by the intersection of two circles with the same radius. At its point of intersection, the center of each circle touches the perimeter of the other. Even more interestingly, *vesica piscis* means, quite literally, "the bladder of a fish," because it resembles the shape of the dual air bladders found in our aquatic friends. Sacred nuts and fish bladders. (Bet you've never read those two phrases in the same paragraph before.)

Mandorlas appear on street corners, corporate slide presentations and commercials, and in widely recognized brands such as Audi, Mastercard, and the Olympics—even the biohazard symbol has them. So does the flag of Greenland. Our eyes resemble the shape. So do our lips. You might find them in the wallpaper pattern in your hotel lobby, the shape of a light fixture in your home, or in the carpet pattern at your office. Like the arrow in the FedEx logo, once you see them, you won't be able to un-see them. Mandorlas are everywhere.

Throughout the centuries, artists have sought to express the stories of God through vivid pictures and rich symbolism. Christian art has been displayed in cathedrals, chapels, and churches around the world. Through the centuries, stained glass windows have been called the poor man's Bible, as these colorful panes told the stories of Scripture visually for a population which was largely illiterate. Stained glass artists often placed Jesus inside a mandorla, believing it was the clearest way to express accurate theology in an aesthetically pleasing manner. Jesus, the perfect embodiment of the overlap of heaven and earth, squeezed into human form. The Divine became human, the Alpha and Omega, the beginning and the end, God and man, full of grace and truth.

Illumination of Christ in Majesty from Codex Bruchsal 1, BL. 1v, dated 1220

Christ in Majesty from Chelmsford Cathedral in the UK

Mandorla held by two angels, Cathedral of St. Martin, Lucca, Italy

Christ in Majesty surrounded by the symbols of the Evangelists from the Westminster Psalter, 13th century

You'll observe Jesus smack-dab in the middle of that sacred nut shape on the large 11th-century Byzantine mosaic on the façade of the basilica of San Frediano in Lucca, Italy. A Roman-style fresco in Catalonia created in 1123 placed Jesus in the mandorla in the apse of Sant Climent de Taull, as does the stone frieze above the entryway into Chartres Cathedral. A 900-year-old illustrated Gospel book has Jesus etched in the mandorla with four small circles in each corner, each containing an image of one of the Gospel writers.

The Eastern Orthodox tradition is rooted in deep wonder at the mystery and ambiguity of God. Eastern Orthodox Christians are not turned off or scared away by the mystery of faith; it's this mystery that draws them further *into* faith. They see overlaps in every area of life. St. Gregory the Theologian wrote that faith is found in this "productive tension that is paradoxical, preserving the mystery without resolving it."[5]

For several centuries, Eastern Orthodox artists have depicted this *both/and* reality through beautiful icons which reflect the depth, complexity, and overlapping identity of Jesus. It was an attempt to visualize (often inside a mandorla) the mysterious holding together of two elements of Christ that seemed to be opposed to one another, a way to express the image of the invisible God (Col. 1:15). God creates not as a scientist but as an artist, which opens up a wide variety of visual expressions of God's mystery, bridging the chasm of many of the paradoxes of God and his existence.[6]

When they paint Jesus, Eastern Orthodox artists utilize an artistic technique called Christ Pantokrator, where Jesus is painted while seated on a throne, holding up his right hand in a blessing and holding a book or scroll in his left hand. My guess is that you've seen a few of these images before. In Istanbul, I stood, awestruck, in the famous Hagia Sophia church, looking up at a large, old, surprisingly well-preserved icon. As I looked closely, I noticed that the facial features of Jesus were asymmetrical. The eyes differed in shape, size, and color. The lips and mouth seemed slightly off. Much to my surprise, I learned that the asymmetry is intentional. If you were to look at a Christ Pantokrator icon, taking each half of the face of Jesus individually, you would see two entirely different depictions of

Mosaic from Hagia Sophia, Instanbul, Turkey

Jesus. In fact, the contrast between the two halves could hardly be more pronounced.[7] As I stood there looking at the image above in the Hagia Sofia, I thought, *What a beautiful way to express the overlapped Jesus on a canvas: fully God, fully man, yet one Jesus.* Paradox, mystery, juxtaposition, divine polarity. All of this does not imply division; the Orthodox community is completely comfortable with the ambiguity in God's nature, and art can bring together two seemingly opposite qualities or concepts into one unified reality.[8] Our Eastern Orthodox friends have much to offer to us.

But the trajectory of this book reaches far beyond mathematical diagrams, footballs, nuts, fish bladders or lessons on Christian art, interesting as those may seem. All of this points us toward Jesus, who embraced and embodied life in the overlap.

When I think of Jesus, I think of my ninth grade Spanish class. During the food unit, we learned about *hamburguesas, fresas, queso,* and *papas fritas.* I vividly remember learning the phrase *chile con carne*—chili with meat. Christian scholars have used the term *incarnation* to describe God's presence manifested on earth when he wrapped himself in a fragile blanket of skin, entered human history, and was given the name Jesus. Heaven and earth overlapped, embraced, and kissed; it was the presence of God among his people in the form of a human being. *The Message* translates Paul's famous words in Colossians this way: "We look at this Son and see the God who cannot be seen. We look at the Son and see God's original purpose in everything created" (Col. 1:15–16). *Dios con carne.*

From what we can tell, there wasn't anything particularly inspiring about Jesus' upbringing. I've often wondered why the Gospel writers were silent about Jesus' life during his teens and twenties. Maybe it's because his growing up years were similar to yours and mine: ordinary. No miracles. No powerful teachings. No large crowds gathering around him. No Olympic records. He grew up in the ordinary town of Nazareth, which most likely had a population of less than 400 and was never featured on the front of a tourist brochure. The Gospel writers record that the residents of Nazareth were surprised by the way Jesus taught—so much so that they rejected him and even tried to kill him. Maybe it's because they understood the ordinariness of his upbringing better than anyone else.[9]

The four Gospel writers don't mention a single detail about Jesus' physical features, either. Jesus' growing-up years and his appearance were probably normal, just like yours and mine. And the Gospels record that Jesus acted as human as you and me.

He was tired.

He became angry.

He wept.

He sang.

He asked questions.

He laughed.

He was quiet.

He became frustrated.

He dozed off to sleep.

He told jokes.

One of my favorite details in the Gospels is that Jesus *sighed deeply* (see Mark 8:12). What human doesn't sigh from time to time, either out of exhaustion or frustration? When Jesus was growing up, he probably tripped and fell while playing with his friends. He probably had bed head, body odor, and bad breath. If these thoughts are jolting, maybe it's time we take a closer look at how we see Jesus. Yes, he was fully God, but he was fully human, too. The Messiah in jeans and a flannel.

Jesus was the Great Mandorla—the Son of God *and also* the Son of Man, the Lion *and also* the Lamb, the Alpha *and also* the Omega.[10] He was both tender *and* firm, both full of grace *and also* truth, the Prince of Peace who also said that he did not come to bring peace on earth, but instead to bring division (Luke 12:51). He was committed to justice *and also* grace. Being in very nature God, he took on the nature of a servant made in human likeness (Phil. 2:6–7). He taught people to give to Caesar what is Caesar's *and also* to God what belongs to God. He suffered *and also* it is his wounds which ultimately heal us. When creating 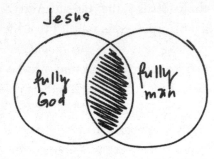 his band of disciples, he invited a card-carrying member of a Jewish terrorist organization (Simon the Zealot) *and also* extended an invite to a corrupt official who worked for the Roman government and was seen as a scandalous traitor (Matthew the tax collector). Jesus showed up at dinner parties attended by seedy prostitutes *and also* esteemed seminary professors. He entered Jericho and loved the oppressed (blind Bartimaeus) *and also* the oppressor (traitorous Zacchaeus) all in the same visit (Luke 18–19). Jesus lived a healthy tension-filled life.

He valued, honored, and invested in men *and also* women. He showed compassion for the Jews, God's chosen people, *and also* loved the Samaritans, whom the Jews despised and regarded as half-breeds. He called people to live lives of holiness *and also* he was accused of being a glutton and a drunk. He was revered as the Messiah *and also* called a friend of sinners. Let that sink in: *a friend of sinners*. The kinds of people many believers work hard to avoid, Jesus welcomed. He lived in the overlap in order to build bridges to bring them—all of them—together.

When we are afraid to live in the middle of all the tension, conflict and mess, we must remember Jesus still lives in the morass, and he's unafraid. Jesus never seemed to be uncomfortable living in this tension, nor did he try to tidy up the mess of these uncomfortable contradictions. In fact, he used each one as if it were a rung on a ladder, enabling him to climb even higher in piquing people's interest and revealing his authority.[11] As Jen Pollock Michel wrote, Jesus is the "Great I And."[12]

My friend Michael is a Methodist pastor in Florida and is quite a character. He always preaches barefoot, has tattoos on just about every square inch of his body, and has enough kids to legally create a small nation state. He loves Jesus deeply. While Michael and I were in Indianapolis one beautiful October Saturday, training a roomful of pastors, he introduced me to a curious little phrase: *conjunctive theology*. The overlapped understanding of Jesus is found in this little conjunction—*and*—which can hold seemingly differing thoughts together as one thought.[13] Saint Ignatius of Antioch wrote about the conjunctive nature of the incarnation: "fleshly and spiritual, begotten and unbegotten, God in man, true life in death, both of Mary and of God."[14] The theology of John Wesley, the founder of the Methodist movement, was described as possessing a *both/and* theology.[15] While many have claimed Christianity is built on the foundation of *either/or*, there is a surprising amount of *both/and* to be found.

During Advent, we light candles on a wreath and read passages from the First and Second Testaments in order to reflect on Jesus as *Emmanuel*—God with us. As Teri Hyrkas said, it seems *with* is Emmanuel's middle name.[16] *With* is one of the most powerful metaphors in all of Scripture. It is not us with God, but *God with us*. No social distancing required.

This is what we read about in the first chapter of the Gospel of John: The Word became flesh and dwelt among us. Jesus chose to come down in human form as the catalyst for human redemption. As translated in *The Message*, "And the Word became flesh and blood and moved into the neighborhood" (John 1:14). The Word didn't become more words. Instead, the Word became flesh. God tucked his glory into a suit of skin and loved us.

God doesn't save through principles. God saves through coming as the living Word.[17] He backed up the U-Haul, unloaded boxes, and moved into the neighborhood. He moved into *our* neighborhood. *God enfleshed.*

A few years ago, I was invited to speak at an event at Wheaton College in the leafy suburbs of Chicago. During a break in the event, I walked over to meet my friend Tracy, who worked in the Billy Graham Center at Wheaton. On the third floor, at the end of the hall, Tracy showed me an art installation, an almost-life-size charcoal gray crucifix hanging on the wall. He summoned me to step in further to get a closer look. It took me a moment to realize what was going on with the piece. It was different from any crucifix I had ever seen. Leaning in to within a few inches of the piece, I noticed clumps of hair, balls of lint, flakes of dead skin, dirt, small bits of trash—even clipped fingernails. The placard on the wall stated that the artist, David JP Hooker, had collected the contents of vacuum bags around campus and incorporated them into the piece. The bottom of the placard read, "For our sake he made him to be sin who knew no sin, so that in him we might become the righteousness of God—2 Corinthians 5:21."

Tracy smiled. I stood silent and still, both engrossed and grossed out. My mind raced as I thought about all those fingernails and hair follicles and who they used to belong to—professors, students, administrators, parents visiting their kids during the weekend—and whether they ever imagined that one day, remnants of their bodies would be made into a piece of art and hung on the wall of the university. Few pieces of art had moved me like this one. *The incarnation—this is what it means*, I thought. *It is Jesus who takes all of our messes upon himself.* A God who came down; who possessed fingernails, hair, and skin cells; and who took on our stuff in order to love us. He became like us so we might be like him.

God didn't need us. Instead, he chose to spend time with us, to be among us. God loved us enough to be near. This up-close, *God-with-us* Jesus, the one who knew love cannot be done well from afar, wrapped skin around himself to be with us.[18] If we've grown up in church, sometimes the wonder of this miracle can lose its sheen. It was author C. S. Lewis, in his classic work *Mere Christianity*, who helped me grasp just how profound the incarnation actually is:

> The Eternal Being, who knows everything and who created the whole universe, became not only a man but (before that) a baby, and before that a fetus inside a woman's body. If you want to get the hang of it, think how you would like to become a slug or a crab.[19]

A slug. A crab. The savior who messed his diapers.

Incarnation assumes identification. God's love was so penetrating, he wanted to identify with us intimately, even if it came at an immensely personal cost. Over 1,500 years ago, the great theologian St. Augustine from North Africa wrote:

> Man's maker made man that He, Ruler of the stars, might nurse at His mother's breast; that the Bread might hunger, the Fountain thirst, the Light sleep, the Way be tired on its journey; that Truth might be accused of false witnesses, the Teacher be beaten with whips, the Foundation be suspended on wood; that Strength might grow weak; that the Healer might be wounded; that Life might die.[20]

To understand this idea of the overlapping of God's space with our space, we have to grasp the concept of temples. In the ancient world, people experienced God's presence by going to a temple, the physical place where God was present on earth. For the Israelites in the time of Moses, it was a tabernacle, a portable tent which held the divine. Smoke covered the tent when God's presence came down to be among his people, Israel.[21] What's truly fascinating is that in the original language, the word *dwelt*, is *eskenosen*, which literally means "to put up his tent." We could translate Jesus' arrival as "tabernacling" (as in *Jesus tabernacled among us*). God dwells among us. Emmanuel.

Much later, God commanded that a permanent structure be built for his presence. The inner sanctum of the Temple, where God's presence existed, was referred to as the Holy of Holies. The Book of John describes Jesus as a temple. Not only that, Jesus was also described as the *temple sacrifice*, the lamb of God which takes away the sins of the world. Without both of these realities, we would have no forgiveness of sins and, ultimately, no hope.[22] The temple *and* the tabernacle reveal a God of stability *and* mobility.

Recently, I was with a group of friends who gathered together to read and discuss the passage about Jesus raising Lazarus from the dead. My oldest son, Carter, a sixth grader, read the passage from John 11 aloud. Lazarus became sick, and his two sisters sent word to their friend Jesus to come and heal their brother. Even though Jesus loved them, he took a few days longer than most expected before heading to Bethany. When Jesus finally arrived, his friend had already been dead and in the tomb for four days. What could have been more important than visiting a close friend on his deathbed? Martha confronted him first, then Mary, both asking essentially the same question: *where were you—and what took you so long?* "Lord, if you had been there, my brother would not have died." The guilt trip of all guilt trips.

Jesus saw Mary weeping. The Jews who had come to comfort Mary also wept. And Jesus was "deeply moved in spirit and troubled" (John 11:33). Other translations read that Jesus was angry. And then Scripture says Jesus wept.

The people took Jesus to the tomb where Lazarus lay. Scripture says when they arrived at the tomb, Jesus was still angry (John 11:38). Jesus wanted the stone rolled away, despite the pleading of Martha, who argued that the acrid smell of her brother's decaying body would be too much for anyone to bear. Then Jesus called Lazarus out of his tomb. Lazarus stumbled out, joints stiff, hands and feet wrapped with linen strips, a cloth around his face, like something out of a first-century science fiction film—except it was real. "Take off the grave clothes," Jesus said, "and let him go" (John 11:44).

The magnitude of this story leaves me with so many unanswered questions. Why did Jesus wait several days to come to Bethany? What was he doing? When he arrived in town, what was he so angry about? What did Lazarus do during those four days? What happened to his soul? What did that first whiff of the tomb smell like the moment the stone was rolled away? What did Mary and Martha say to Jesus after seeing Lazarus hobble out from the tomb with his hands, feet, and face covered with cloth? And, if I was Lazarus, what would I possibly be afraid of during the rest of my days on earth?

What strikes me most in this story is the presence of Jesus' divinity *and also* his humanity, all within just a few verses. We see God's space (referred to as heaven or the kingdom of God) and our space (referred to as earth or this present age) overlapping in the same place.[23] Like any human, Jesus became angry, he wept, he talked, he walked. And like no human to ever live, he raised his friend from death to life even though he had died a few days prior. We may be tempted to overemphasize Jesus' divinity, thus underemphasizing his humanity (or vice versa). Without understanding the sacred overlap effect of the incarnation, we can't fully understand the power and the hope of Christmas *and also* Easter. We can't fully understand the power and hope of the gospel.

As the divine Son of God, Jesus could have cocooned himself and hung out only with the righteous. I once heard someone say that we should never show only one cross with Jesus on it. Jesus did not die alone; he died between two people—criminals at that. He died as he lived: in the company of criminals. It is not only how he came to earth in a humble birth that matters but also how he left this earth in a gruesome yet redeeming death.

The word *Trinity* is not found in our Bibles, but has been used for centuries to describe the mysterious relationship between the Father, the Son, and the Holy Spirit. In its most basic form, orthodox Christian belief embraces a Trinitarian God, who consists of three distinct beings and yet, at the same time, one single essence. The early church apologist Tertullian (AD 150–225) wrote that the Father, Son, and Spirit are inseparable yet distinct from each other; distinct in person, yet still one God.[24]

Centuries later, the Trinity was described with a fancy hundred-dollar word: *perichoresis* [peri-kor-EE-sis] which literally means "dancing around." The Trinity is the divine dance of God. I don't love dancing, but I love the thought of God on the dance floor, moving rhythmically and gracefully, where Father, Son, and Spirit—with smiles on their faces and sweat on their brows—clasp hands and spin joyfully, moving gracefully around the room. As if in a square dance, they each move in unison, at times graciously allowing each other to take a turn as the primary focus of attention while the others look on, smiling, clapping, and encouraging one another in their unique expressions. But *perichoresis* implies more than just dancing: there is no God-ness without the three, no essence that each part of the Trinity possesses by itself. Each absolutely depends upon the others. God is community of the deepest, most connected and interactive kind—beyond full description. Countless volumes throughout the centuries have been written to try to explain the Trinity. All of these writings may be exhausting, but they certainly are not exhaustive. Our finite ways will always fall short when we attempt to describe a wild, uncontainable, and mysterious God. It is a mystery that we apply by analogy only. In true mandorla form, God in his immense love allows himself to be accessible and known. And yet, in all his greatness and vastness, he will never be fully known.

One analogy which has been immensely helpful for me in my understanding comes from Russian painter Andrei Rublev. His famous fifteenth-century icon of the Trinity resides in a museum in Moscow, as well as on my iPhone home screen. The painting is strikingly beautiful and theologically rich. It is referred to as *The Holy Trinity* (or *The Hospitality of Abraham* based on the story of the three angels visiting Abraham in Genesis 18). Rublev painted these three angels sitting in a circle around a table (which looks like a Communion table). Their gazes are turned toward each other, with a bowl of roasted lamb in the center of the table. The house in the background, we can assume, is Abraham's.

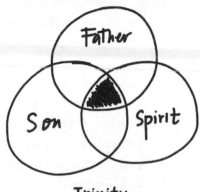

Trinity

The three angels, with halos around their heads and wings protruding from their backs, are widely understood to represent the members of the Trinity. Despite being winged creatures capable of flying, they each hold a staff. Why would three flying angelic beings carry walking sticks? Because the Trinity isn't detached from our lives, flying high above us in the ethereal clouds. Father, Son, and Spirit join us on our sacred-and-mundane journeys, gallivanting around with us in our everyday lives.

A well-recognized visual representation of the Trinity is a

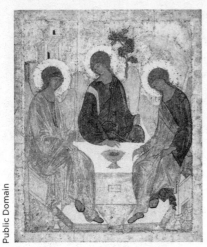

Icon of the Holy Trinity, State Tretyakov Gallery, Moscow, Russia

simple three-class circular Venn diagram. The oldest recorded use was found in a thirteenth century manuscript in Chartres, France.[25] Despite the complexity and the mystery of the doctrine of the Trinity, the symbol is simple and clear. In Celtic Christianity, artists created the *triquetra*, also called the Trinity knot, a three-leaf-shaped symbol. Celtic artists took only the overlaid parts of the three circles as the foundation of their distinct Trinitarian expression.

A few years ago, I took the plunge and got my first tattoo: three simple overlapping circles just under my right tricep. When I comb my hair after a shower or brush my teeth before bed, I catch a glimpse of my tattoo in the bathroom mirror, a daily reminder of the Trinitarian reality in which I live each and every day. I begin my day by being reminded that God the Father, Son, and Spirit, three-in-one and one-in-three, is present here, and I have nothing to fear. I end my day remembering the triune God is present and I recount God's presence made manifest over the past sixteen or so sacred-yet-ordinary hours—my personal dermatological liturgy.

But you don't have to get inked to be reminded daily of the Trinitarian reality. Every day, this three-in-one God makes himself present in our

Celtic Triquetra

lives in various expressions, popping up at various times, even in the seemingly run-of-the-mill cracks and crevices of our day. When we sit in traffic, look at spreadsheets, fold laundry, check email, mow the lawn—all of these are opportunities to be aware of God's presence.

God wrapped flesh around himself and came down in the form of a human being in order to love us, rescue us, and redeem us. He wasn't 95 percent God with a body. He was fully God *and also* fully man. I love the way Paul wrote about it: "In him, in bodily form, lives divinity in all its fullness" (Col. 2:9 NJB). His love couldn't be expressed from afar. He not only had to be near us, he had to be *with* us. The God-with-us Jesus moved into the neighborhood, just as winged angels with walking staffs join us in our daily adventure of faith. The triune God, readily willing to become a slug if he needed to in order to love us—fingernails, hair, dead skin cells, and all. If we are to follow Jesus faithfully, it will require a daring pilgrimage to the center of the mandorla. It's there, and only there, where we will be able to make any sense of his daring mission. God moves from dwelling *among his people* in the Tabernacle to dwelling *in the Temple*—and then, *in a human body*. But the incarnation becomes even more personal: God moves from *dwelling among his people* to now *dwelling inside of them*. God moves in. *Dios con carne.*

The Father *and also* the Son *and also* the Spirit. Jesus as fully God *and also* fully man. The overlap of heaven *and also* earth. The incarnation *and also* the resurrection. Sacred nuts *and also* fish bladders.

Who knew one little shape could communicate so much?

CHAPTER 2

SCANDALOUS MISFIT

Hanging with Saints and Sinners

"Why does your teacher eat with tax collectors and
sinners?"

—MATTHEW 9:11

We are more sinful and flawed in ourselves than we
ever dared believe, yet at the very same time we
are more loved and accepted in Jesus Christ than
we ever dared hope.

—TIM KELLER

Two things have messed with my theology more than anything
else: reading my Bible and following Jesus. The more I read my
Bible the more I see a Jesus who is quite different than the one I've
made him out to be. And the more I follow him, the more messing
he does with me.

When I seem to have Jesus figured out, he baffles me. He
provides me with the comfort I need *and also* ushers in discomfort
I do not want. This used to frustrate me; now I'm coming to see it's
what makes him so brilliant, so fascinating, so attractive.

Two of the greatest forces in the world are shame and fear. The more I talk with people, the more I realize just how much shame dominates our lives and controls our circumstances. Shame is when we want to run and hide, when we dash to our closet and frantically search for a mask we can yank off the shelf and strap on in order to conceal who we really are. As the Swiss psychologist Carl Jung said, shame is a soul-eating emotion. It is emotional sunburn on the skin of our souls.

For three-and-a-half years, I was paid to wear a mask. As a side gig, I worked as Sox the Fox, the mascot for the Colorado Springs Sky Sox, the former AAA minor league baseball affiliate of the Colorado Rockies. Pastor by day, mascot by night. The players gave me the nickname Reverend Sox. I high-fived kids, tossed T-shirts into the crowd between innings, signed autographs, pinched umpires' butts for a laugh, cheesed for pictures, and likely gave some unfortunate young children nightmares for months. Mascoting, for all its fun, is physically grueling work; I've never sweated so much in my life as when I was in that suit. I was rolling in the dough at fifty bucks an appearance (thirty-six after taxes), but it was well worth it. I never once felt like I was working. In that mascot suit, I learned an important lesson about life and how people treat you when you wear a mask, how they ignore you when you don't, or shun you if you wear the wrong one. When we experience shame, our first instinct is to reach for a mask. It's how we learn to hide. It takes courage to be who we truly are, and despite the vulnerability involved in exposing who we really are, it's incredibly freeing to live without faking it. Spiritual formation in a life-size fox suit.[1]

As I've thought about shame and fear, I've also pondered the word *disgrace*, defined as a loss of reputation or respect, especially as a result of a dishonorable action. But we don't need a dictionary to know what it means; we've all felt it. Many of us have felt the unsettling horror of disgrace, the erosion of our worth and dignity. Discovering a spouse has been unfaithful. Infertility, a miscarriage, hidden physical abuse, an abortion nobody knows about. Being browbeaten by a boss. An incarcerated family member. Sexual abuse. A hidden addiction that's lasted years. Unemployment, and failure to find another job. Adult children who've turned on you. Being told as a child, "You're not good for anything, and you'll never amount to anything in your life." Perhaps it's taken decades of work and countless dollars spent in counseling to try to dig out of that emotional hole. These are not theoretical issues, mind you. These are stories of real people, each one with a name, a face, a heart-rending story. When these are our stories, we are tempted to put on a mask to hide our shame and disgrace.

Throughout the biblical story, we read that God has a soft spot for the disgraced and the broken. The Bible mentions disgrace over eighty-five times. God's story is full of disgraced—and disgraceful—people whom he rescued and then used in his grand redemptive story. Moses' anger was so great it led him to murder, which he tried to cover up. When exposed, he ran away. That's when God showed up in the burning bush. Elijah, a great prophet, was so depleted and upset that he was suicidal and told God he felt there was no longer any point in living. God ministered to him, restoring him with sleep, food, water, and his presence. Jeremiah felt so disgraced by his unfruitful ministry that he blamed God, calling him a liar. Then God affirmed his ministry. The psalmist regularly screamed prayers like, "Lord, don't allow me to be disgraced! Bring disgrace to my enemies, but do not put me to shame!" And God listened.

Maybe the reason Jesus loved to hang out with (and even touch) misfits—the prostitutes, the lepers, the poor, the desperate, the invisible, the young—is because they were the ones who felt most disgraced. Maybe he had a soft spot in his soul for the disgraced because it was his story, too. Have you ever noticed how much disgrace is a part of Jesus' life? Disgrace even shrouds his birth story. Mary found herself in a disgraceful situation: engaged and pregnant. What does this do to a teenager who holds a positive pregnancy test in her hand?

I was in the Charlotte airport not long ago and bumped into someone who used to be a part of our church but had moved out of the area. I hadn't heard from her in a long time, so it was good to spend a few minutes chatting. After the smiles and the hugs and the shock of seeing someone you know in a place you never expected, I asked her how she was doing. "Well," she said, "I'm still single . . ." Her voice trailed off, then she looked down at her belly and slowly rubbed it with her hand. That's when I noticed the bump. She looked back up at me, then quickly turned her face away and down toward the well-worn gray airport carpet. I could tell it was painful and awkward for her. She tried to smile, but she couldn't hide her fear, uncertainty, and shame.

I realized the best thing I could do in that moment was to say nothing, so I kept my mouth shut. I felt compelled to wrap my arms around her and hug her tightly. I was hoping she would feel Jesus in that hug, right there in the middle of Terminal D. And as I hugged her, I wondered if my friend's shame was similar to what Mary might have felt in public. *How will I tell Joseph? He will never understand or believe me . . . How will I tell my parents? They'll literally kill me—or at least disown me. Where can I run away and hide for nine months—or the rest of my life?*

The text tells us, "Because Joseph her husband was faithful to the law, and yet did not want to expose her to public disgrace, he had in mind to divorce her quietly" (Matt. 1:19). It seems strange to us due to the vast cultural differences between the first century and our world, and it's difficult to even imagine it, but the most gracious act Joseph could possibly have done in that situation was to enact a quiet divorce. It would have inflicted the least amount of shame upon her. Mary would have been protected to some degree, although Joseph would have lost face and experienced disgrace himself. Had her pregnancy story not worked out the way it did, Joseph may never have had the opportunity to remarry because of "the Mary situation." I wonder if Jesus was ever teased by schoolyard bullies as a kid much like the slight he received as an adult when he was told he was a bastard child. Even in debates revolving around theology, religious leaders dragged his salacious birth story into the discussion (John 8:41).

Jesus' earthly parents weren't the only ones to experience disgrace. His relatives Zechariah and Elizabeth, parents of John the Baptist, felt it, too. Zechariah, a religious bigwig who served as a priest in the temple, and his wife Elizabeth (Mary's cousin) struggled with the harsh reality of infertility. In those days, infertility was considered a curse from God. How could a priest be called to serve God while also experiencing God's curse?

An angel comes to Zechariah and tells him that, despite their advanced age, Elizabeth is pregnant and will give birth to a son, and they are to call him John. The priest of God doubts the promise of God and, because of his lack of faith, loses the ability to speak until his son is born. A disgraced priest. How can you fulfill your duties as a priest in the temple of the Lord if you can't even speak? How can you act on God's behalf if you don't believe God's promises?

Elizabeth finds out she's pregnant and exclaims, "The Lord has done this for me. In these days he has shown his favor and *taken away my disgrace* among the people" (Luke 1:25, emphasis mine). Elizabeth is no longer barren, no longer suffering under the ostracizing weight of infertility. John the Baptist, who would grow up and pave the way for Jesus' ministry, is born in the midst of a context filled with disgrace.

But let's back up just a bit here. Jesus' family tree was decorated with plenty of disgraceful characters who would have made things painfully awkward at Thanksgiving dinner. The Book of Ruth recounts the story of Naomi, a disgraced widow—rejected, stuck in the culture with no way to move upward. Her daughter-in-law, Ruth, has also lost her husband. Through a series of miraculous events, Ruth meets a man named Boaz, who she finds out is a distant relative, and who ultimately ends up marrying her and providing her with an opportunity and a future.

You remember who Boaz's mother was, right? Rahab. Yes, her—the infamous woman from Jericho. What was her profession? Prostitution. Right there, in the middle of Jesus' family tree, is a call girl. Ruth and Boaz have a son and name him Obed. Can you imagine Obed as a little squirt asking, "Grandma, what do you do for a living?" Obed grows up and becomes the grandfather of King David, and it was prophesied that the Messiah would come from the line of David. What's mind-boggling to me is not that the Bible mentions Rahab's faith; it's that her faith made her eligible for enshrinement in the Faith Hall of Fame because she welcomed spies into her home in Jericho (Hebrews 11). A Hall of Famer who engaged in solicitation. A misfit.

Now, back to Jesus' family situation. Joseph and Mary are in the lower end of the socioeconomic tax bracket. Luke 2 records a minute yet significant detail: Mary and Joseph went to the Temple to dedicate their newborn son Jesus on the eighth day of his life, like all pious Jews would do. They brought a sacrifice of "a pair of doves or two young pigeons." If you have a Bible with cross-references in it, you're bound to find a reference to Leviticus 12:7-8: "These are the regulations for the woman who gives birth to a boy or a girl. But if she cannot afford a lamb, she is to bring two doves or two young pigeons." Jesus' parents were too poor to bring a lamb to sacrifice at the Temple, so they brought a lesser gift. Jesus is born into a poor Jewish family, a minority group living under the heavy oppression of Roman rule who had to flee the country for their own safety.[2] Refugees. Cultural misfits.

And he's born in a disgraceful location: a manger—a wooden (or possibly stone) trough used to hold animal feed. Many scholars believe Jesus was born in a cave (most likely not an above-ground wooden structure like we display each year in our nativity scenes) somewhere in the hillsides of Bethlehem; the cave most certainly would have smelled of mold, smoke from torches, urine from sheep, and feces from cows, a less-than-ideal place for a woman in labor.

The first humans to hear and feel the seismic tremors of the good news of the Messiah's arrival were shepherds. Despite our images of cute kids in Christmas pageants with hand towels tied around their heads, shepherding was a disgraceful profession in the first century. They were not the key influencers of the day. They were seen as dirty, untrustworthy, irreligious, wandering vagrants who rarely attended synagogue (their flocks demanded their around-the-clock attention out in the fields). Of all the people on God's green earth who could have delivered breaking news of the Messiah's arrival, he chose the equivalent of pawn shop owners. Misfits.

But it wasn't just his sketchy family tree and disgraceful birth story; much of Jesus' life was full of disgrace. He was rejected by those in his own town of Nazareth, which wasn't exactly a cultural hot spot in Palestine. A town like Sioux City, South Dakota; Gary, Indiana; or Cedar Rapids, Iowa. His own family didn't believe him, thought he needed to be institutionalized. There were several plots to kill him—not by the irreligious, but by the religious elites. He was rejected by the people he loved and came to save. Arrested, beaten, spit upon, mocked with a crown of thorns. Betrayed by his closest earthly friends. Even Peter, the captain of the team of disciples, swore he'd stick by his side—then shortly thereafter swore on his life, multiple times, that he didn't even know him. They hung Jesus on the cross with a sign above his head to mock him: *King of the Jews*. Even the criminal crucified alongside of him heaped insults on him. Passersby hurled insults at him, throwing his own words back in his face. The chief priests and teachers of the law chided him that he could save others but not himself (Mark 15:25–32). His last words before his death were asking God why he had been forsaken.

Jesus hung naked on a cross before others in the cruelest and most inhumane form of public execution. Have you ever had a mortifying dream in which you were naked in public? Have you ever actually been naked in public? Have you ever been naked, bloodied, beaten, and unable to breathe, hoisted high in the air on a cruel instrument of execution in public? Now *that's* disgrace. So disgraceful, in fact, that Christian artists have always placed a loin cloth over Jesus' genitals because to not provide a covering would feel profane. It's disgrace to us, even two thousand years later.

A disgraceful man born in disgraceful surroundings to a disgraceful family with a disgraceful lineage experiencing a disgraceful pregnancy in a disgraceful socioeconomic situation. Jesus grew up in disgrace and experienced disgrace all the way until his last breath. Why would Jesus hang out with, care about, and die for the disgraced? Because he was one himself. God's cosmic rescue plan travelled along the path of deep disgrace.

While two of the most powerful forces in the world are shame and fear, there are two forces even more powerful than these: love and hope. Who were the people who rushed toward Jesus and wanted to spend time with him the most? Some of the most disgraceful of people, including prostitutes (like one of his own relatives), a woman who had five husbands, a demon-possessed man, a widow subject to chronic menstrual bleeding, the poor, desperate parents with ill children, the crippled, and lepers, who were physically deformed as well as relationally and culturally excluded. Why did they flock to Jesus? Because Jesus loved them as they had never been loved before and offered hope they had not known was possible. Why did the disgraceful come to him? To be *re-graced*.

Author Brant Hansen points out that in the Sermon on the Mount, Jesus listed the kinds of people who should be blessed—happy—about the reality of the kingdom of God: The spiritually bankrupt. The grieving. The humble. Those who had experienced injustice. The merciful. Those in desperate need of peace. Those who suffered not for doing what was wrong, but for doing what was right.[3]

Genesis 3 records sin entering the world for the first time. Adam and Eve are told not to eat the fruit from the tree, but they did anyway. They rebelled—and everything changed. They realized that they were naked, and they felt shame and hid. They felt disgraceful. Ann Voskamp, in her children's Advent book *Unwrapping the Greatest Gift*, wrote:

> When we've fallen, and when we're lost, God comes with one question. Not the question "Why did you do that?" Not the question "What did you do wrong?" The very first God-question of the Old Testament, of the whole Bible, is a love question howling out of God's heart: "Where are you?"[4]

While the first question of the Old Testament is "Where are you?" the first question of the New Testament is: "Where is *he*?" The magi go to Herod and ask where this saving baby can be found. Wise men and women still search for the one who can handle our disgraceful state and offer us love and hope in the midst of heartbreak, shame, and spiritual disappointment. Jesus re-graces the disgraced, rubbing soothing aloe vera on our sun-blistered souls.

A few years ago, I stumbled upon a painting created by Sister Grace Remington in Iowa, titled, *Mary and Eve*. It's a simple yet theologically dazzling painting, an image always within close reach in my mind. Eve and Mary stand facing each other. Eve's head is tilted downward, her cheeks red with shame and guilt, the serpent wrapped round her right leg and much of her left. Her right hand clutches a half-eaten apple, and her left hand holds Mary's left hand, which is resting on her pregnant belly. Mary's head is also pointed downward, and she is smiling slightly, a confident, hope-filled smile. Her right hand rests on Eve's cheek, comforting her. What I find most striking about this intimate portrait is not Mary's face or hands, but her left foot, which is crushing the head of the serpent. Another sister at the abbey wrote this brief poem to highlight what Remington created:

> O Eve!
> My mother, my daughter, life-giving Eve,
> Do not be ashamed, do not grieve.
> The former things have passed away,
> Our God has brought us to a New Day.
> See, I am with Child,
> Through whom all will be reconciled.
> O Eve! My sister, my friend,
> We will rejoice together
> Forever
> Life without end.[5]

Mary, the pregnant teenage misfit, is consoling the universe's first misfit, telling her of the soon-arriving Christ child, a misfit in his own right, who would rescue all the other misfits in the world. Disgrace *and also* hope; guilt *and also* redemption. The tightening squeeze of a snake wrapped around the legs of one disgraced woman while its head is being crushed by a formerly disgraced—yet now hope-filled—woman.

The story of Good Friday is that Jesus died. He died as he lived: in the company of bad people. The great misfit died so other misfits could truly live. In his life, Jesus drew a dangerously eclectic group of misfits to the table: terrorists, traitors, professional fishermen, men who used to be disciples of another rabbi, and one who would betray him for money. He called members of Jewish ISIS and Edward Snowden onto the same team. Judas sat next to Jesus during the last supper. It amazes me that Jesus gave him a chance to sit and talk—all the way to the bitter end. He offers us the same opportunity.

Printed out and stuck inside my Bible is a tattered piece of computer paper with a few paragraphs from Dallas Willard's book *The Divine Conspiracy*. I read it on occasion, and I choke up almost every time:

> The flunk-outs and drop-outs and burned-outs.
> The broke and the broken.
> The drug heads and the divorced.
> The HIV-positive and herpes-ridden.
> The brain-damaged, the incurably ill.
> The barren and the pregnant too-many-times or at the
>   wrong time.
> The over-employed, the underemployed, the unemployed. The
>   unemployable.
> The swindled, the shoved aside, the replaced.
> The parents with children living on the street, the children
>   with parents not dying in the "rest" home.
> The lonely, the incompetent, the stupid.
> The emotionally starved or emotionally dead.
> And on and on and on.
> Jesus offers to all such people as these the present blessedness
>   of the present kingdom—regardless of circumstances . . .
> Even the murderers and child-molesters.
> The brutal and the bigoted.
> Drug lords and pornographers.
> War criminals and sadists. Terrorists.
> The perverted and the filthy and the filthy rich . . .

Can't we feel some sympathy for Jesus' contemporaries, who

huffed at him, "This man is cordial to sinners, and even eats with them!" Sometimes I feel I don't really want the kingdom to be open to such people. But it is. That is the heart of God . . .

If I, as a recovering sinner myself, accept Jesus' good news, I can go to the mass murderer and say, "You can be blessed in the kingdom of the heavens. There is forgiveness that knows no limits."

To the pederast and the perpetrator of incest.

To the worshiper of Satan.

To those who rob the aged and weak.

To the cheat and the liar, the bloodsucker and the vengeful: Blessed! Blessed! Blessed!

As they flee into the arms of The Kingdom Among Us.[6]

Grace rarely fits into our nice, tidy categories. It's large and expansive and disruptive. It's scandalous. Thank God for it, because the disgraced Misfit was exactly what was needed in order for the rest of us misfits to be *re-graced*. Grace is the banquet meal for misfits, nourishing, edifying, and keeping us alive. The good news: even though we were misfits, now we find our sense of belonging in the family of God because of him.

No more masks are needed for the misfits; let the re-gracing begin.

CHAPTER 3

DOUBLE-MAJOR JESUS

Embracing Justice and Embracing Grace

Love is the motive, but justice is the instrument.

—REINHOLD NIEBUHR

True godliness does not turn men out of the world, but enables them to live better in it, and excites their endeavors to mend it.

—WILLIAM PENN

She carries a pearl
In perfect condition
What once was hurt
What once was friction
What left a mark
No longer stings
Because Grace makes beauty out of ugly things
Grace finds beauty in everything
Grace finds goodness in everything.

—"GRACE," U2

During the fall semester of my junior year of college, I studied abroad in Jerusalem at a school on Mount Zion. During our time at Jerusalem University College, my three roommates and I refused to cut our hair or shave. By the end of the semester, we all looked like Old Testament prophets or the Unabomber—we weren't quite sure which. We not only learned about the cultural, historical, and biblical stories of Israel/Palestine; we lived them. We occupied a room called The Tomb Room, where my bed literally rested above a several-hundred-year-old tomb. (It's not as creepy as it sounds; the body was exhumed many years prior.) We kept our textbooks in a niche carved in the stone wall, originally used to store feed for animals before they converted it into a dorm room. It's hard not to have a spiritually impactful semester abroad when you wake up in an empty tomb and grab your textbooks out of a manger on your way to class.

Our field trips included jaunts to places like the Sea of Galilee, the Elah Valley (where David killed Goliath), and to Jordan to see the ancient stone city of Petra. On weekends we'd hitchhike through the Negev wilderness, bribe commercial fishermen to let us spend the day out on the Sea of Galilee, and watch the sun rise over Mount Sinai in Egypt. Once we even assisted a Bedouin shepherd, who knew no English, with the birth of one of his lambs. Some mornings we'd grab a handful of piping hot pita, trudge through the cool, refreshing waters of Hezekiah's Tunnel, and hustle back to our dorm rooms just in time to change clothes and dash to class with wet hair. After class, we'd walk to the Western Wall to people-watch or head to Jaffa Gate to sip Middle Eastern mint tea from the second story balcony of a café overlooking the Tower of David.

One of my regular exploits each week was to Shorashim, a store in the Jewish quarter of the Old City, about a six-minute walk from campus. The store was owned and managed by two brothers, Dov and Moshe Kempinski, who are also trained as Pharisees. These brothers generously made themselves available to whomever happened to wander into their store, patiently answering tourists' questions about Judaism and Jewish practices. About once a week, I'd find myself engaged in deep conversation with one or both of them about life and God and Jesus and the Torah—and how we reconcile our religious differences. They were kind, patient, warm, and engaging, always leaving me with questions I hadn't previously considered and pushing me to think differently.

One afternoon, I ambled down to the shop, pulled up a stool, and sat with Dov, who explained to me the importance of *shalom* in the story of God. When we speak of Yahweh's view of justice, Dov told me, we can't speak of it without including *shalom*. *Shalom* is the Hebrew word understood as perfect harmony, rightness, perfection, and settledness. All is right; all fits.

In the Christian story, *shalom* existed in the pre-sin Garden of Eden, and *shalom* will be present again, as we read at the end of Revelation. But for now, we live in the land of in-between, the *shalom*-shattered, sin-scarred world. We know of no other exist-ence. And yet, in Christ, we have an instance and an experience of the future now.

Dov also shared with me that justice in Hebrew is the word *tse-daqa* [tse-da-KAH] or *mishpat* [mish-PAHT], terms used to describe making something right or returning it to its original ideal. We sometimes translate this as *righteousness*, or even just *rightness*. Justice as rightness or righteousness makes sense, for when God's *shalom* is present, it is just right. Kingdom justice, then, is the res-toration of humanity to both God and others, a return to *shalom*. It is making us whole by putting all the broken pieces back together once again.[1] As Dov shared, I was reminded that this is why the promise of Jesus in Revelation is not to make all new things, but to make *all things new*.

I don't know a single follower of Jesus who believes justice or righteousness is a bad thing. But I am challenged by Jesus' words in the Beatitudes, where he says, "Blessed are those who *hunger and thirst* for righteousness, for they will be filled" (Matt. 5:6). Often, I think rightness and justice are a good idea, but what I need God's help with is in developing a hunger for it, like I hunger for food after a day of fasting. This kind of longing—a desire to strive for justice and rightness—is the kind of life Jesus desires for his followers.

After Jesus was tested in the wilderness by the devil, he returned to the region of Galilee in northern Israel. Luke records that Jesus taught in the synagogues and everyone praised him (4:15). He traveled to Nazareth, the place of his upbringing and, like a good Jew, went to the synagogue on *Shabbat*. Designated to read Scripture that day, he stood, unrolled the Torah scroll, and found his place in the book of Isaiah:

> "The Spirit of the Lord is on me,
>> because he has anointed me
>> to proclaim good news to the poor.
> He has sent me to proclaim freedom for the prisoners
>> and recovery of sight for the blind,
> to set the oppressed free,
>> to proclaim the year of the Lord's favor." (Luke 4:18–19)

My friend Adam is a deeply committed follower of Jesus who is passionate about helping churches find the appropriate posture and pursuit of biblical justice. In his book, *Becoming a Just Church*, Adam highlights that Jesus purposefully chose the Isaiah passage and read it in the synagogue on that fateful *Shabbat* day as a defining element of his mission and ministry. The timing of Jesus' reading of this passage was no accident.[2] He rolled it up, handed it back to the attendant, sat down, and began to teach. Then Jesus uttered a detonating statement: *The passage I just read: that's me.*

The Holy Spirit, he pronounced, was upon him, commissioning

him to proclaim this good news to those on the margin, to announce freedom for those who had not experienced it, to give sight to the sightless and freedom to those who were under oppression. I doubt anyone fell asleep in the pews that morning.

After stating this, Jesus briefly recounted two Old Testament stories, Elijah with the widow in Zarephath, and Elisha and the Syrian leader Naaman. These stories were as hard as buckshot. A near riot broke out in the synagogue; they wanted Jesus killed. Two stories, comprised of just four sentences total. When a few sentences don't come out of my mouth just right in a sermon, I might receive an email or two from concerned congregants seeking clarification. With these four sentences from Jesus, the Jews wanted him dead. So what exactly happened between the beginning of the passage, when they were praising him, amazed by his gracious words, and the end of the passage, when suddenly they wanted an execution?

The impoverished widow and the leprous leader were Gentiles, from outside of Israel—and, in the minds of pious Jews, outside of God's blessing. This was unimaginable, incomprehensible, utterly offensive. How could God's justice include Gentiles? God would never love any people but the nation of Israel, his chosen ones. How could he care for *those people* when Israel, God's chosen, were in desperate need of justice from the oppressive rule of Rome? They were furious enough to want to run him out of the synagogue—and right off the side of a cliff.[3] Issues of justice are emotional. They always have been.

What, exactly, are we talking about when we talk about embracing justice *and also* embracing grace? When and where did Jesus exhibit both justice and grace? These terms, simple as they may seem, are emotionally charged words with wildly varied meanings, depending on who you talk to.

Where justice feels stalwart and brazen and deserved, grace

feels tender and gentle and, at times, even scandalous. Many people view mercy and grace as being synonymous. They are similar, yet distinct. Mercy is not getting what we deserve, whereas grace is getting what we do not deserve. We see mercy in the Old Testament, but we don't get a full glimpse of grace until the coming of Jesus Christ in the New Testament. It is then that we see God's grace is finally revealed in high definition through his own self-giving. Grace builds its house on the foundation stones of mercy.

The Hebrew word *hesed* can be translated as "lovingkindness" or "loyal love." It is the closest word to the New Testament concept of grace, which is often translated as *charis* (where we get the word *charisma*, meaning "gift"). *Hesed* is the kind of love found in the emotional metaphor through the agonizing marital dynamics of the prophet Hosea and his unfaithful wife, Gomer. Grace is not a willy-nilly, shoulder shrugging, yeah-I-guess-I'll-forgive-you kind of approach. It's rooted in an unwavering love which cannot be derailed. Even the teenage Mary, when she found out she was pregnant, belted out a song of spontaneous joy, in what is called the Magnificat, as she pondered God's *hesed* (Luke 1:46–56). Zechariah's song, a few verses later, reflects the same sentiment (Luke 1:78). God remained faithful to Israel, even when Israel had been unfaithful to him. In fact, *hesed* is the central term which describes Israel's relationship with Yahweh. Jesus is the fullest expression of God's *hesed*.

Anne Lamott said that grace is like spiritual WD-40, a lubricant loosening the bolts we never thought would budge.[4] We can hardly turn a red-lettered page in our Bibles without reading an example of Jesus extending grace to others, often to the horror, shock, and outrage of the religiously entitled. Jesus railed against the proud spiritual elites with acrid words in Matthew 23, when he called the religious leaders hypocrites. They tithed but neglected justice, mercy, grace, and faithfulness. Instead of practicing *either/or*, Jesus told them they must practice *both/and* (Matt. 23:23). In his most famous sermon, Jesus said the merciful are blessed because what goes around comes around (Matt. 5:7). And more than once Jesus spoke of Jonah, a dramatic and satirical book depicting an angry prophet who was offended that God's *hesed* included the people of Nineveh, Israel's bitter enemy.

The mission of God is to double major in justice and grace, like fraternal twins from the same womb.[5] God loves justice and hates injustice. Scripture also teaches that Jesus desires mercy and grace, even above sacrifice. I love the image in Psalm 85:10–11: "Love and faithfulness meet together; righteousness and peace kiss each other." Brazen *tsedaqa* and gentle *hesed* embrace in affection. When *mishpat* and *hesed* overlap, they create a sense of the shalom God desires for the world.[6]

In my seminary courses, I begin every class by asking my students to stand, and together we recite the *Shema*, a passage found in Deuteronomy 6:4–5:[7]

> Hear, O Israel: The LORD our God, the LORD is one. Love the LORD your God with all your heart and with all your soul and with all your strength.

Shem'a is the Hebrew word for "hear" or "listen"—the first word in this passage. Hearing in order to comprehend and then to act is a frequent theme in the Bible. Hearing is a crucial element of spiritual growth.

We also recite the Shema of Jesus. When Jesus was questioned by the religious leaders who asked him what the greatest commandment was, he responded:

> "'Hear, O Israel: The Lord our God, the Lord is One. Love the Lord your God with all your heart and with all your soul and

with all your mind and with all your strength.' The second is this: 'Love your neighbor as yourself.' There is no commandment greater than these." (Mark 12:29–31)

Jesus' response is distinct, but it wasn't the first. Rabbi Hillel and other Jewish sages have stated that this love-God-love-others approach was the proper summary of the Law. But what Jesus did was deny that the first commandment, when there is conflict, overtakes the second one. He added to the original text which commands us to love God with all our minds, stating we are also to love our neighbor as ourselves. He saw right through the religious leaders' *either/or* thinking and expanded the discussion to a *both/and* reality: the greatest commandment is actually *two* commandments. How do we show justice *and* grace? By loving God *and* others. We shouldn't be forced to choose one or the other. We need both. Loving others includes brushing up against the thorns of injustice in society. Love wants them removed.[8] When my students and I stand and recite the Shema from Deuteronomy, followed by the Shema of Jesus, it forms us to be equally committed to loving God and loving others without being tempted to believe we have to choose between the two. You don't have to be a student enrolled in seminary to do this; you can do this as a lifelong student of Jesus enrolled in the school of discipleship. Try reciting these prayers at the beginning and the end of your day. Over time, you will find they form you into a double-majoring student of Jesus.

The most impressive architectural feature in Jerusalem during the time of Jesus was the Temple Mount. It's one of the most impressive archaeological features in Jerusalem. Today it remains under Muslim control, and tourists are able to visit the temple area under tight security. While the wait time can be quite long, it's still worth it. It was on the Temple Mount that my mind's eye envisioned Jesus sauntering around, worshiping, teaching, engaging in theological debates, and turning over tables. In John 8, we read that in this Temple area, religious leaders brought before Jesus a disgraced woman caught in the act of adultery. Although many scholars believe this story is apocryphal, indicated in our Bibles with italics or a footnote at the bottom of the page, there are many who still believe this to be an authentic expression of how Jesus lived the sacred overlap. What we see in this story gives us a clear glimpse and a consistent image of the nature of Jesus' ministry.[9]

With an air of repugnance, the Pharisees placed her before Jesus and said, "Teacher, this woman was caught in the act of adultery. In the Law Moses commanded us to stone such women. Now what do you say?" (John 8:4–5). It was an *either/or* scenario devised to trap Jesus and further shame the woman. They were waiting, ready to pounce. I imagine these tawdry Pharisees with legs crossed and clipboards steadied on their laps, looking over the top of their glasses, waiting for Jesus' response. At first, Jesus didn't speak. He bent down and started writing. Names, specific sins, a verse from the Law, stick figures—we don't know exactly what he scribbled in the dirt. He then straightened back up and challenged any sinless person to start throwing stones. One by one, the stones dropped. People slowly slunk backwards as subtly as possible. Finally, only two remained: Jesus and the woman. While the religious leaders talked *about* her, Jesus began to speak *to* her and *with* her, saying, "Woman, where are they? Has no one condemned you?" (John 8:10). The questions were a build-up, a pregnant pause waiting for the payoff, like a comedian about to deliver the punchline of a joke. But this was no comedic performance—this was her life hanging in the balance.

> "No one, sir" she said.
> "Then neither do I condemn you," Jesus declared. "Go now and leave your life of sin." (John 8:11)

Those who enjoy majoring in grace and minoring in justice are quick to point out that Jesus did not condemn the woman—which is absolutely true. But we can't forget the follow-up line: "Go now and leave your life of sin." The whole scenario was a test to see which one Jesus would major in: *tsedaqa* or *hesed*. The religious leaders wanted all justice and no grace. Conversely, all grace but no justice would have shown Jesus' disregard for the Law. The only proper response for Jesus was justice *and also* grace. No condemnation—*and yet* he called her a sinner and told her to stop. Jesus refused to live in the oppressively constraining *either/or* paradigm when it came to loving God and loving neighbor, choosing instead to live in the spiritual and relational world of *both/and*. He announced the kind of forgiveness that alone can deal with both the sin of the woman *and also* of her accusers. God's grace covers over adultery *as well as* all the sin of arrogant judgmentalism. The overlay of justice and grace always gives people dignity and affirms the image of God in others.

The posture of presence is why this worked. Presence shows value and gives dignity. Jesus offered the woman worth and meaning (something the religious leaders never imagined doing), and he forgave her (thus angering the religious elite even more), but he also challenged her lifestyle, telling her what she was doing was sin and telling her to stop doing it (something which would have surprised and startled the irreligious). Reflecting on this story, Howard Thurman wrote, "He placed a crown over her head which for the rest of her life she would keep trying to grow tall enough to wear."[10]

But there's an important detail which is easy to miss here: the text says Jesus bent down and wrote with his *finger* on the ground (v. 6). Then it says that once more, he bent down and wrote on the ground. Again, we don't know what he wrote, but that may not be the point. It may simply be important *that he wrote*. Jesus often employed a Jewish teaching tool called a *remez*, a Hebrew word meaning "hint." Assuming their listeners knew the Torah intimately, rabbis would drop hints throughout their teachings to help people see a deeper meaning in the teaching than what lay on the surface. Jewish audiences would hear these clues and make the connection, but many of us in the twenty-first century West miss them entirely.[11]

Could it be that as John records this story for his readers, he wants us to see the *remez*, not in what Jesus is writing in the dirt, but what he is using to write with—his own finger? Maybe this is the reason Jesus bending down and writing is mentioned twice here. In the Old Testament, we see the finger of God mentioned in the giving of the Ten Commandments (Ex. 31:18). During the ten plagues in Egypt, God provided the plague of gnats, and when Egyptian magicians were unable to duplicate the feat, they told Pharaoh it was the finger of God (Ex. 8:16–19). We also see the importance of fingers in offering sacrifices in the Temple (Ex. 29:12; Lev 4:6, 17, 25, 30). We see God's fingers mentioned in the works of his creation (Psalm 8:3). The Gospel of Mark records the detail of Jesus inserting his fingers in the ears of a deaf man in order to heal him (Mark 7:33). Jesus mentions using the finger of God to cast out demons as a way of signaling that the kingdom of God had arrived (Luke 11:20). Putting rings on people's fingers was a sign of family belonging and identity (Luke 15:22, Gen 41:42; Esther 3:10).[12]

But what do fingers have to do with mandorlas? Well, maybe quite a bit. Could it be that John wants us to see that through Jesus, there is healing *and also* the giving of the law *and also* sacrifice for the forgiveness of sins *and also* identity and belonging? Could Jesus, through the use of his finger, be giving his listeners a *remez*—that he, like his Father, cares about justice *and* grace?

Jesus doesn't just model this for us; he commands we live into it as his followers. And he doesn't tell us to do this in ethereal and generic terms. In the Sermon on the Mount, he gives specific, practical ways to do this. Rejoice when you are persecuted. When you are struck on one cheek, offer the other cheek as well. When you are forced to walk one mile, double-knot your laces and walk another. It is easy to love our friends. Jesus even said so. It's our natural proclivity, the gravitational pull of our hearts. But to *love* our *enemies?* To *pray* for those who *persecute* us? To *bless* those who *curse* us? *Are you kidding me?* If Jesus can love Samaritans, Greek pagans, oppressive Roman soldiers, Judas, the religious leaders— now, *that's* radical. Not as a doormat or a punching bag, but as hope-filled, faith-saturated men and women.

Scot McKnight reminds us that talking about social justice makes a lot of churches and a lot of Christians nervous. They worry that striving for social justice means running the risk of getting lost in the "love others" stuff, as they've seen happen with some people. But others worry about the "love God" people who don't often look to serve and love their neighbors.[13] This justice/grace conversation not only makes a lot of Christians nervous, it also makes many of us emotional, defensive, and afraid. We fear we may lose the way forward, that the wheels of justice and grace might shake uncontrollably, a death wobble on our theological longboard. Any time we are afraid, we experience a primal reaction where we want to fall back into *either/or* thinking. Maybe this is one of the reasons the Bible tells us time and time again not to fear. And maybe this is why Jesus said perfect love casts out fear. When we're afraid, *either/or* becomes our default mode as we seek to assuage the pain of uncertainty. Love is where we live between the extremes, not in the mushy middle.

The purpose of finding the overhang of justice and grace is not to yell, "They deserve it!" Instead, it is to say, "This is the way God's world should be." The Christian is called to participate in actions that anticipate the way God's world *will* be.[14] Assuredly, living in the midst of the tension takes a great deal of energy, thought, courage, prayer, and conversation with others. It can be exhausting. Was Jesus' mission on earth primarily about justice or primarily about grace? Yes. The point is, we miss the point if we make it an *either/ or* proposition; it's *both/and*.

Injustice, then, is the breaking or thwarting of the process of *sha-lom*—a theft by the strong from the weak, by the rich from the poor.[15] There are two primary camps in which Christians reside when it comes to addressing and combating injustice in the world. The first is to state that if Jesus is the wild revolutionary, then the mission of the Christian faith is to build the kingdom right here on earth through a variety of social, political, and cultural meas-ures. Those taking this approach, sometimes dubbed social justice warriors, are passionate, engaged, and at times romantic, rallying around causes in an effort to eliminate injustice once and for all. Picket signs, petitions, and bullhorns in hand, they often major in zeal but minor in love.

The second group, on the other end of the spectrum, are those who throw their hands in the air in apathy or despair and claim there is simply nothing that can possibly be done to make a real difference this side of heaven. Evil is too prevalent, Satan is too dangerous, and the structures are too rooted to bring about any real, lasting change, so we just ignore it altogether.[16] We'll just run a few soup kitchens and wait it out until God comes and sorts out this one big cosmic mess, they say. These kinds of people major in reality but minor in hope and faith.

Many conservative churches I know hear the word "justice" and slap labels like "progressive" or "liberal" on it. It's unfortunate and ironic, because Jesus spoke about justice as a crucial part of his kingdom to be manifested in the world. Somewhat surprisingly, Jesus taught his followers to pray specifically for God's kingdom to come to earth, just as it exists in heaven, but not that the church would grow. It's not that the church isn't important, but it's not to be our *primary* pursuit and motivation. It's all in our perspective. Howard Snyder's words are a gift:

> Kingdom people seek first the Kingdom of God and its justice; church people often put church work above concerns of justice, mercy and truth. Church people think about how to get people into the church; Kingdom people think about how to get the church into the world. Church people worry that the world might change the church; Kingdom people work to see the church change the world.[17]

Church, of course, is a significant expression of God's mission for the world. The church was his idea, after all. But it is not the same thing as the kingdom. We are kingdom people first, not church people. Jesus, in the Sermon on the Mount, did not tell people to seek first the church; instead, he said, our first pursuit should be God's kingdom. But with our eyes and hearts firmly set on the kingdom, we can live into the fullness of all Jesus imagined by *being* the church. It is why Dallas Willard wrote that the local church should be a beachhead for kingdom activity.[18] While the kingdom and the church are not wholly the same thing, they certainly overlap. And justice is certainly a crucial part of that sacred overlap, too.

If we do not get this right, we will never get our motivations to pursue justice right, either. I love the imagery of the righteous man Job used, showing us how righteousness and justice overlap:

> I put on righteousness as my clothing;
> justice was my robe and my turban.

> I was eyes to the blind
> and feet to the lame.
> I was a father to the needy;
> I took up the case of the stranger.
>
> (JOB 29:14-16)

If we believe what we pray, then as Christians we cannot ignore the areas of injustice where they exist. This means we must reject the arrogance and triumphalism of the first approach of revolution and reject the defeatism of the second approach of indifference.[19] We are summoned to learn to love and live out *both* the Great Commandment *and* the Great Commission.

My friend Adam rightly points out that justice in many churches is reduced to an optional outreach strategy. When justice is framed as one of the options on the outreach menu, where Christians can tick a box to sign up for opportunities to "do justice," it means justice is optional for everyone. In the kingdom of God, justice is not an optional outreach strategy; it is a way of life for the people of God. We are called to be merciful gardeners of *shalom* in a world of injustice.[20] It is at the heart of God's cosmic redemption project. Adam wrote that God designed his church to be a living parable of his intent, people who embody and embrace God's tomorrow, today.[21]

The early Christians knew about this balance of embracing justice and embracing grace. In fact, it was a part of their evangelism strategy. Sociologist of religion Rodney Stark shared how the radical and peculiar love of the early Christians was the driving force behind the growth and expansion of Christianity:

> Christianity revitalized life in Greco-Roman cities by providing new norms and new kinds of social relationships able to cope with many urgent urban problems. To cities filled with the homeless and the impoverished, Christianity offered charity as well as

hope. To cities filled with newcomers and strangers, Christianity offered an immediate basis for attachments. To cities filled with orphans and widows, Christianity provided a new and expanded sense of family. To cities torn by violent ethnic strife, Christianity offered a new basis for social solidarity. And to cities faced with epidemics, fires, and earthquakes, Christianity offered effective nursing services.[22]

That is peculiar. And it is radical.[23]

When people hear the name of our church, The Renew Community, for the first time, they often furrow their brows, cock their heads, and purse their lips in confusion. "The Renew Community?" they ask. "Shouldn't it be The *Renewed* Community or maybe The *Renewing* Community instead?" One gentleman made it a point to tell us that the name of our church doesn't make grammatical sense. I assured him we were fully aware of this when we chose the name. We wanted people to trip over our unique name because we find ourselves smack-dab in the middle of the past, present, *and* future tenses of God's grand story. We have been renewed to the saving work of Jesus. We trust God's promise for the future, that all things will one day be made new again. But we also believe God is all about the renewal of all things—*even in the present*—and he wants us to participate with him. We see our church, along with other local Jesus communities, as active participants in the R & D department of the kingdom of God. We are seeking to embrace God's tomorrow, today—a living parable with bad grammar.

It's not about us wringing our hands and pacing the floor while we wait it out until God returns someday. *God has brought the future right here into the present through Jesus Christ.* He wants that future to be fleshed out more and more today, right now, right here.[24] There are people throughout history who have embraced God's tomorrow, today—people like William Wilberforce, who helped abolish slavery in England and paved the way for its abolition years later in America. Like William and Catherine Booth, co-founders of the Salvation Army. Like Dr. Martin Luther King Jr., who shed a bright light of resolute hope on the issue of civil rights in the United States. Like Gary Haugen, founder and president of International Justice Mission. Like Bryan Stevenson, attorney and founder of the Equal Justice Initiative, who works to keep Dr. King's hope and vision alive today. These people—and many others—would tell you that striving for justice might sound sexy, but it's exhausting and complicated and, at times, terrifying. Issues of justice can sometimes get us wrapped around the axle, but it's still worth it.

Part of double-majoring in justice and grace is taking Jesus' words seriously and being proactive makers of peace. Not only is it a good idea, Jesus said it's how we are identified as God's kids: "Blessed are the peacemakers, for they will be called children of God" (Matt. 5:9). I notice Jesus isn't blessing the restlessly violent, nor is he blessing the helplessly passive peacekeepers. It's those who strive to make peace who are counted as the blessed gardeners proactively pursuing God's *shalom*. God's not after creating a spiritual U.N.; he truly wants us in the pursuit of God's tomorrow, today. The closer we get to peacemaking, the closer we get to the heart of God and vice-versa. Because in making peace, we are modeling what God, through his Son Jesus, did for us. He made the first move. He came to us, to rescue us. We did not initiate; we simply responded. I keep a quote from St. Bernard of Clairvaux next to my desk: "If God did not love his enemies, he would have no friends." This is the ultimate model of peacemaking.

Peacemaking is not only messy business; it's also serious business. Yitzhak Rabin, Martin Luther King Jr., Gandhi, Jesus—all were peacemakers whose lives ended through terrible, violent action. Peacemakers go to war, but not against people. They war against division, hatred, death, hopelessness, and the numerous pervasive evil powers which exist in the world.

But we don't have to travel overseas or be known around the world or uproot our families and live in a war-torn country in order to be peacemakers. The most powerful means of peacemaking can come in the simplest and most ordinary of ways: we can commit to "living gently in a violent world."[25] We can embody *hesed* (lovingkindness, committed and loyal love) and *tsedaqa* (justice, rightness)—the expression of God's re-*shaloming* work.

If we gather in Jesus' name but don't follow in his way, we are not mandorla people.

If we raise our hands in worship but do not lift a finger to serve the least, we are not mandorla people.

If we attend church frequently but don't attend to the needs of the poor regularly, we are not mandorla people.

If we feed the hungry but our motive is not rooted in love, we are not mandorla people.

If we attend a Bible study but refuse to participate in a Bible doing, we are not mandorla people.

If we participate in social justice projects yet refuse to share the hope we possess, we are not mandorla people.

We're called to live with kingdom dexterity, where we double-major in right belief *and* right action in the school of Jesus.

PART 2

WHEN JESUS BLOWS UP YOUR EITHER/OR LIFE

The real voyage of discovery consists not in seeking new landscapes, but in having new eyes.

—MARCEL PROUST

I am the Alpha and the Omega, the First and the Last, the Beginning and the End.

—REVELATION 22:13

CHAPTER 4

ORTHOPARADOXY

RIGHT BELIEVING AND RIGHT LIVING

We don't believe something by merely saying we believe it, or even when we believe that we believe it. We believe something when we act as if it were true.

—DALLAS WILLARD, *RENOVATION OF THE HEART*

The best theology is a lifeology—a life well-played, well-prayed, well-spent.

—LEONARD SWEET

The word *orthodoxy* means "right thinking" or "right believing"— and think and believe rightly we should. Throughout the centuries, the church has painstakingly developed creeds and confessions for this very reason: to be clear and unified in what we actually believe. We get our word creed from the Latin word *credo*, which means "I believe."

One of the most famous creeds, the Nicene Creed, was created at the Council of Nicaea in the summer of 325 A.D. This first ecumenical council was an effort to preserve the unity of the church around key doctrinal points. The Roman emperor Constantine gathered over three hundred bishops from all over the world to discuss the Church's official stance, most specifically on the doctrine of the Trinity. One leader in attendance, Arius, argued that Jesus was not equal in status to the Father; this was referred to as the Arian controversy.[1]

These councils that developed creeds and confessions were deeply important (though certainly not as exciting as what presumably happened at Nicaea), as they preserved the unity of the beliefs of the Church. As important as they were—and, in many ways, still are—they have their limitations for two reasons. One, what is puzzling about these creeds, helpful as they may be, is they skip over about three decades of Jesus' life and ministry. For example, a few lines of the Apostles' Creed read:

> I believe in Jesus Christ, God's only Son, our Lord,
> who was conceived by the Holy Spirit,
> born of the Virgin Mary,
> suffered under Pontius Pilate,
> was crucified, died, and was buried;

It jumps rather quickly from Jesus' birth to his arrest. The greatest man to ever live, the Savior of the world, and in one short line we jump from his birth to his death. Where are the references to his miracles, his teachings and healings, the stories and parables he told about the kingdom of God? Why are they not in the creeds? And two, what about the shared commitments of how we live *because of* what we believe? How are we to know how to live like Jesus if we cut out the stuff about his life and teachings? How beneficial is belief if we don't know how to act upon what we believe?

The word *orthopraxy* (from the Latin, *praxis*, where we get our word practice) means "right living"—and live rightly we should. Despite the creeds and confessions being almost entirely about what we believe, the Third Lausanne Congress on World Evangelization convened 4,200 Christian leaders from almost two hundred countries in Cape Town, South Africa, in October 2010. These kingdom-minded mission leaders drafted what was called The Cape Town Commitment. Part 1 of the document established biblical convictions as found in the Scriptures; part 2 sounded the call to action. Right thinking *and also* right living.

One of the elements which makes the Sermon on the Mount so rich is Jesus' dual emphasis on right thinking and right living. His teaching didn't remain in some ethereal space up in the clouds. He taught that because the kingdom of God, his rule and reign, is present, we must think differently than before ("you have heard it said . . . but I tell you . . ."). This right thinking flows naturally into how we live and how we treat others. And Jesus was pretty specific about it: don't speak poorly of others; don't degrade the image of God in others by lusting after them sexually; settle disagreements outside of court, keep your marital commitments; say what you mean and mean what you say; lend to others without expecting a return; love and pray for those who don't reciprocate; give to the underprivileged secretly; fast discreetly; live without worrying; don't have a judgmental spirit. Jesus was about right thinking *and also* right living. I think it could be dubbed The Mandorla Manifesto.

Mahatma Gandhi was gripped by the life and teachings of Jesus, most specifically what he read in the Sermon on the Mount. He studied Christianity closely and observed the lives of Christians he saw in Great Britain. He famously stated that if Christians lived out the beliefs they had in Christ, everyone would be a Christian, including him. It was the fragmentation, the incongruent living, the duplicity that he found unreconcilable. The orthodoxy did not match the orthopraxy.

Halakhah [ha-la-KAH] is the noun form of the Hebrew verb meaning "walk." Jewish Law is almost exclusively an explanation about how a good Jew is to live and behave. The *Halakhah* guides religious beliefs, but it also guides everyday activity. To Jews, walking with God referred to the 613 laws of the Torah, 248 positive ("thou shalt") and 365 negative ("thou shalt not"). To pious Jews, the *halakhah* was—and still is—crucial. But *halakhah* can also be translated as "the way to act," or "the practice." How we live—how we practice our faith—matters in Judaism.

Early Christians had their own *halakhah* of sorts called the *Didache* (DID-a-kay) meaning "the teaching." This anonymous first-century document was written in an attempt to provide a practical guide to help the early Jewish Christians think through how they followed Jesus in their everyday lives. It spelled out specific instruction for elements such as how to baptize (immersion), how to participate in Communion (as an entire meal), how to pray (recite the Lord's Prayer three times daily), and how to fast (on Wednesdays and Fridays). We aren't sure if this ever tipped into legalism, but it was helpful guidance for early Christians who were trying to match up their orthodoxy and their orthopraxy in consistent, congruent ways. Some even call this one of the first instances of the development of a Rule of Life.

This orthopraxis is both individual *and* collective. We don't have a Didache for Christians today, but when the Church takes orthopraxy seriously, it is expressed fully in upward, inward, and outward dimensions. All three dimensions are crucial to live robustly as an operating center of kingdom activity. One of three or two of three just won't cut it; the church will be malformed. We need all of them.

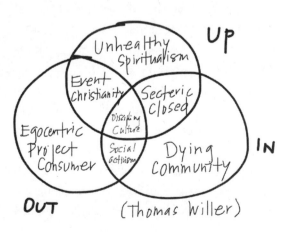

Our beliefs should always inform our actions. Churches usually skew one way or the other in their prioritization of either right doctrine or right living. Just like we need *both* justice and grace, we need *both* orthopraxy and orthodoxy working together symbiotically. This is what James communicated when he wrote, "Do not merely listen to the word, and so deceive yourselves. Do what it says" (James 1:22). As author Skye Jethani writes, orthodoxy without orthopraxy is nothing less than hypocrisy.[2] Additionally, Jesus tells a parable in a way which often makes many Christians squirm: it is our right *actions*, not our right beliefs, which separate the sheep from the goats (Matt. 25:31–46). And yet Romans, Galatians, and Ephesians reveal it is our faith in Christ Jesus' work on the cross, not our doing, which saves us.

So which is it? Does our salvation come from right believing or right living? The book of James wrestles through this tension (James 2:14–26). It was C. S. Lewis who answered this by stating it's like asking which blade in a pair of scissors is most necessary.[3] Both, of course. My favorite verses are 1 John 2:5–6: "This is how we know we are in him: Whoever claims to live in him must live as Jesus did." Too much orthodoxy and not enough orthopraxy leads

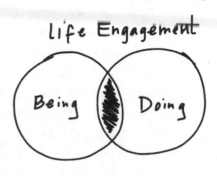

to hypocrisy and a lack of credibility; too much orthopraxy and not enough orthodoxy is dangerous. In order to cut, we need both blades of the scissors. As Jim Wallis often states, *faith works*. This ultimately leads us to an important question: is orthodoxy really orthodox if it does not lead to right action?

It is a mystery, this sacred overlap. How can two things be joined together as one? Orthoparadoxy.[4]

In order to trust God, we must learn to trust his paradoxical nature. As Alan Hirsch and Mark Nelson wrote, we will never understand any of these foundational truths about God if we cannot learn to live and love both mystery and paradox. What seems at first to be absurd or self-contradictory actually proves to be true. How? By holding what seem to be irreconcilable forces in tension.[5] Any attempt to resolve the paradox makes it untrue. God simply cannot be pinned down. He is bigger and greater and more wonderful than we can imagine him to be. It's truth and goodness and beauty. It's faith and hope and grace. It's love and truth and obedience. It is forgiveness and reconciliation and adoption into the family. It is restoration and mission and wholeness.[6] It is wonderful. It is perplexing. And that's the point. Krish Kandiah, in his book *Paradoxology*, sums it up best in these six questions:

> What if the tension between apparently opposing doctrines is exactly where faith comes alive? What if this ancient faith we call Christianity has survived so long not in spite of, but precisely *because of* its apparent contradictions? What if we have settled for neatly packaged, simplistic answers, instead of seeking out the deep and rich realities of our faith? What if it is in the difficult parts of the Bible that God is most clearly revealed? What if it is in and through our doubts that we learn the meaning of true relationship with the God who created us—of true worship? What if Christianity was never meant to be simple?[7]

Paradox is in our DNA, and the taproot of all of this is mystery. The basis of our Christian faith rests upon it.

One of my new favorite words is *portmanteau*, a large leather suitcase with openings in two equal parts. But this French word has another meaning: the seamless blending of two words or sounds to create an entirely new word—like brunch, motel, spork, manscaping, or edutainment. This overlaying existence gives us the opportunity to becoming living, breathing portmanteaus. For example, the mystery of this almond-shaped life means our days will be brimming with *simplexity*, both simplicity and complexity.[8] Living the *both/and* life can leave us feeling uncertain and vulnerable. And, as my brother says, when we believe rightly and also act rightly, we often end up feeling *terricited*.

CHAPTER 5

RESIDENT ALIENS

Too Christian, Too Pagan

> I didn't go to religion to make me happy. I always knew a bottle of Port would do that. If you want a religion to make you feel really comfortable, I certainly don't recommend Christianity.
>
> **—C. S. LEWIS, *GOD IN THE DOCK***

> I believe this moment is unlike any other time in history. Its uniqueness demands an original response. If we fail to offer a different way forward, we risk losing entire generations to apathy and cynicism.
>
> **—GABE LYONS**

I have friends who are considered aliens.

The United States IRS tax code uses an archaic term to designate foreigners who are legally granted permission to reside in the country while retaining citizenship in another: *resident aliens.* As great as these people are, and despite my best efforts, when I hear the word "aliens," I just can't fully scrape away the childhood mental images of green, one-eyed extraterrestrial creatures with antennae. As strange as this phrase may sound to my ears, it helps us capture the spiritual tension in the sacred overlap.

It was Paul who wrote in his opening greeting of his letter to the Ephesians "to God's holy people in Ephesus, the faithful in Christ Jesus" (1:1), emphasizing their dual earth/heaven identity as people who possessed an earthly ZIP code while still belonging to Christ. The apostle Peter also understood that the early followers of Jesus felt out of place and urged them to live faithfully in a pagan culture. He used a similar phrase, often stated in various Bible translations as *strangers, pilgrims, foreigners, sojourners, temporary residents,* or *exiles* (1 Peter 2:11). A few translations still retain the phrase "resident aliens." I wish more translations would use that phrase. But this is not just a New Testament reality. In the Old Testament, the nation of Israel was in bondage in Egypt and later hauled off into exile in Babylon, living as resident aliens in both places.

Stanley Hauerwas and Will Willimon address this topic in their book *Resident Aliens*. Though written a few decades ago, it has proven itself to be prescient. The authors write that when followers of Jesus Christ are baptized, their citizenship is transferred from one dominion to another; in the process they become resident aliens in the surrounding culture.[1] In our baptism, when we come up out of the water, dripping wet with matted hair and soaked clothes, it's as if the church hands us our green card.

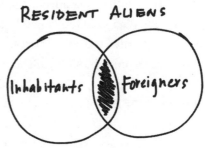

God's people, Israel, felt this disorienting displacement and the subsequent push-and-pull of their identity. Israel had left slavery in Egypt via the dramatic parting of the Red Sea. They were no longer slaves in Egypt, but they were not yet residents of the promised land. Instead, they wandered in the wilderness *for an entire generation.* The story of Israel, God's people, and their we're-not-slaves-but-we're-not-quite-fully-free identity is a mandorla story itself. Then, finally, freedom. Land. Home.

Generations later, the people of Israel were hauled off into exile in Babylon, a pagan country. We see in the Book of Jeremiah that God's call to Israel was to retain their foundational identity as God's people even though they were resident aliens in a foreign land. Christians tend to put a lot of focus on one particular verse from the twenty-ninth chapter of Jeremiah—verse eleven. Yes, God loves us enough to give us a hope and a future. And while it sounds wonderful and inspirational in a graduation card, sadly, this verse is often taken out of context. God wasn't promising graduating high school seniors they'd thrive as they head off to college in the fall; he was speaking directly to a large group of weary exiles living in a pagan land and wondering if God was still in control—and if he *was* in control, whether he still cared about them.

Despite their status as exiles, God tells them to stay put—put down roots, build houses, plant gardens. Get married, and put down roots. Have a family, raise your kids, and encourage them to bring grandchildren into the world. Seek the peace and flourishing of the local culture because if the local culture is at peace, you will be too (Jer. 29:5–9). God called Israel to build, to engage the culture with a posture of settled rootedness, even as they were living amidst the same people who hauled them off into captivity. God exhorted them to seek peace and pray, to live in a way which was focused on *shalom* in the present while also focusing on God's future intent.[2]

We, too, are spiritual exiles and resident aliens. We live here, but we don't really belong here. As C. S. Lewis wrote, if we find in ourselves a desire which no experience in this world can satisfy, the most probable explanation is that we were made for another world.[3] When we live faithfully in the way of Jesus, we feel tension: while we have a mailing address, the world is not our home. It is not the kind of tension we feel in situations of conflict or an emotionally charged conversation; it is much more like the tension that occurs when you stretch a rubber band. Neglecting to stretch the band means it will never serve its purpose, but stretch it too far, and it will snap. This is the kind of tension we feel when we wonder if we've gone too far—or not far enough. When we wonder aloud if we're doing it right—if we're being too Christian or too pagan— maybe that's exactly the space where we need to dwell.

Here we must pause and consider: is the world to be despised, dismissed, and disregarded as evil, or does God love the world, giving us license to enjoy much of what he has created? We must hold in tension the inherent goodness of creation—of what God himself made—and the subsequent moral corruption brought on by humanity. How are we to live in the midst of this reality? We don't write off the culture entirely, but we don't endorse it *carte blanche*, either. Thus, as resident aliens, we need wisdom to navigate the tension, knowing when to use the gas pedal and when to hit the brakes. The apostle Peter wrote this in one of his letters: "Live such good lives among the pagans that, though they accuse you of doing wrong, they may see your good deeds and glorify God on the day he visits us" (1 Peter 2:12). The faithful way of life in exile is to live *among* the pagans, not apart from them. But even as we live this good way of life, we need to come to expect that pagans will be upset with us. We will be misunderstood, our words will be misconstrued, our motives will be questioned—and we will be accused of wrongdoing because we will be disrupting and critiquing the status quo.[4]

But Peter also knew that retreating and sticking one's head in the sand was not the way to faithfully follow the risen Christ either. It's a different, more extreme position. It is the way of prophetic witness, which not only faithfully represents Christ to the world but also works to renew others within the community. We don't reject every element of the world in which we live (there are many good elements which exist, of course) and yet we don't fall madly in love with the world, either.

One of the vocational hats I wear is that of a leadership coach. As I work with hungry leaders around the country—pastors, attorneys, college vice-presidents, directors of nonprofits, church planters, Chick-fil-A operators—even a professional disc golf world champion—I have a series of incisive questions I ask to help leaders remain focused. One of the questions I ask frequently, which I've adopted from Andy Stanley, is "Is this a problem to be solved or a tension to be managed?" I ask this because *living the sacred overlap is seldom about fixing problems and almost entirely about living in the tension.* To the Pharisees and experts of the Law, religion was about solving moral and social problems. To them, the woman caught in adultery was a moral problem. To them, the woman wiping her hair on Jesus' feet was a social no-no. To them, Zacchaeus was an economic, political, and nationalistic problem. But Jesus didn't see people as problems. He came to do away with claustrophobic religion in order to give people true life and freedom. This drove the Pharisees and religious leaders up the wall because, in doing so, Jesus actually created *more* problems they felt the need to attempt to fix. And so their grandest idea for solving the problem of Jesus was to kill him.

What does all of this mean? How do we navigate between complete separation from the world and complete and mindless engagement with it? I've always been inspired by people who are fluent in other languages. I recently met someone in their twenties who knew six languages. *Six.* I have a hard enough time wrestling with words and putting them in proper order so that they make sense in English. But this mandorla life requires that we be fluent in the language of the kingdom *and also* the language of the culture. We are called to be bilingual.

Sometimes people use the word *exegesis* when talking about the

Bible. To *exegete* something means "to analyze or accurately interpret a word or passage and be able to explain it clearly to others." Seminaries work to train future pastors in biblical exegesis. Many healthy churches work to equip God's people in this, too. But not much energy or attention is given to teaching *cultural* exegesis. This requires a keen awareness of culture and forces us to engage in dual listening, where we study and perceive Scripture as well as study and perceive culture. This requires listening to the Spirit *and also* listening to the culture with a sound mind and a discerning heart. It's cross-cultural ministry without leaving your neighborhood. We don't have to memorize a thousand verses or have a degree in Old Testament theology, but we do need to be biblically and culturally bilingual.

I find myself returning to the book of Daniel frequently. As I read through it, I am growing to believe more than ever before that this book in particular needs to find a more central place in the lives of God's people. If we can release the sanitized Vacation Bible School versions of the stories from our mental cages—the fiery furnace and lions' den—we can begin to see the inspiring examples of those who lived in the tension of faithful obedience on the foreign soil of a pagan culture and see how these stories have implications for us today. Few books in our Bibles give us a clearer or more compelling vision of the mandorla life in our current cultural moment.

Daniel and his faith-filled friends remained steadfast against the Babylonian king's unfair and unjust laws, which ran counter to God's purposes. This put them at risk of losing their jobs, their reputations, and even their lives. Everything about Babylonian culture was different for them: a new place, new language, new customs, new diet. They were even given new names. Yet they handled themselves with grace, did their jobs professionally, and possessed great courage to stand up against these issues. They didn't complain, and they didn't act like victims. They suffered admirably but boldly. And with God's involvement, they rose to the top of the org chart. Daniel, a resident alien, resolved not to defile himself with the choice food and wine provided by the king (Dan. 1:8) and he spoke to the king with both wisdom and tact (2:14). Respect *and* conviction. Confidence *and* humility. Polite *yet* unwilling to obey the king.

A few years ago, during a trip to Kentucky, I met with the president of a Christian college who gave me a small print by British painter Briton Riviere, a riveting piece painted in 1890 titled *Daniel in the Lions' Den*. Free from any schmaltzy sentimentality, Riviere portrays in astounding detail the hungry lions, most notably their eyes. Just feet away from these beasts, Daniel's hands are bound behind his back. His head is lowered, and he exudes peace and calm. Riviere painted the scene again two years later, in 1892, titling the second piece *Daniel's Answer to the King*. Lions circling around him, Daniel stands with his hands bound, looking up into the light, from which we can assume the king's voice is coming. Daniel once again exudes confident tranquility. I carry these paintings with me in my mind, using them as triggers to prayer, that I may live with this same God-honoring tension.

But Daniel and his Jewish brothers weren't the only ones who lived as resident aliens in a virulent land. Jesus and his family lived as exiles in the land of Egypt.

The church is the place of belonging for resident aliens. It exists, as Hauerwas and Willimon write, as "an adventurous colony in a society of unbelief."[5] But it should not be as a colony seeking to huddle and cuddle and hope the world just leaves us alone. "When we are baptized," write Hauerwas and Willimon, we "jump on a moving train . . . We become part of a journey that began long before we got here and shall continue long after we are gone."[6] The train has been rumbling down the tracks for quite some time, and yet it bids us to run hard, grab hold, and hop on.

Living in this confusing space, we may at times experience some sort of identity crisis. Peter instructed resident aliens to avoid sin, living such upright and different lives that those around them would see their way of life and praise God because of it (see 1 Pet. 2:12). It sounds like he's advocating for a separatist approach here, but his encouragement is to submit to the government rulers in the land *and also* to live as free people. Live freely, he writes, but don't use it as a license to do whatever you please. Love your fellow believers, worship God, honor the emperor (2:13–17). That's a lot of embodied tension as resident aliens. But how would they know how to live this way? He instructed them to look to the example of Christ. He lived, he died, and he suffered. He bore our sins so we might die to sin and live honorable, holy lives. His wounds were the resolution, the healing for our wounds. It is within the context of the church that resident aliens become rooted in their identity in Jesus.

The church, immersed in God's story and commissioned to participate in God's mission, takes context seriously, committed to seeing the story of Scripture come alive in our current culture. Author and practitioner Mark Scandrette leads a Jesus community in San Francisco called ReImagine. Mark and other leaders convene on a regular basis to explore how to help committed followers of Jesus grow spiritually while at the same time engaging with others who are not yet on an expedition with Christ.[7] In order to explain their approach, they refer to each of these two spaces by colors. Yellow space refers to situations where Christianity focuses primarily on the personal world of faith. This includes individual rhythms, practices, and spiritual disciplines (reading Scripture, praying, participating in a church, etc.). Blue space refers to the times and places that are primarily others-focused (social justice, service, outreach, activism, etc.). ReImagine realizes that these spaces are not divided; they overlap. The community refers to those overlapping spaces of blue and yellow as green spaces and those who are committed to those spaces as green people, where context is both individual and collective, internally oriented as well as externally oriented, and where both the religious and the irreligious find connection, meaning, and commonality.[8] Green people who have been issued green cards.

It's no secret that the church in North America has lost a great deal of its cultural, moral, and spiritual influence over the past few decades. Because of this, we must boldly become green people. It has been said that the seven deadly words of the church are: *we've never done it that way before.* To paraphrase this kind of thinking, we have no interest in becoming green. It's too dicey. We'd like to remain yellow, thank you very much. As North American Christians, it's time to convene a family meeting to remind ourselves we aren't called to be docents of our denominational museums. We can no longer afford to remain yellow.

But there is hope on the horizon. Several churches are growing tired of embracing the church-as-we've-always-done-it approach. A growing number of them are stepping out of maintenance mode thinking. They are drawing on courage, wisdom, and compassion, moving toward and embracing this new way. They are turning those seven deadly words around and saying, with great joy and anticipation, "We've never done it that way before," and adding, "Let's try it and see what happens."

Instead of simply cloning existing forms of church, we need to cultivate and embrace new Jesus-saturated postures and approaches that meet people where they already are. The last thing I want to do is be a part of managing the decline of the Western church over the next several decades. But when we submit ourselves to the creative Holy Spirit and seek to plot good kingdom mischief on his behalf, the triune God smiles in agreement.

During our senior year of college, my then-fiancé (now my wife) and I went on a weekend winter retreat for college students at Spring Hill, a large Christian camp in central Michigan. We joined hundreds of college students from around the region, playing broom ball on an outdoor ice rink and listening to live music while we sipped lattes and hung out with friends late at night, only to rise the next day at the crack of noon. But the weekend retreat also included sessions with a speaker named Dick Staub. What he shared has stayed with me for almost two decades. Dick said that Christians often respond to culture in one of three inaccurate ways: we *withdraw*, where we retreat to our protective cocoon of comfort and when that comfort is threatened, we *combat*, spending our time intensely engaged in the culture wars; or we *conform*, assuming a chameleon-type posture in order to fit seamlessly with the culture around us. But he offered another option:

> Most Christians are either too Christian or too pagan. The Christians who are too Christian are very comfortable within the Christian subculture and are ill at ease when in the world. On the other hand, Christians who are too pagan are at ease with the world but fail to integrate their faith into their everyday life. Taking Jesus into our world requires fully engaging both our faith and the world, yet few of us have learned to live a fully integrated life of faith and the world. Paradoxically, in my experience those who wholeheartedly embark on this path will end up seeming both too Christian for their pagan friends and too pagan for their Christian friends.[9]

The too-pagan people think you've lost your mind; the too-Christian crowd thinks you've lost your faith. When our Christian friends question why we seem to be pushing the envelope so much while, at the same time, our friends who describe themselves as not very religious think we're taking this Jesus thing a little too far, we're probably in a place of healthy tension. Staub concluded: "The Christian who is too Christian doesn't love the world enough to enter fully into it, and the Christian who is too pagan doesn't love Jesus enough to make a difference while there."[10]

Being too Christian *and* too pagan is the essence of living in the midst of extremes. Similarly, the late Anglican priest, scholar, and author John Stott wrote that much of our troubles occur when we either pursue Christ and withdraw from the world, or we become preoccupied with the world and forget that we are also in Christ. We must remember we are in Christ *and also* in the world, where God has placed us on purpose.[11] What we are after is incarnation—a rejection of *excarnating* the gospel (completely retreating) and *carnalating* the gospel (doing as we please as we gorge ourselves at the all-you-can-eat moral buffet).

As Staub pointed out, the problem is that many Christians often don't have any irreligious friends and thus have an us-versus-them mindset. This leads to a whole array of distortions, not the least of which is how we think about our friendships. If we do have irreligious friends, we tend to see them as projects to complete rather than people to befriend and love.

But when the pendulum swings to the other side, we have the compromising (or accommodating) approach, a chameleon-like conformity to the ways of the world, which is equally problematic.[12] Paul addressed this head-on in his first letter to the Corinthian church. Man, did those early Christians have problems! Corinth, a city in Greece about an hour west of Athens, was a thriving metropolis in the first century. It boasted temples, theaters, baths, and markets. Over a thousand cult prostitutes were available to help people worship the goddess Aphrodite in the massive temple at the top of the hill. It was like the Las Vegas of the ancient world. What happened in Corinth stayed in Corinth.

Paul pleaded with these Jesus followers to make Christ central to their lives and practices. But Paul wasn't happy, especially when he learned that a man in the church was sleeping with his stepmom (1 Cor. 5:1–2). Paul chastised the church: they were to be set apart and different from the rest of the licentious Corinthians. They were to love those who sinned without entering into sin.[13] Instead of the little Jesus community being an example of hope for the world, the world had shaped and molded it into something it was never intended to be. Paul never asked the Gentile believers to become Jews. He encouraged them to keep their own identity. Yet he also knew a morally compromising approach just wouldn't cut it. When the church accommodates and compromises, it becomes, as Hauerwas and Willimon wrote pointedly, "a dull exponent of conventional secular political ideas with a vaguely religious tint."[14] *Too pagan.*

Fortunately, this has been modeled for us by Jesus, who was too religious for some and not religious enough for others. Jesus was a raging non-conformist. Nobody seemed to be able to put him into a box. When people tried to force him into one, he'd ask a deflecting question, tell a provocative story, throw down a theological hammer, or commit some social or religious *faux pas* on purpose, which sent religious leaders hissing. Jesus didn't fit in the pagan world, nor did he ever feel completely comfortable hanging out with the religious leaders of his day. The Pharisees and Sadducees looked down their noses because Jesus stayed out late partying with the irreligious. These were the spiritual leaders, the ones who asked, "Why does your teacher eat with tax collectors and sinners?" (Matt. 9:11). To the religious leaders, Jesus was a moral square peg in a religious round hole. But he responded by saying you don't go to the doctor when you feel healthy. "I have not come to call the righteous, but sinners," he said (Matt. 9:13). Jesus saw sick people and wanted to bring them health; the religious leaders saw healthy people and sought to make them religiously impressive yet spiritually sick.

The irreligious loved hanging out with Jesus—that is, until he tightened the screws by challenging them to a different way of life. At times, Jesus seemed to land on neither side of an issue, never fully pleasing the religious *or* the irreligious. He taught and interacted with saints in the synagogue *and also* clinked glasses with his buddies at the local brewery during happy hour. He kept the Torah *and also* ripped into the religious leaders. He hobnobbed with the rich and the powerful, and also touched lepers and allowed his feet to be anointed by a dishonorable woman. He intentionally healed people on the Sabbath in order to get a rise out of the religious elite. Is this maddening paradox, frustratingly confusing contradiction, or faithful overlapped living? Maybe it's all three. Jesus' perplexing peculiarity was the very thing which made his life so attractive, alluring, and impossible to ignore. Clearly, he was too much of a saint; and, in the eyes of the religious elites, he was also too much of a sinner.

In theory, it's easy for me to accept that Jesus doesn't seem to fit tidy categories, but when I think about the implications, it requires me to step back and assess my life in a way which often makes me squirm. Why? Because I, like most people, want to fit in. I don't want to stand out, be different, be on the receiving end of stares. If I am to receive Jesus' invitation, it will require me to give up my desire to live a normal life. Much of the time, that requires just about all the faith I can muster. But in moments of greater clarity, I remind myself that a normal life isn't what inspires me or others. On the days I am sane enough to speak the whole truth, I can admit I really don't want to live a normal life.

There is a real danger with true Christianity. When it's real, it's not safe. If we find ourselves following a safe Christ in a safe Christianity, we can be fairly certain we are not embracing the kind of Christianity Jesus offered. It can feel safe to live in a religious cocoon; it can be equally safe to claim to be a Christian but demonstrate no distinction in how we live compared to our non-Christian neighbors, friends, and coworkers. But living in God's Venn diagram involves much more. It reminds me of what Annie Dillard wrote in her book *Teaching a Stone to Talk*:

> On the whole, I do not find Christians, outside of the catacombs, sufficiently sensible of conditions. Does anyone have the foggiest idea what sort of power we so blithely invoke? Or, as I suspect, does no one believe a word of it? The churches are children playing on the floor with their chemistry sets, mixing up a batch of TNT to kill a Sunday morning. It is madness to wear ladies' straw hats and velvet hats to church; we should all be wearing crash helmets. Ushers should issue life preservers and signal flares. They should lash us to our pews. For the sleeping god may wake someday and take offense, or the waking god may draw us out to where we can never return.[15]

Christianity is a risk-filled adventure, indeed—crash helmets, life preservers, signal flares, and all. It's one of the reasons Jesus prayed specifically for his followers. He prayed that they would not be taken out of the world, but instead would engage with the world differently (John 17:11–19). It's from this passage where we get the well-worn phrase *be in the world but not of it*. Jesus' prayer is needed, especially in a religious landscape dominated by the two camps of legalism (keep the rules) and licentiousness (what rules?). Jesus knew we couldn't navigate this by ourselves. He knew he had to talk to the Father about our need for help. The way of Jesus is nestled between the extremes of enslaving legalism and mindless moral laziness.

Resident aliens live as green people in green spaces with our green cards firmly in hand.

CHAPTER 6

BEING PECULIAR

Inhabiting the Space between Normal and Weird

No man is strong unless he bears within his
character antitheses strongly marked.

—BLAISE PASCAL

How can you do things in the world that cause others
to write a cheerful question mark over your life?

—GRAHAM SMITH

Keep Portland Weird. If you've ever visited Portland, Oregon,
you've probably seen the billboards, bumper stickers, and
mugs proclaiming this motto. Portlanders are especially proud of
the unique cultural personality of their beloved city. Vermont and
Austin, Texas have gotten in on the fun and adopted their own
version of the phrase as well.

Michael Frost is a professor, writer, and key leader in the missional church movement of the past few decades.[1] A few years ago,
he wrote a short book titled *Keep Christianity Weird*, tipping his hat
to the Portland phenomenon. It's a helpful book, one I recommend,

and I see what he is going for with the title of his book. All too often, Christians are known for being too conventional, sitting down and mindlessly slurping the thin soup offered by the culture around us. Jesus did not have normal in mind when he was calling people to live under the new rule of the kingdom. Had reporters walked around the streets of first-century Galilean villages and asked residents to describe Jesus' life and teachings, nobody would have described the rabbi as being fairly conventional. I wholeheartedly agree with Frost on the point that we should *not* be normal. Paul, writing to the Christians in Rome, who lived at the epicenter of worldly culture of their day, challenged the faithful to make sure they weren't thoughtlessly being shaped into the likeness of Rome:

> So here's what I want you to do, God helping you: Take your everyday, ordinary life—your sleeping, eating, going-to-work, and walking-around life—and place it before God as an offering. Embracing what God does for you is the best thing you can do for him. Don't become so well-adjusted to your culture that you fit into it without even thinking. Instead, fix your attention on God. You'll be changed from the inside out. Readily recognize what he wants from you, and quickly respond to it. Unlike the culture around you, always dragging you down to its level of immaturity, God brings the best out of you, develops well-formed maturity in you. (Rom. 12:1–2, MSG)

Our calling is, as Dr. Martin Luther King Jr. wrote, to be *transformed non-conformists*.[2] Sadly, for the most part, Christianity in Western culture has largely become a confirmation of the status quo and business as usual.[3] Our kingdom orientation necessitates that we push against the status quo. For a long time, we've been purchasing our mental furniture from the factories of Hollywood and Silicon Valley. The world most definitely does *not* need more normal Christians around.

And yet, it's the last word of the title of Frost's book I just can't quite embrace. I don't believe *weird* is what we're after. Many people already perceive followers of Jesus to be far from normal. They see Christians as Bible-toting Oompa Loompas, as people who are in need of doubling their medication. The world doesn't need a growing supply of religious people who were normal three cats ago. Put me down as someone who thinks one snake-handling church is one too many.

When I think of weird, I think of Burning Man, IKEA shopping carts, goat yoga, and how asparagus makes your urine smell. When I think of weird people, those who still have active Juno email accounts immediately come to mind. So do people who use only their index fingers when using air quotes, adults who go to amusement parks by themselves, and those who like kombucha but not fish tacos. On occasion, *weird* is a compliment, but not most of the time. Weirdness can make me chuckle at times, but when things are truly weird, I tense up. I'm not entirely afraid of weird people, but I wouldn't say I'm calm or relaxed around them, either. My initial subconscious reaction is to pull back. *Weird* is often synonymous with *bizarre, strange, creepy,* or even *repulsive.* Just because we seek to live lives shaped like an almond doesn't mean we have to be nuts.

Frost affirms that we aren't to be zany or wacky—and he's right. The world, he says, is getting tired of stupid stunts and religious mania. Christians have been more than willing to look like maniacs.[4] Conventional Christians, no. But *weird* Christians? Not that, either. Maybe my blade is just a bit too sharp here in splitting hairs—if so, forgive me. I get the heart behind what Frost is saying, but what if there's a space *between* normal and weird? I believe there's a better word out there for us to hang our collective hats on.

To be fair to Frost, he introduced me to the insights of Richard Beck. Beck uses a word to describe our Christian identity which I find fits a bit better: *eccentric.*[5] The word comes from two Greek words—*ek* (out of) and *kentron* (center). To be eccentric is to be *out of the center.* In the late Middle Ages, the word was used mostly as an astronomical term to describe the orbit of planets and the fact that the earth was not at the center of the universe. Scientifically speaking, Copernicus' theory of the earth revolving around the sun was seen as eccentric. But more than astronomy, it has also carried geometric connotations which imply a location outside of the center of an object, most often a circle.[6] When Jesus becomes the center of our lives, it seems everything else in our lives becomes off-centered; in essence, we become eccentric.

As Frost points out, to live this way is a new orbit, where we are displaced—and replaced—by God at the center. And, he says, in this displacement followers of Jesus act in strange and unusual ways in relation to the current cultural norms. When we do this we live questionable lives.[7] In addition to using the word *weird,* Frost describes God as being eccentric:

> God is not an American or Australian. God is not middle class. God is not black. Or white. Or poor. Or rich. Or Southern Baptist. Or Pentecostal. Or Republican. Or Democrat. Or any of the other containers we try to put him in. He's an eccentric God, and an eccentric God is free—truly, utterly free.[8]

The word eccentric is better than weird, but it's still not quite right. I'd like to propose another word instead: *peculiar.* Yes, technically, the definition of peculiar can connote weird, but in its culturally nuanced form, peculiarity is much more about being *unique, uncommon, unusual, different,* or *distinctive.* It is a radically distinctive orientation—more

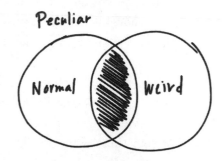

whimsy than strange. When I smell something peculiar, I'm not turned off; instead, I'm intrigued and want to keep smelling it until I figure out its source, to discover exactly what it is and where it's coming from. Certainly, we are not the center of the universe (though sometimes we behave like we believe we are), but we shouldn't live at the center of the circus ring, either. Frost writes that we should seek to be winsome and weird.[9] Maybe being peculiar is nothing more than to be charmingly eccentric, whimsical, and distinct.

Pastor and author Tim Keller wrote about the peculiar nature of the early church:

> The early church was strikingly different from the culture around it in this way—the pagan society was stingy with its money and promiscuous with its body. A pagan gave nobody their money and practically gave everybody their body. And the Christians came along and gave practically nobody their body and they gave practically everybody their money.[10]

Outside of Jesus and my family—and maybe fish tacos—I have three passions: to equip and invest in hungry leaders, to grow fruit on other people's trees, and to collaborate to create good kingdom mischief. When I mention that last one to people, they often cock their heads, furrow their brows, and ask, "Good kingdom mischief?" Yep. I like to make messes and start crazy things so that Jesus is honored and the kingdom is more fully realized on earth. In a sense, even my passions are peculiar—and I love that. It's a blast. You don't need a special job to do stuff like that. You can just follow Jesus in the overlap.

Idiosyncratic faith is found in the overlap in that it's both normal and weird—*it doesn't fit into either category perfectly*. People often fear "weird," but "peculiar" incites curiosity and interest. There is something about peculiar people that is intriguing. When

I leave their presence, I continue thinking about them. I notice they are different. I am unable to put them into a clearly defined category. *Why are they the way they are? Who are they, really?* They don't seem to fit the mold; they don't quite fit the status quo. I am not turned off by them. In fact, it's quite the opposite; usually I want to know more about them and what makes them tick. These people raise my level of curiosity. They always force me to ask more and deeper questions than before. It's because there is an attractiveness, rather than a repulsion, to peculiarity. When we live with faithful peculiarity, it offers the world an alluring tableau of Christ and his kingdom. We are off-center from fitting in seamlessly with culture, and yet we aren't so off-center that we're seen as weird. When we live as kingdom agents, we are not normal, but people often want to engage further with us and know more about us. As Stanley Hauerwas and Will Willimon write, we are a people who follow an odd God, and the church's oddness is essential to our faithfulness.[11]

Finding the tension point that enables us to live a peculiar life requires large doses of emotional and contextual intelligence. Emotional intelligence is the ability to be aware of other people's perceptions and to control our actions and emotions in order to manage relationships with empathy and tact. With low emotional intelligence, our best efforts can be interpreted by others as awkward, annoying, or offensive without us even knowing it. It's deeper than mere wisdom; it's keen self-awareness. We've all been around kind people who are socially tone deaf, failing to realize what everyone else knows: they are way off-key. Contextual intelligence is similar: we must be aware of our surroundings, aware of the connections, networks, rituals, and rhythms of the people around us, and be keenly aware of how our actions are impacting others and vice versa. Yes, be different, but by all means please don't be *weird*. Be child-like, not childish.

While *weird* and *eccentric* aren't words you'll find in Scripture, the word *peculiar* can be found in Scripture. First Peter in the KJV translation reads, "But ye are a chosen generation, a royal priesthood, an holy nation, a peculiar people" (1 Peter 2:9). How was the nation of Israel to be a peculiar people? By living differently from their surrounding pagan neighbors, with the posture of resident aliens.

When I read the Gospels, I'm led to believe that people weren't attracted to Jesus and his ministry just because he was full of compassion and grace. They were also attracted to him because he was peculiar—he was different from anyone they had ever met before. He was intriguing and unforgettable. He incited curiosity. The only way people could begin to understand Jesus was to engage with and experience him firsthand. Because of his peculiarity, people told others, you are just going to have to experience him yourself. Come and see. One problem today is that the church often runs after popularity but seldom considers what it would mean to strive for peculiarity.

Jesus tells us we should live our lives in such a way that we don't fit in with the ways of the world. We *should* stick out. We are to be as shrewd as serpents and as innocent as doves. Dr. Martin Luther King Jr. penned, "We must combine the toughness of the serpent and the softness of the dove, a tough mind and a tender heart."[12] King stated that if God was only toughminded, he would be a cold, passionless despot. If he was only a tenderhearted God, he would be too soft and sentimental to do anything when the world went wrong. But the good news is that God is both. And when God's people are both toughminded and tenderhearted, we become something the world has rarely experienced: snakes *and* doves. Thus, we become peculiar.

In the Sermon on the Mount, Jesus unpacks how his peculiar people are to live. When God's rule and reign are on display and the kingdom is present, it means rejoicing, even in the midst of persecution and suffering. It means forgiving and embracing the other. It means turning the other cheek rather than striking back.

It means cheerfully giving away your coat, going the extra mile when you don't have to. What makes it even more peculiar is he urges us as peculiar people to participate in his peculiar mission.[13] When Christians live with appropriate peculiarity by representing the peculiarity of Jesus, we carry ourselves differently. People raise their eyebrows and cock their heads, often not because we are offensive or annoying, but because we don't fit into their preconceived notions. Our lives should incite curiosity. When you're peculiar, you are categoryless.

Emmanuel Katongole wrote about the role of the church after the horrific genocide of 1994 in his homeland of Rwanda:

> The community in Antioch brought together Jews and Samaritans, Greeks and Romans, slaves and free, men and women in a way that was so confusing that people around them didn't know what to call them. So they called them "Christians." The only way they knew how to describe their peculiar actions was to say that they were followers of an odd preacher from Galilee. The world is longing for such new and odd communities in our time. . . . I pray the time is now and that the resurrection might begin in us.[14]

To be peculiar is to be, quite literally, uncategorizable.

So how exactly do we become peculiar without being weird—yet without being normal, either? How do we find the sweet spot in the midst of the tension? These are important questions for us to explore. But before we do this, we have to talk about assumptions and values.

As we explored earlier, posture matters. If you have ever taken a communications class, you may remember there are three forms of interpersonal communication: verbal, paraverbal, and body language. UCLA psychology professor Albert Mehrabian published a famous study which found 7 percent of our communication is verbal (our words), 38 percent paraverbal (our tone, timbre, and pitch) and a whopping 55 percent of our communication is non-verbal (our body language).[15] It's often referred to as the 7/38/55 rule, or the Mehrabian rule, although calling it the rule of communication has made some a bit uncomfortable. Our words reveal what we know, but our tone and body language reveal what we actually *believe*—our values and our priorities. Indicators of non-verbal communication are often referred to as *tells* because they do just that: they tell others a great deal about what we think and feel. The Puritan Joseph Hall had a profoundly simple phrase Dr. Mehrabian would appreciate: *God loveth adverbs.* Not just what we do but *how* we do things matters to God. It matters to people, too. If we speak of Christ's love for the world and for the people around us but our posture reveals condescension and judgment, the world becomes confused by what we are saying. Our posture must match our words, and our words must match our posture.

One of the verses I find myself repeating most frequently is James 1:5: "If any of you lacks wisdom, you should ask God, who gives generously to all without finding fault, and it will be given to you." If we don't know what to do or how to say it or when to act on it or whom to speak with, we are to ask the Father, who is generous and faultless and promises to give to those who ask. This promise is available to us as we try to navigate this new way of living. In fact, it is impossible to live the God-honoring *both/and* life without wisdom.

But we need more than just wisdom; we need the courage to act. To live holy lives, as we are called to do, means to be separate, different, distinct, set apart from the rest of the world. This is part of what it means to live into our sacred eccentricity. But this way of life means more than simply living in our camps, checking our moral boxes, and pointing fingers at The Other. It means being holy *without* being holier than thou.

As a white American male, I don't pretend to believe I'm the expert in mandorla living. Our African American brothers and sisters are often exemplars in this way of life. You can't read books like Howard Thurman's *Jesus and the Disinherited* without feeling the pain of his collective experience and also feeling inspired by the hope and the courage of living in the middle.[16] African Americans have been—and sadly, often continue to be—socially, legally, economically, and politically marginalized. Being told you are less than human, while at the same time retaining your identity in God as treasured sons and daughters of the King, takes extraordinary courage. As Thurman wrote, "The awareness of being a child of God tends to stabilize the ego and results in a new courage, fearlessness, and power. I have seen it happen again and again."[17]

I find myself praying often, asking God to give me appropriate measures of both wisdom and courage. Even so, I feel my life lacks robustness. If I live wisely and courageously but lack compassion, my witness falls flat. It can feel self-serving and people can feel taken advantage of—a seemingly well-intentioned but dissonant cymbal. Wisdom without courage is riskless, and courage without wisdom is reckless, but wisdom and courage combined with compassion is priceless.

We need wisdom, compassion, and courage—but we also need a guide to make the sojourn with us: the Holy Spirit. Some of you may be thinking, *Oh, no. Here comes the kooky stuff.* Let me try to settle your nerves a bit. I get it. Maybe you grew up in the kind of church I did, where the Trinitarian expression of God's essence was the Father, Son, and Holy Scripture (or maybe for

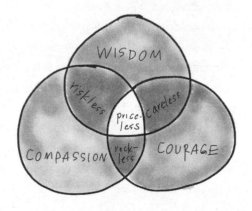

your faith tradition it was Father, Son, and Self-Reliance). Sadly, I spent many years of my life in fear of the Holy Spirit. Instead of believing the Spirit was peculiar, relational, and good, I was led to believe the Spirit was downright weird, moody, and untrustworthy. Cherith Fee Nordling describes people who believe in the Father and the Son but minimize the role of the Holy Spirit as "binitarian" Christians.[18] Nobody taught me this overtly, but I picked it up through the actions, inactions, and parenthetical statements of people at my church. I learned to believe that a Spirit-filled time at church might lead people to feel such deep emotions that they might be tempted to stand up and run around the sanctuary naked during worship. So I kept my distance.

Fortunately, over the past decade of my life, there's been no area of my adventure with Jesus which has grown more than in learning to trust and experience the Holy Spirit. I've been able to see the truth of the Spirit and let go of the numerous deep-seeded lies and fears I'd held to. I've come to grips with the fact that I can experience freedom in the Spirit and not have my brains fall out.

When I began to understand the Trinitarian reality, I realized *everything the Spirit does is an effort to point people toward Jesus.* Since the Trinity cannot be in conflict with itself, everything the Spirit does is Jesus-centered. With this, I could begin to relax. Sure, there were—and are—uncomfortable moments when I'm trusting the Spirit, but *those moments are still centered on and rooted in truth and Jesus.* Looking back, I don't know how I was able to live all those years without an awareness of the role of the Spirit in my life. Certainly, the Spirit was present, working patiently behind the scenes, accommodating my misunderstanding, helping me grow. I just didn't realize it at the time. I don't know how *any* follower of Jesus can live faithfully and freely without full, daily submission to the Spirit and an awareness of his presence in our lives. When new wine is being poured, we've got to be willing to offer new wineskins to hold what the Spirit so graciously offers (Matt. 9:17).

Jesus tells us in John 14 he has entrusted his followers with a Paraclete. The Greek word *parakletos* [para-CLAY-tos] doesn't have a one-to-one translation in the English language, but its essence can be understood as a kind of combination of teacher, friend, encouraging guide, and emboldener. The Paraclete is a good counselor, one who guides us in those extreme tensions. We're also told the Spirit is the comforter. For years I took this to mean he was my holy security blanket, to which I could cling when I was scared, anxious, or overwhelmed. I could run to my bed and pull the Spirit covers over my head and hide. While the Spirit does comfort in times of worry and fear, I've come to see the Spirit as one who provides comfort through encouragement, one who *emboldens* his followers to keep going. Like a trainer at a boxing match, the Spirit is in our corner, working with us, persuading us not to give up. Between rounds, the Spirit refreshes us, reminds us, encourages us, gives us perspective, and helps us remain hopeful and faithful. Sometimes the Spirit wipes our face with a towel; other times we're handed the spit bucket. Openness and surrender to the Spirit is what adds to our peculiarity.

Avoid being weird and stay away from being normal.

Being peculiar is what we're after.

FAITHFUL WITNESS

Living the Right Preposition

We must live in the kingdom of God in such a way
that it provokes questions for which the gospel is
the answer.

—LESSLIE NEWBIGIN

———

Let love and faithfulness never leave you;
bind them around your neck,
write them on the tablet of your heart.

—PROVERBS 3:3

I never imagined someone would want to kill me; I also never imagined someone would admit it to me over breakfast.

On a recent Saturday morning at the park, I bumped into a man who, two years prior, had informed me he was so angry with me, he wanted me killed. It was, needless to say, a brief and awkward conversation. He doesn't attend our church anymore, and fortunately, he doesn't feel the same way about me now (at least, that's what he told me).

At the time he told me he wanted to kill me, I had just returned from a three-month-long pastoral sabbatical. This man had stored up so much venomous hatred toward me, he hoped I would not return to the church after my sabbatical. He distrusted my leadership and was bitterly displeased with the vision and direction of the church. He hoped—even prayed—I would quit ministry or take another position elsewhere. When he learned I would continue serving in my role as pastor, he wanted to kill me.

He shared this with me, man-to-man, over pancakes, bacon, and less-than-memorable coffee. The conversation, however, was unforgettable. It wasn't the playfully hyperbolic *I'm-gonna-kill-you* we yelled as kids when we chased our friends around the playground. This was real. Our table at that diner became his confession booth. He was vulnerable and remorseful for what he had seriously considered doing to me.

A mentor once told me that when I entered the ministry, I must be ready to preach, pray, and die at a moment's notice. I'd done the first two, and I wondered if maybe my time had arrived for the third. I told the man I appreciated his repentant heart (for many reasons, some of them selfish), but his confession had cracked and scrambled my emotional eggs. It left me shaken for weeks. In the aftermath, fear would work its way into my mind, wash over me, and at times overwhelm me. *Somebody wanted me dead.* As someone who already lives with a natural propensity for fear and anxiety, I found it deeply unsettling. I was so rattled, I hardly told a soul. It took me three weeks and a two-pound bag of Twizzlers to finally work up the courage to tell my wife. Years afterward, I could still sit down at my kitchen table, reflect on the event, and cry.

When I bumped into him that Saturday morning in the park, with our jackets zipped up and our winter caps pulled snug over our ears, I tried to bracket my discomfort, but all the details of our breakfast conversation charged back into my mind. The confession, the look on his face, even the bad coffee. As we finished our brief but awkward conversation, I wondered if maybe, just maybe, I had been doing something right after all. Maybe the point isn't to spend our days in futile attempts to please everybody. Anyone who tries to please everyone is asking for trouble. The evidence of a life of sacred overlap is learning to expect that people will be intensely angry at times. It may even mean people on *both sides* of an issue won't like you (but hopefully not to that level of intensity).

Our brief conversation also made me think a great deal about people, especially religious leaders who live with death threats every day. One of my professors in seminary had served as a missionary for several decades in two hostile countries in South Asia. In class, he told stories of the death threats he received and what it was like to learn of the horrific news of his colleagues who had been murdered. Jesus lived under the regular threat of death, from religious leaders no less, who plotted to kill him (and in the name of God). Even Jesus' friends, fearing for his safety, pleaded with him to avoid certain places at certain times. He was a marked man. Paul was under constant threat of arrest and death as well.

As rattled as I was by my would-be killer's diner confession, and as much as I'd never wish such an experience on anyone, maybe when we're following Jesus in between the extremes, these kinds of things come as counterintuitive affirmation of a mandorla life. Maybe I shouldn't be all that surprised.

Jesus desires to establish his rule and reign from heaven to earth, and he's chosen an instrument by which this is to happen: the church. His vision is to use faithful followers who long to see this heaven-to-earth-right-now reality occur. This is revolutionary.

The word radical comes from the Latin word *radix*, meaning "root." *Radicalis* meant "of or pertaining to the root, or having roots" and was used primarily in agrarian contexts. When someone declares they are making a radical change, it means they want to get to the root of the issue. About a year ago, I came across a book titled

The Quest for the Radical Middle, which recounts the history of the Vineyard, a movement of Spirit-led churches over the past few decades under the leadership of the late John Wimber. I did not grow up in a Vineyard church, but learning about the movement through friends in seminary compelled me to pick up the book. The "radical middle" is not some wishy-washy fad or neutered version of a Christianity which can't make up its mind or take a truth-grounded stand on issues. Neither does it suggest we strive for some sort of meet-in-the-middle compromise in an attempt to appease everyone. The radical middle is actually about living into *both* realms—which actually requires more courage, not less.[1] What makes it so radical is how difficult it is to remain in it over the long haul. Christians throughout history have found this difficult to do, tending to pull toward one extreme or the other. We're often pushed to choose in order to minimize uncertainty and discomfort. But living in the radical overlap is learning to discern and embrace both God's *yes* and God's *no* at the same time.

The Vineyard Movement, as far as I can tell, continues to look to Jesus, who modeled for humanity that the Word and the Spirit are in proper relationship to one another, as its model for living in the tension between the extremes. The words are in the midst of the voice of the Spirit, and the Spirit blows in accordance with the parameters of the Word. Both live in dynamic tension. From the beginning, Satan's strategy has been to challenge these tensions. Satan attempts to pit the Word against the Spirit, reason against experience, organization against organism. Yet the challenge remains to make sure the affirmation of both the Word *and also* the Spirit lands in the radical middle.[2]

This resonates with me, yet it reminds me once again that this way of living leaves us vulnerable to being misunderstood and disliked, to not having a tribe or even a trench into which we can retreat when situations get dicey. It not only leaves us vulnerable, it can also leave us exhausted. My buddy Jon used to like the phrase "the radical middle," but now he's replaced it with "the time-intensive middle" instead. This space requires us to take more time to think and listen, more time to pray and converse. It necessitates greater compassion. The *both/and* life isn't fast, efficient, or easy. It requires excruciating patience.

If we're to live between the extremes, we have to possess a compelling *why*. If not, we'll buckle and retreat to the trenches of one of the extremes. At times, this can sound appealing.

We can have all the right information; we can do all the right things, crossing our theological t's and dotting our moral i's; but if we fail to understand that posture is crucial in this space, we will be ineffective, unfruitful, confusing, unloving and, at times, offensive. *Why* is crucial, but so is *how*. Posture isn't about what we know; it's about how we feel, about what is important to us. Posture is about our values, priorities, and motivations—the emotional, social and, yes, sometimes audible, tone in which our lives speak. This, of course, involves our physical posture as well.

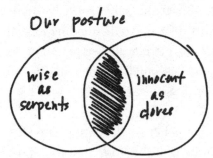

At times, Christians (me included) have done a poor job of stewarding the message of the good news of Jesus. The primary turnoff hasn't necessarily been what we've said, but *how* we've said it; our overall attitude leaks out of our disposition, whether we realize it or not. Should we be surprised when the world becomes confused if we speak of a loving God with a hostile tone or we speak of a humble Jesus in a condescending manner? With a nod to Marshall McLuhan, the postural medium is the theological message. Why the disconnect? *Incongruence.* Our posture has not matched our message.

When we live as carefully and soulfully as possible, our posture is more important than we often realize. I like the posture of The Meeting House, a church in Hamilton, Ontario, which states that it is boldly honest, eagerly hopeful, and relentlessly Jesus-centered. When Christians talk about evangelism, we don't talk often enough about the vital importance of posture. If we believe people are projects to be won over or agendas to be conquered, it doesn't matter what we say or how well we say it; our posture will communicate to others that we are disconnected and disingenuous, thus making our message unappealing. If we are angry or afraid of our neighbors, our posture will communicate to them more than enough before we open our mouths.

In first-century Palestine, there were four main Jewish sects: the Pharisees, the Sadducees, the Zealots, and the Essenes. The Pharisees believed that the way to love Yahweh was to keep the Law perfectly, separating themselves from immorality. The Sadducees believed the Temple was the center of Jewish life (which is why, when the Temple in Jerusalem was destroyed, much of the sect fell apart as well). The Sadducees didn't believe in the supernatural—angels, demons, resurrection, heaven, hell, miracles, healing, etc. They were religious sellouts, accommodating and making deals with the Roman Empire in an attempt to preserve power.

The Zealots were driven by pragmatism and violence, believing it was their God-given duty to kill anyone who interfered with the establishment of a religious kingdom on earth or who treated God's people poorly (which, in the first century, would have been the Romans). They hid daggers in their clothes and sought to bless God by taking out the Romans when situations presented themselves. They were like the Jewish version of ISIS and the Taliban. And lastly, there were the Essenes, which were like the Amish of the first century. Even the religious nature of Jerusalem was too liberal for them. Disgusted by what they saw, they sought to escape and retreated, quite literally, from the culture. They established their own remote religious colony down by the Dead Sea to remove themselves from the impurities of the world in order to remain pure and worship God faithfully.

The Pharisees were the sect Jesus slammed the most in the Gospels. And yet, what's most interesting—and disorienting—is that the group Jesus was most closely aligned with theologically was the Pharisees. Ironically, Jesus didn't spend a great deal of time railing against their *theology*. Jesus taught his followers that they should be careful to do everything the Pharisees tell them to do, but he also added, "But do not do what they do, for they do not practice what they preach" (Matt. 23:3). Do as they say, not as they do. Jesus' main issue with the Pharisees and teachers of the Law was not the content of their teaching; it was their *posture* and *attitude*. Their hearts were incongruent with their beliefs. Doing the right thing the wrong way can quickly become the wrong thing. Quite simply, Jesus said, *how* matters.

While our posture matters, so do our prepositions. Skye Jethani has said that when we get our prepositions wrong, we get Christianity wrong. We are tempted to do things *for* God, and we live our lives with the hidden (and sometimes not-so-hidden) motivation to impress God, trying to get him to raise his divine eyebrows and nod with approval. By looking to impress God, we are tempted to believe that if we work harder or do better or we pray more or fill-in-your-own-moral-blank-here, he will love us a little bit more than he did yesterday. This is religion, but it is most certainly not the Gospel.

Instead, the Gospel is fleshed out as we live *with* God. When I am stuck in prayer, feeling as though my words are useless and bouncing back at me like tennis balls on the side of a brick wall, I simply remember that prayer—and life—is assuming a *with God* posture. If I can eliminate *for* and insert *with*, I begin to understand the kind of freedom Jesus so freely offered to us. But living with God doesn't mean we don't do anything. It was Dallas Willard who often liked to say that grace is not opposed to *effort*; it is opposed to *earning*.[3] The Gospel is not against work; it is against the motive of seeking to earn God's favor. In fact, in Scripture we're told we *should* work hard, for we are co-laborers with Christ (1 Cor. 3:9). Work is not bad; what are often wrong are our motivations for why we do what we do. How wonderfully freeing it is when I actually grasp that this is the way of Jesus.

It's tempting to bifurcate our work between the secular and the spiritual, but in doing so, we can become theologically claustrophobic—even heretical. In the first century, a heresy emerged called dualism.[4] This approach divided the world into two antithetical parts or principles, believing one part of our lives is spiritual, while the other part is not. It is the foundation stones of *either/or* thinking. In doing so, we are led to ask, what does worship have to do with work?[5] Over the years, people have often said to me self-deprecatingly that they are "not a pastor like me." They are "just" an electrician or an insurance agent or a teacher or an engineer or a stay-at-home mom. I smile but politely correct them: "You are not *just* a fill-in-the-blank. In the eyes of God, nobody is a *just somebody*." In Hebrew, there's no word for "spiritual." The mindset of the authors of Scripture is that there's no dividing out certain areas of our lives and throwing them into bins marked either *secular* or *spiritual* (although our actions can be either sacred or desecrated).

With a vision of the *both/and* life, we possess dignity in our work. We are not merely checking things off a to-do list or fulfilling our job descriptions; instead, we are joining with God and his mission even as we go about our daily activities. I respond to the people who tell me they are *just somebodies* by reminding them they are beloved children of God, that they are missionaries cleverly disguised as people who install electrical wiring in office buildings or who change dirty diapers. Some have called this vocational holiness, which is a theologically fancy way of saying that we take God with us wherever we go (or, maybe better stated, God takes us with him wherever he goes). We don't do this in some nebulous or general way. I love the way author and theologian Tish Warren Harrison writes about this:

> We grow in holiness in the honing of our specific vocation. We can't be holy in the abstract. Instead we become a holy blacksmith or a holy mother or a holy physician or a holy systems analyst. We seek God in and through our particular vocation and place in life.[6]

The Benedictine monks used a Latin phrase to describe their life's work: *ora et labora* (prayer and work).[7] We are likely to have the mental picture of monks walking around old monasteries wearing brown bathrobes, sporting bad haircuts, and chanting off-key prayers. However, we have much to be grateful for in what these monks can teach us about our work; none of us is a *just somebody*. The monks possessed—and still possess—a strong work ethic and believed their work should honor God as much as their prayers. A fourteenth-century monk by the name of Walter Hilton exchanged letters with a man who felt he was a *just somebody*; the man was convinced he should leave his current life and go live in a religious community, believing it would make him more spiritual, more connected to God. But Hilton encouraged him to stay put, right where he was, to live "a third way, a mixed life combining the activity of Martha with the reflectiveness of Mary."[8] Work and worship are not separate; they are complements. God wants us to *ora*, no matter where we *labora*.

God values his creation so much that he not only blesses us, but he also sends us. It's part of his nature. We are blessed and sent in our jobs, roles, and responsibilities. The mission of God doesn't just shape our lives; it shapes our work, too. The mission of God in the everyday.

Three mornings a week, I swim at the Y. Every Monday, Wednesday, and Friday, I enter the pool area, my nostrils recognizing the pungent smell of chlorine and my skin detecting a level of heat and humidity in which one could grow orchids. I chat briefly with Bob, head coach of the Lansdale Catholic High School swim team, who take up most of the lanes in the winter months. While they seem to skim effortlessly across the top of the water like a pod of dolphins, I bob sluggishly like a stiff manatee. I share a lane with Morgan, who swims much faster and much longer than I do; we're the only swimmers in the water who aren't teenagers. I always feel rather old and slow. Truth be told, I *am* rather old and slow.

As I tie the strings on the waistband of my swimsuit, press on my goggles to enhance the suction around my eyes, and slide into the chilly water to begin another workout on my liquid track, it gives me space and time to think and pray about the day ahead, brainstorm new ideas, and reflect upon complex problems. Several of the ideas in this book were developed between flip-turns. My brain, and my life, often have too many tabs open at the same time, and swimming helps me exit out of a few of the unnecessary ones. My prayer life is usually pretty sharp during these times, too, where I ask God for the gracious provision of my needs—most notably, oxygen—between my gasps for air.

Last week I was deep in thought, somewhere between lap twelve and thirteen, about how we can best discern how to live in the *and also* life. I realized once again that this kind of life requires—and embraces—tension. Everyone seems to avoid tension, but new solutions are found in the midst of tension, not apart from it. Between strokes I pondered questions: *How are we to live in the midst of the tension between being overly structured on one end and just winging it on the other end? How are we to bring the extremes together in a kind of tension which is good and healthy?* If life is full of paradox, then we'll need regular helpings of wisdom to help us discern how to live in the midst of these sacred ambiguities. As I swam, and Morgan passed me yet again, I thought about the *either/or* dynamic found in Scripture, most specifically in Proverbs. The rhythmically poetic words of chapter 10 contrast the wise and the foolish, the righteous and the wicked. But there are other proverbs which don't follow this *either/or* mentality. I remembered two oddly placed proverbs, back-to-back, in Proverbs 26:

> Do not answer a fool according to his folly,
>   or you yourself will be just like him.
> Answer a fool according to his folly,
>   or he will be wise in his own eyes.

Yes, answer a fool. No, don't do it. Is this relational inconsistency? Biblical schizophrenia? We can't slap a lifeless and thoughtless paint-by-numbers approach onto godly living. As I spent lap after lap pondering this, I realized it requires a life of discerning, assessing, and living in the tension. I wonder if Olympic swimmers think such thoughts as they swim laps at 6 a.m.

Embracing the *ora et labora* of the *missio dei* ("mission of God") means we have to live in the mess, with a lack of certainty much of the time. And the messiness will mess with us. Messiness is hard for me. I'm an Enneagram 1, if you're into that sort of thing. These kinds of messes have ruined many potentially good nights of sleep. They hold my thoughts and feelings hostage and demand a steep ransom. I want peace and certainty and clearly defined perimeters in my life. I want to tighten things, clarify the uncertainties, and fix the problems as quickly and efficiently as possible. And yet, when I reflect upon my life, I realize that if I truly want to submit to God in all areas of my life—not just the easy ones or the areas that make sense to me—then I will embrace being well outside my climate of comfort. The sacred overlap is, to coin a term, *messesary*. Several years ago, pastor and author John Ortberg taught on servant leadership (a mandorla approach itself) and shared four tensions we all must live in: (1) decisive submissiveness, (2) tough-minded accountability and tender-hearted compassion, (3) resourceful dependence, and (4) embracing a posture of relaxed urgency.[9] As great as these tensions sound, we need discernment to know how to navigate in the ambiguities with faithfulness, conviction, and love.

Several years ago, our church developed an intentional—and intense—men's discipleship initiative. We invite a group of spiritually hungry guys to press into Jesus and into each other for several weeks. It's been one of the most fruitful initiatives we've created. When a new cohort of men completes the process, we welcome them to a night of celebration. Before the night begins, we supply them with the address of a restaurant and one cryptic piece of instruction: wear a white-collared dress shirt you don't mind throwing away. This usually raises quite a few eyebrows. What they learn later is that we've reserved the upstairs room at a restaurant known for its hot wings. We contact the restaurant ahead of time and give specific instructions: set the tables *but do not put out napkins.*

When the men arrive, they are greeted by other men who've previously completed the discipleship program. Each alum congratulates and hugs the new graduates, and when we are all seated, ready to enjoy all-you-can-eat wings, we inform them there are no napkins. We tell them not to ask the wait staff for any; the only napkins available to us are the white shirts of the men to our left and to our right. We eat, we laugh, we tell stories, and we make one big mess. It's one of our favorite nights of the year. Guys intentionally pat each other on the back, smear barbeque sauce on their neighbors' sleeves, and draw smiley faces on the backs of other dudes' shirts. I wear the messes of the guys next to me; they wear my messes, too. It's a wild time. No matter how many showers we take, the smell of wing sauce lingers for at least three days. The waitstaff loves it (especially since we assure them we'll tip well for the extra mess we end up making). We cast the vision to continue to live into this Jesus way of life. We pray for each guy at the table. Before the evening officially concludes, we gather for a group photo, the picture usually taken by one of the waitresses, who giggles between takes. All of us look like we just returned from a war zone. And in a sense, we *are* engaged in a battle.

We want the men to know—and embody—that we're called to wear the messes of others. As we sit around the table, wreaking and dripping of wing sauce, we recognize we are living metaphors of the Christian life. We tell the men gathered in that upstairs room that healthy community is not the absence of conflict, but the presence of Jesus in the midst of it.

Gabe Lyons, founder of Q Ideas, wrote that Christians can live in the messy tension between the two extremes by living as *restorers*, which he defines as:

> Provoked, yet not offended.
> Living as creators, not critics.
> People who are called, not merely employed.
> Grounded, but not distracted.
> In community and not alone.
> Those who remain civil, but are not divisive.
> People who are countercultural, but not "relevant."[10]

A significant part of faithful witness, of course, involves *faith*. But what do we do in those times when we don't feel so faith-filled, when we're caught in the angsty middle between faith and doubt? Faith and doubt are strange bedfellows. Even though, on the surface, they don't seem to mix, the truth is that we can't truly put our faith in anything until we have first possessed doubt. There are a lot of churches I know that simply dole out kitschy, pale spiritual advice like *just pray more* or *doubting makes you weak* or *just believe*. But we know the reality that it's just not that simple much of the time.[11]

The Scriptures tell us that if we doubt, we are like a wave tossed by the wind and shouldn't expect to receive anything from the Lord when we ask (James 1:6–8), and yet the little Book of Jude urges readers to be patient and merciful to those who doubt (chapter 22). Heck, even Jesus' cousin John the Baptist, who uttered such bold declarations about Jesus being so great that he was unworthy to stoop down and untie his sandals in his presence, doubted from his cramped and lonely prison cell (Matt 11:2–3). As Hebrews 11:1 states, faith is the substance of things we hope for and the evidence of what cannot be seen. Faith *assumes* that doubt must be present to begin with. Krish Kandiah, author of *Paradoxology: Why Christianity Was Never Meant to Be Simple*, writes that "the paradoxes that seem to undermine belief are actually the heart of our vibrant faith, and that it is only by continually wrestling with them—rather than trying to pin them down or push them away— that we can really worship God, individually or together."[12]

One of the most strikingly ironic themes in the Gospel of Mark is how frequently Mark notes that the demons understood immediately who Jesus was and how much power and authority he possessed, yet Jesus' ever-present disciples were the slowest to realize he was who he said he was. The demons get it; the disciples are out to lunch. Right before the Great Commission passage in Matthew 28:18–20, where Jesus sends his disciples out to make new disciples, Matthew adds this often-missed line: "When they saw him, they worshiped him; but some doubted" (28:17). The disciples had been with Jesus and seen his miracles, heard his teachings and even had backstage passes—yet some still doubted. What is wildly comforting for me is that *Jesus still chose to commission them to go make disciples, even in the midst of their doubt.*

Another story comes to mind: Mark records a dramatic and emotional interaction between Jesus and a father whose son is demon possessed. As a dad of two sons, I can't imagine the heart-breaking horror I might experience by seeing my son, quite literally, out of his mind in fits of rage and insanity with no cure or solution. The desperate father begs Jesus to do something:

> Jesus asked the boy's father, "How long has he been like this?"
>
> "From childhood," he answered. "It has often thrown him into fire or water to kill him. But if you can do anything, take pity on us and help us."
>
> "'If you can'?" said Jesus. "Everything is possible for one who believes."
>
> Immediately the boy's father exclaimed, "I do believe; help me overcome my unbelief!" (Mark 9:21–24)

I love that raw and honest prayer: *I do believe; help me overcome my unbelief!* Sometimes it's freeing to say what everybody thinks but nobody has the courage to say aloud. In my most honest moments, this is the struggle I feel. I seem to be full of faith and full of doubt at the same time. How does it all work out in our adventure with Jesus? Everything is possible for those who believe, but is anything possible for those who don't fully believe? I don't always know myself. I know my mustard seeds are small, and sometimes that's all I've got. But I am grateful that in the midst of my faith *and also* my lack of faith, Jesus is present, willing to be patient with me and humbly show himself to me. I doubt, yet he still loves.

Mother Teresa of Calcutta, known for her small stature and huge heart for the poor, also struggled with her faith. In one of her letters, published after her death, she wrote, "Jesus has a special love for you. As for me, the silence and emptiness is so great that I look and do not see, listen and do not hear."[13] One of my favorite prayers, filled with gut-wrenching honesty, uttered about five hundred years ago by another St. Teresa—the spunky Spaniard, Teresa of Avila—expressed another sentiment. She prayed:

> Oh God, I don't love you. I don't even want to love you, but I want to want to love you![14]

Some things are so honest and vulnerable you can only voice them to God. If these Teresas struggled with faith and prayer, then it's understandable that we will struggle at times, too.

So much of faith includes doubt.[15] Both are central to the spiritual life. I am not trying to encourage you to doubt your own faith; I simply want to acknowledge the role doubt plays in faith. Ironically, doubt must precede faith. It's what poet Robert Browning wrote:

> You call for faith: I show you doubts,
> To prove that faith exists.
> The more of doubt, the stronger faith, I say, if faith o'ercomes doubt.[16]

Faithful witness is sometimes seed-sized, and in his immense grace and patience and goodness, Jesus still uses it. Faith and doubt may be strange bedmates, but they certainly share the same king-sized mattress.

My sons' elementary school is just a block from our house; it appears to inhale students every morning and then cough them out in the afternoon. On spring mornings, when the windows in my office on the third floor of our house are open, I can hear the bustling as kids chat and squeal with their friends. When I look out the window, I can see the minivans lined up in the carpool lane, waiting to be waved forward by students on safety patrol. When the weather is nice, I often take a walk around the block at midday, to clear my mind or pray. When I pass the school, all is quiet outside the building; there's not a sound or person in sight. And then, at 3:40 every afternoon, kids begin trickling out a few at a time. This builds to a crescendo, as the building spews out one large, chaotic rush of students with noise, laughter, excitement, and relief. Some kids run to hug their parents or jump in their parents' cars, while others sprint to throw the football on the playground. Each weekday morning, York Avenue Elementary School, like most schools around the world, inhales deeply, holds its breath for several hours, and then exhales its students.

I often think of church as a pulsating heart, which expands and constricts to push blood through the veins and arteries of the body. Or, better yet, a living, breathing entity that inhales her people, holds her breath, and then exhales them out, scattering them as missionaries disguised in various vocations, roles, and responsibilities throughout the world. Of the forty miracles found in the book of Acts, all but one of them occurred *outside* the walls of a religious building.[17]

This idea of a breathing church is quite theological actually. The Hebrew word for spirit is *ruach*. (To say it properly you have to say the end of the word—the *ch*—as if you are clearing your throat.) *Ruach* means "spirit, breath, or wind." If you step outside on a frigid January day and utter the word *ruach* aloud, you quite literally see the meaning of what you are saying. In Greek, the word is *pneuma* (said with a silent p), which also means "spirit, mind, or breath." It's where we get our word *pneumonia*, the condition where you have trouble breathing. To be a faithful church, we take our cues from this holy wind-breath. We read in the Gospels that the first apostles were told by Jesus himself they could not begin his ministry until—and only until—they had received the gift of the Holy Spirit (Luke 24:49). Don't do anything until the Spirit comes. Stay put. Maybe we should take note, too. In the book of Acts we see that the Spirit is the chief player in the mission of Jesus' church, the director of this entire venture which points the world toward Jesus.[18]

As members of Jesus' church, we are both blessed *and also* sent. We are called to gather in Jesus' name *and also* scatter in it. If all we do is gather, singing our songs and saying our prayers and listening politely to sermons without any intent to live all of it outside the church, it would be like taking a deep breath and never exhaling. It's exhausting, unhealthy and, eventually, we'd turn blue and die. If all we do is scatter, busying ourselves with service projects, community events, and other meaningful endeavors, it would be like we're exhaling and exhaling until there is nothing left in the tank. Eventually, we'd turn blue and die. Gathering for worship is vital because it's where we center around the life, death, and resurrection of Jesus and respond to his great love for us. But ninety minutes spent in worship every Sunday only equates on average to a mere 1.3 percent of our waking hours in a given week. If we believe this space will be sufficient to mold us into fully formed, fully matured Christlikeness, who are we kidding? We need to gather together in worship, but we also need to learn to engage with God and others in various forms of worship, formation, and mission during the other 98.7 percent of our time.

This approach of only inhaling (or only exhaling) is never the vision or intention of the church. If we have either one without the other, we cannot faithfully express God's purposes in and for the world. It's spiritual pneumonia. But when churches find the sweet spot in the midst of this healthy tension, they develop strategies for both gathering *and also* scattering in order to bless the world. Doing both means we value the activities of the church without neglecting those outside the church. Inhaling and exhaling with regularity and intention, we allow the Spirit to work in our communities of faith in naturally supernatural ways. Being present and committed to the local church is an important priority, but sometimes this also means you gotta just skip the

Wednesday service to hang out with your neighbors to enjoy a cigar and some scotch.

This is what pastors and authors Hugh Halter and Matt Smay describe in their book as the power of the *and*. The right things are centralized *and also* decentralized. Resources of people and money find a blessed blending of maintenance *and also* mission, survival *and also* sending, tradition *and also* innovation. Fans are turned into followers, disciples are made into apprentices, and consumers become missionaries.[19] It reminds me of Jesus' words in Matthew 13 where the owner of a house brings out of his storeroom new treasures *as well as old*. The kingdom is not always *either/or*; it's often *both/and*.

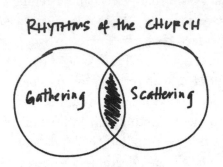

Jesus' intent is to create little pockets of heaven where people can be in God's presence, but he does it out here in the middle of the world, in the middle of sin and death.[20] I'm certainly not saying this is easy. Admittedly, many Christians find church to be the most difficult aspect of being a Christian.[21] As a pastor, I have found this tension to be tough work, like walking a tightrope; sometimes it feels like I am about to throw up (especially when I'm told by someone over breakfast that he wishes I wasn't alive anymore).

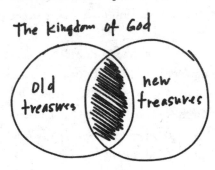

The church stands as an alternative and prophetic space, a colony of heaven in a country of death.[22] We don't have to be seminary trained or overly religious to participate in this. As Eugene Peterson wrote, church is "a congregation of embarrassingly ordinary people in and through whom God chooses to be present to the world."[23] We long for things to be made right and to be put back together in the *shalom* of God, yet we live in the midst of a world at war with itself.

When we started our church over a decade ago, I asked our core team why we existed, why we would go to the trouble of setting up chairs and singing songs and listening to sermons. I wasn't against these activities; I believed they were important. But if we didn't clarify *why* we were doing these things, we could fall into the trap that perpetuates the unhealthy mentality that we're just in this for ourselves. Without focused and intentional conversation and communal discernment, we could run the risk of becoming a church who inhaled and held its breath for dear life. During the weeks those conversations took place, trying to clarify exactly why we would gather each week as a community of Jesus followers, we eventually landed on the phrase *formation for mission*. We realized that we gathered to be formed in order to be sent. We realized that, in our own way, we were articulating the blessed-and-sent posture. The purpose of our singing and prayers and Communion and storytelling and sermons was to form us in order to allow the Spirit to exhale us into our various contexts, not as *just somebodies*, but as God's deeply loved children sent to represent Christ well in the world by living the *with God* life.

I wish I could tell you that everything is wonderful for our church. It's not. We have disappointed people on both sides. Those entrenched in their spiritual ideologies have left. Families who demanded we take a clear and public stance on every issue at hand felt we were too unstable and loose. They felt we shouldn't just carry our cross; we should wield and brandish it, too. Those longing for frequent pontification about the church's need to continually fight the culture wars didn't last. But those who have stayed have been a beautiful representation of what it means to live gritty, imperfect, and bruised-yet-free lives. Inhaling *and also* exhaling, blessed *and also* sent, studying God's Word *and also* following God's Spirit.

It's messy and costly and time intensive. But it's worth it.

CHAPTER 8

THE PRAYER OF SACRED OVERLAP

How Jesus Teaches Us to Pray

"Our Father in heaven,
hallowed be your name,
your kingdom come,
your will be done,
    on earth as it is in heaven.
Give us today our daily bread.
And forgive us our debts,
    as we also have forgiven our debtors.
And lead us not into temptation,
    but deliver us from the evil one."

—MATTHEW 6:9–13

Before we can pray, "Lord, Thy kingdom come," we must be willing to pray, "My kingdom go."

—ALAN REDPATH

I still remember the first time I was prayer-shamed.

At the end of fifth grade, I switched schools and began attending a Christian school across town. I was relieved that the transition to the new school went smoothly and that I was able to make friends quickly. But I was not prepared for what happened in English class during the first week. Our teacher, Miss Scully, began class by encouraging us to stand and recite the Lord's Prayer together. As the class intoned the prayer in unison, I looked around and, to my great surprise, everyone knew the words but me. Although I lived in a Christian home, I wasn't all that familiar with the prayer. *Where did they learn this?* I thought. *At church? I go to church. How did I miss this?*

Everyone finished with *Amen*, the more reverent pronunciation, with the long "a" sound, where the beginning of the word looks and sounds like you're yawning—*ahhmen*. Miss Scully asked if any of us did not know the words. She must have seen me. Timidly, I raised my hand. Giggles rippled throughout the classroom. My seams were showing; I'd been exposed. The girl sitting at the desk next to me turned and asked incredulously, "Seriously, you don't know the Lord's Prayer?" I most certainly did not. I had been prayer-shamed. It may not seem like a big deal to you, but in that moment it felt like I had been left in the middle of the Indian Ocean without a life raft, shivering and disoriented.

For whatever reason, I stuffed this memory in my emotional carry-on bag and have lugged it around with me through the airports of my life all these years. Just thinking about it makes my eye twitch. Miss Scully certainly did not intend to embarrass me. In fact, she asked the class so that if any of us did not know it, she could print it out and give it to us to tuck inside the front flaps of our Trapper Keepers for quick reference. But it was too late; the shaming had already left its searing mark. True to her word, the next morning Miss Scully handed me a slip of paper. I took the slip home and had it memorized by bedtime. I wasn't going to risk any more prayer-shaming in English class.

It still amazes me, all these years later, how often I think about that day in Miss Scully's class when I recite the Lord's Prayer. Now I recite it confidently and with ease; several years ago, I taught a series on it at church. I say it aloud in the morning as I sit on the couch while the house is dark and quiet. Ever since the novel coronavirus hit the US in the spring of 2020 and we all learned to wash our hands much more frequently, I've engaged in the practice of reciting the prayer as I scrub. I still do it to this day. I had my sons learn it, and they could recite it before they entered elementary school. Maybe it was my subconscious desire to protect them from any potential prayer-shaming experiences.

Earlier, I mentioned that every week during my seminary classes, I have my students stand, and we recite the Shema from Deuteronomy 6:4–5 as well as the Shema of Jesus together. At the end of each class time, we stand and recite the Lord's Prayer. (I put the words on the screen, just in case). We engage in this practice because the Shema and the Lord's Prayer serve as wonderful bookends for what we learn during each class. To pray and live the Shema naturally flows to praying and living the Lord's Prayer.

Before we begin reciting, I tell the students there are only two rules. First, pray it like you believe it—and if you struggle to believe it, I won't force you to recite it. And second, unless you speak like Shakespeare in everyday conversation, say *you* and *your*, rather than *thee* and *thine*. Doing so forces us to shift out of spiritual autopilot and re-personalizes both prayers. It takes the religious stiffness out of our joints and becomes a more personal and accessible space for conversation with God.

The church father Tertullian wrote that the Lord's Prayer is a summary of the whole gospel. But there is danger when we thoughtlessly recite the Lord's Prayer. We often fail to ask what it really means. The Lord's Prayer is not intended to be recited only on a Sunday morning sitting in a pew, or in seminary class, where we might be tempted to make ourselves sound super-spiritual. It provides a framework for prayer, hooks on which we can hang our praises and requests. It was a structured (but certainly not rote) conversation with God intended to remind Jesus' followers of his priorities.[1]

When we say it, we petition our Father about his name, his kingdom, and his will—expressing that our concern is with God breaking into history in order to make the world right again. One of the elders at our church, Dennis, describes the Lord's Prayer as a dance. You're in heaven, Father—come join us down here. Forgive us, God, *and also* we commit to forgiving others, too.[2] Don't let us be tempted, Lord, *and also* deliver us from the Evil One. Give and take. One step in, one step out. I take your hand, you take mine.

When we see its power in its original setting, even the prayer's first line is jolting: *Our Father.* The disciples are encouraged to address the God of the universe in an expression of intimacy. In addressing God as our father, we are recognizing that Jesus is also our brother. We are sons and daughters.[3] Jesus invites us to pray, quite literally, in the language and with the posture of a child. Jesus would later go on to define what he meant by "father" by telling the story of the prodigal son found in Luke 15. He breaks the mold of human patriarchy and instead presents an image that reaches far beyond what first-century Middle Eastern culture expected from a human father. He created a new mental image in the minds of his listeners—an image of a loving God.[4]

Prayer can be difficult, even for pastors. It's strange to admit this, but I confess it's true. A few years ago, during a particularly dry prayer season, I realized I needed some scaffolding for my prayers, something to propel me into further and deeper conversation with God. So I made it a practice to say, pray, and ruminate on one short phrase of the Lord's Prayer each day of the week. I've continued the practice to this day:

On Mondays, I center on *Our Father in heaven.*

I focus on the reality of a Father who loves us, cares for us, and rules in power, reminding me I don't have to worry. He is *our* Father, not merely *my* Father. Right from the beginning, we learn that prayer is relational. On Mondays, I am reminded of the opportunity for relational closeness with God while also remembering he rules from heaven, not just from my living room couch.

On Tuesdays, I pray *hallowed be your name.*

I contemplate the ways in which I can cherish, honor, and revere God's name because he is good, faithful, and powerful. I ponder my words, actions, and thoughts about God over the past week as I drive across town, or when I throw the football in the backyard with my sons or stand in line at the post office, considering where I may have cheapened the use of his name in some way—and if so, I enter into a time of confession.

Wednesdays take me to *your kingdom come, your will be done, on earth as it is in heaven.*

This nudges me to look for the kingdom of God at work in the ordinary details of my day. Author Reggie McNeal wrote about the times he said bedtime prayers with his young daughter and how he noticed she always kept her eyes open. When he finally asked her why, she said she didn't want to miss anything while praying.[5] Wednesdays help me to pray with my eyes open, so I don't miss something important.

Thursdays bring me to *give us our daily bread.*

I thank God for his provision of my basic needs, especially the ones I can so easily take for granted: our warm home, a pantry full of food, clean drinking water from the tap. This line helps me see leftovers for lunch as the visible, tangible grace of God providing me with the nourishment I need while I watch the countdown timer on the microwave. Every meal, all bread, is a sacred gift. St. Augustine wrote in his commentary on the Sermon on the Mount that this line reminds us that no matter how rich we may be in worldly wealth, we are still beggars in relation to God.[6] Thursdays force me to come face-to-face with the reality of my own spiritual panhandling.

Fridays are more difficult: *and forgive us our debts, as we also have forgiven our debtors.*

Fridays are, more than other days of the week, when I confess the ways I have failed God and people. It is where I find I still need to work through the act of forgiveness to release any feelings of hatred, resentment, or frustration I still hold over others. Anne Lamott wrote that failing to forgive others is like drinking rat poison and waiting for the rat to die.[7] By praying this line on Fridays, I open the cap, dump the contents of the poison bottle in the toilet, and flush.

Saturdays are *lead us not into temptation.*

I ponder what currently tempts me, big and small. I ask God to show me the truth about my temptations and to provide people who can help me address them head-on. Saturdays are when I become more fully aware that my identity is wrapped up in my job, that I've perceived others as a means to an end, or that I am unable to resist a second (or fourth) bowl of ice cream. I confess my weaknesses and wrong thinking, that I've operated as though it is my world to rule.

And on Sundays I pray *deliver us from the evil one.*

I ask God not only to deliver me from Satan, but also to help me notice when the Evil One whispers lies, even sneaky-good lies that are *almost* legitimate, but are still lies: the truth, plus or minus ten percent.

Even though I know it soundly, pray it confidently, recite it frequently, teach on it regularly, sometimes I wonder if I fully comprehend this powerful prayer of Jesus. How much of its central message might I still be missing? Like the girl who sat next to me in Miss Scully's English class, I think, *Seriously, Briggs, you still don't know the Lord's Prayer?*

What's interesting is that the prayer is for the past, present, *and also* future, for our temporary *and also* our eternal needs. For this earthly life, we ask for the provision of food today, that we can forgive others who've wronged us in the past, and that we won't be led into the temptations looming in the future. But we also offer petitions that are eternal—that God's name would be hallowed, that we would live in the kingdom forever, and that we would do his will. All three of these things will most assuredly last forever. We pray for the overlapping of heaven *and* earth, the present *and* the future.

The words of the Lord's Prayer are found in the biographies of Jesus written by Matthew and Luke. In Luke's account, the disciples come to Jesus and ask him to teach them how to pray. It is the only situation recorded in the Gospels wherein the disciples specifically ask Jesus to teach them how to do something. *The only one.* Not how to preach captivating sermons or how to cast out demons effectively or how to conduct effective pastoral visitations, but how to *pray.* When his disciples ask him how to pray, Jesus doesn't launch into a forty-five-minute seminary-level lecture, nor does he begin the first lesson of an eight-week Sunday school curriculum. He simply prays *for less than thirty seconds.* Jesus invites us to participate in communication with the Father in which our words are few and powerful.[8] This blows my mind. But maybe it shouldn't blow my mind. Jesus specifically told his listeners that when we pray, we shouldn't use many words (Matt. 6:7). Jesus wants us to pray simply, directly, succinctly.

Jesus responds by saying, "When you pray, say . . ." (Luke 11:2). Scot McKnight writes that the word *say* might best be translated *recite* or even *repeat*.[9] Praying the Lord's Prayer with frequency and familiarity has been in the collective DNA of the church for centuries.[10] For Catholics, Orthodox, Protestants, this was the norm until informal prayers took root in the twentieth century. The more I spend time with the Lord's Prayer, the more I realize two things. First, it's a significantly *we*-oriented prayer, quite un-individualistic.

Our Father . . .

Give *us our* daily bread.

Forgive *us our* trespasses as *we* forgive those who trespass against *us*.

Lead *us* not into temptation.

Deliver *us* from evil.

Second, it's a prayer centrally oriented around the kingdom of God. Jesus talked a great deal about the kingdom of God, which is the rule and the reign of God in the world. It was his favorite expression to describe his mission.[11] Throughout Scripture, God's kingdom shows up whenever and wherever his children gather together and submit to his authority.

It is striking how often the early Christians recited the Lord's Prayer, so much so that it dominated the everyday life of the typical Christian. If Jesus made the kingdom central to his mission, wouldn't it make sense for it to become top priority for us as well? Whenever people submit to the king, his kingdom is exercised and recognized. For followers of the Risen Christ, we embrace Jesus' royal words: "Seek first the kingdom and his righteousness, and all these things will be given to you as well" (Matt. 6:33).

The Lord's Prayer expresses the yearning for overlapping worlds. When we recite the line *your kingdom come, your will be done, on earth as it is in heaven*, we are acknowledging the fundamental desire, the thesis statement, of the prayer itself. It remains one of the most revolutionary sentences we could ever utter.[12] There is this paradox that exists: the kingdom has already come, yet it is still in the future. Already, but not yet. The kingdom of God is near, yet it is far away.[13]

When I returned from that trip to Turkey and Greece—the trip that included the trip up the Bosporus Strait I shared earlier—I struggled like many weary international travelers to throw off the dastardly draining effects of jet lag. That disruptive and disorienting experience interrupted my circadian sleep patterns, essentially punching me in the face, and leaving me sluggish and lacking both energy and motivation. I wanted to take a nap right after lunch and was up and ready to go before the sun even thought about getting out of bed in the morning. While my body had arrived back in the States, I felt as though my harried soul was still waiting at some lonely gate in a faraway airport to catch the next flight home. I hoped the flight took off soon, because it was clear that coffee wasn't working. *Come, Lord Jesus.*

My foggy state reminded me of when singer-songwriter Sandra McCracken wrote, "jet lag is one of my favorite embodied metaphors of our spiritual reality." We often experience the tension of living between present promise *and* future fulfillment. We live in liminal space, pulled between two spiritual time zones: we are sojourners who are not yet home. We experience pervasive brokenness in the midst of gospel hope.[14] This can leave our souls feeling a bit disoriented. When we pray that God's kingdom would come to be on earth as it is in heaven, it's a call to ask God to reset our watches and orient our sleep patterns so we can be fully present in the spiritual reality of our everyday lives.

Hope is the same way. The Hebrew worldview divided time into two parts: the present age and the age to come. Hope is what finds us in that sacred overlap. Hope is a dependence upon what God will do, but it is not just future-oriented. It is rooted in the past, remembering what God has done, *and also* rooted in the present. When we look to the past and God's activity, and to the future toward God's promises, we are rooted confidently in the present. Hope.

Shalom is an important component to all of this. As we explored earlier, *shalom* is not just peace or the absence of war or conflict. It is a state of perfect harmony, wherein every single element fits exactly as it should. It is right relationship. The story of God begins in Genesis with *shalom*; and the story of God ends in Revelation with *shalom*. Today, we live between the *shaloms*. Jesus' prayer shows us that these two worlds are not to be kept apart but to participate in as agents of the kingdom. The Celts held a unique set of beliefs: they were convinced that the veil that separated heaven from earth was about three feet thick. They also believed that this veil of separation has worn through in spots, leaving no separation between the two realms. These places of overlap were known as *thin places*. Celtic spirituality believed these thin places existed geographically, like the isle of Iona off the coast of Scotland, as well as on certain days of the year. Thin places can happen anywhere—the treadmill at the gym or in a meeting at work or at the mall (especially if there is a Chipotle in the food court).

Jesus' prayer is modeled closely after a Jewish prayer called the *Qaddish*. Its similar-sounding line reads, "And may he establish his kingdom during your life and during your days, and during the life of all the house of Israel, speedily and in the near future."[15] Kingdom theology is Venn diagram theology. And whether we realize it or not, when we pray the Lord's Prayer, we are praying a mandorla prayer.

This Jesus prayer is filled with gospel aches, especially the ache for the full story to be completed, to end at the place where God is the all in all. This is rooted not in our own moral awesomeness, but in the humble petition where we ask God to act. Earlier, we looked at the Latin term *missio dei*. But even before *missio dei*, theologian Karl Barth used the term *actio dei*—the "action of God." Simply put, the Jesus prayer is a prayer for God to *actio* something, a request that his redemptive power would be at work to manifest heaven's condition here on earth.[16]

Stuck inside the back flap of my leather journal, in which I write prayers and thoughts, is a weathered copy of an alternative rendering of the Lord's Prayer. I don't remember who gave it to me or what its original source is, but the language stirs my imagination:

> *Our Father in heaven, be lifted up today!*
> *Rule over us, we pray, and tear down our idols.*
> *Let your intention be realized completely,*
> *Regardless of what it may cost.*
> *We look to you to feed us, to provide what we need.*
> *For this day, do not worry about tomorrow.*
> *Forgive our sins; erase our debts.*
> *Teach us to do the same for others.*
> *We are weak and prone to wander.*
> *Oh, have mercy, dear Lord.*
> *Find us in our weakness; rescue us in our lostness.*
> *Protect us from the evil one.*
> *We confess you as King of the everlasting kingdom.*
> *The high and omnipotent God, the all-glorious One.*
> *This is how it is and how it will always be.*
> *Amen.*

When we pray the line, "Let your intention be realized completely," we're asking something significant, maybe more than we can fully grasp. We pray, in essence, *God, we know and acknowledge that your reign is fully realized in heaven. May this same reality be fully realized on earth as well—right here in our world, nation, state, county, city— even in my own home.* George Eldon Ladd wrote that when we grasp this, we embrace the *already/not yet* nature of the kingdom of God. It is both present *and also* imminent; it has come *and also* it's not yet here; it is here *and also* near at the same time. I like the way David McDonald titled his book about the kingdom: *Then. Now. Next.* The kingdom exists in the past, present, and future.

If the Psalms are prayers found somewhere in the overlap of despairing realism and assuring hope, then the Lord's Prayer is found in the overlap between faith-filled submission and mission-saturated anticipation. The Lord's Prayer is not useless (no honest prayer ever is). It is not demanding of God or trying to control outcomes. What I find so formative is that when I soak my mind and soul in the waters of this prayer, God teaches me to care more about some things and not as much about others.

If you ask people why they are Christians, they might tell you it's because their sins have been forgiven and when they die, they will spend eternity with God. This is not entirely wrong, but it's significantly incomplete. This approach is what Dallas Willard calls the gospel of sin management, making us vampire Christians, where we say, in essence, "I'd like a little bit of your blood, Jesus, but I don't care to be your student or take on your character. In fact, why don't you excuse me while I get on with my life, and I'll see you one day in heaven." The truth is, we know our sins are forgiven precisely *because* the life of heaven is now, *in us*, where we can learn to live every moment of our lives with God. It's simple, yet profound. It seems to change nothing, yet it changes everything. [17]

What's deeply ironic is that the gospel story we often tell today is significantly different from the message of Scripture. In the common gospel message approach, we often focus so much on the afterlife that we forget there is a whole world for us to participate in right here. Willard used to say with an impish grin that if becoming a Christian is about having your sins forgiven so you get to go to heaven when you die, why wait? Go now. Our posture should not be to see the gospel as an evacuation plan, escape hatch, or impending vacation. We must stand in the middle between the world as it is *and also* the world as it is meant to be. Here's the good news: there's life to be lived in the kingdom of God *right now*—even before we die. It's not just life after death; it's life before it, too.

Here's another highfalutin' hundred-dollar theological word

used to name the mindset of separated thinking and living: *gnosticism*, with a silent *g*. Gnostics see the final goal as the separation of the world from God, of the physical from the spiritual, of earth from heaven. Simply put, this line of thinking believes the world is bad and God is good—and therefore, we shouldn't mix the two. Gnosticism is an *either/or* theology. Christians who possess this narrow way of thinking are all dressed up with no place to go.[18] Much of the Book of 1 John is his attempt to convince people to throw off gnostic thinking. Similarly, Paul states in Ephesians 1:10 that God's design and promise was to bring unity and fulfillment in all things in Christ *in both heaven and on earth*.

The Lord's Prayer is an anti-gnostic prayer. It's not intended to take us *away*, to separate us from earth, but to make us agents of redemption, renewal, and reconciliation *for* this earth. The prayer, when it runs through our collective bloodstream, eliminates any temptation for us to lean out, check out, or wait it out. The gospel is not an evacuation plan to heaven designed for religious people. It is a transformation plan for everyone on earth. Our mission is not to be snatched from this earth and make it to eternity, but instead, to bring heaven here. It's not about abandoning the world, but about building bridges and celebrating God's healing of it. We live fully in the present with the hope and the faith that we will be made fully complete in the future. Throughout Scripture, we see that heaven and earth are made for each other. They are twin interlocking spheres of God's single created reality: we begin to comprehend earth only after we are equally familiar with heaven.[19]

The life Jesus promises us—life to the fullest measure possible—doesn't start when we die; it starts the moment we fully yield ourselves to God and his rule and reign. When we grasp a grander God-shaped, God-sized vision of the kingdom, the kind of kingdom Jesus talked about so frequently, we begin to see that *all* people are graciously summoned by God to participate in his mission by working to *bring heaven now*.

Earlier we referenced Philippians 3:20, wherein Paul reminds the church in Philippi that their citizenship is found in heaven. Philippi was a Roman colony; most of the residents of Philippi were citizens of Rome and knew what citizenship entailed. The purpose was to extend the influence of Rome around the world, creating cells and networks of people who would remain loyal to Caesar. But their destiny was not Rome. The purpose and function of a Roman colony was to *bring the culture of Rome to the city of Philippi, not the other way around.* Paul's words to the Philippian Christians, saying that they were citizens of heaven, doesn't mean that when we're done with this life, we'll lounge around killing time in the next. Paul's message was clear: *bring the culture of heaven down to earth.*[20]

We must be careful to keep the *already/not yet* elements of the kingdom in proper perspective. If we overemphasize the *already* reality of the kingdom and underemphasize the *not yet*, we can see the church as nothing more than a religious social justice organization. If we overemphasize the *not yet* reality of the kingdom and make the *already* element a low priority, we can come to see salvation as a divine fire insurance policy given to us to place in our files in the upstairs closet in case of an emergency. Neither approach is an accurate view of the kingdom. We must learn to live in the *already-ness* and the *not yet-ness.*[21]

I am beginning to realize that what Jesus wants for us is a life of *congruence*, a life in which all the parts fit together seamlessly. This reminds me of the psalmist who prayed for an undivided heart (Psalm 86:11). The Living Bible renders it as, "May every fiber of my being unite in reverence to your name." To live a life of congruence is to ensure that all areas are in alignment. Jesus was often angry at the religious leaders of his day because of their incongruence. He simply couldn't handle their duplicity, hypocrisy, and showmanship—their pristine tombs with rotting corpses inside. The apostle Paul, before his sensational conversion on the Damascus Road, studied at the feet of a brilliant Jewish rabbi named Gamaliel. He, too, believed in congruent living when he wrote, "A disciple, who is not inwardly the same as outwardly, will not be allowed to enter the house of study."[22]

What Jesus desires for us—and what the Lord's Prayer pulls us into—is a life where our Sunday experience matches our Monday through Saturday existence. Jesus even gave us a litmus test for this: feed the hungry, clothe the naked, welcome the stranger, visit those behind bars, care for the sick, befriend the sinners, and side with the weak, the least, and the lost. Whatever you do to the least of these, Jesus says, you do unto me. Do these, Jesus says, and you pass the congruency test.

The Lord's Prayer shows us in high definition that God our Father is good and loving and patient and trustworthy. But for many of us, the opposite comes to mind when we think of him. Anne Lamott wrote that many people think of God as a high school principal in a gray suit who never seems to remember your name but is always leafing unhappily through your files.[23] But if we have a loving father who is in control and reigns in heaven, whose name is hallowed and good, we don't have to succumb to the fits of worry which besiege us on Monday mornings. He loves us deeply and he desires for the values of heaven to be the values here on earth. We can desire that, too.

The Lord's Prayer also makes it clear that *forgiveness is a big deal to God.* Jesus' directives in the Sermon on the Mount can seem daunting. Do not pay back wrong for wrong. When cursed, bless. Do not take revenge. *Really?* In the fourth century, St. Gregory of Nyssa wrote that the most difficult element of Jesus' prayer is when we speak of asking for and extending forgiveness to others.[24] This can feel at times like a punch in the stomach. I want to receive forgiveness much more than I wish to extend it. It's why C. S. Lewis wrote that forgiveness sounds like a great idea unless you're the one who has to do it.[25]

But which is it: do we forgive others because God forgave—and forgives—us? Or do we forgive others so that God will ultimately forgive us, too? Or does God forgive us and then we are able to forgive others? Well, yes.[26] But I tend to believe a better translation of this line might be "Forgive us, Lord, as we are in the process of forgiving others." Forgiveness, it seems, is not a one-time dramatic event where we check the box on the to-do list once and for all. It's an ongoing, daily process where we extend and ask for grace and mercy in order to participate in the mending, repairing, healing process. The process of forgiving others never ends; neither does the need to ask God to forgive us. Forgiveness, according to Jesus, is like breathing: we can't do it just once and expect to live very long.

Depending upon your faith tradition, you might ask God to forgive "our debts," "our trespasses," or "our sins." Matthew uses the word *debts* to imply the unfulfilled obligations of God, while Luke uses both *sins* and *debts*. Whenever I pray with a group, I find I hesitate for just a split second when we get to this line, wondering which of the three words will be used most prominently by the group—and if I have chosen correctly. Presbyterians, for example, traditionally have used *debts* while others, like Episcopalians, seem to use *trespasses*.[27] But whether we utter *debts, trespasses,* or *sins,* they all do the trick.

I oscillate between reciting *trespasses* and *debts.* When I pray that line and choose to utter "trespasses," I often think back to my semester abroad in Israel. One weekend, my buddies and I trekked around the Golan Heights, just north of the Sea of Galilee. Because of the wars fought decades prior in the region of the Golan, enemy forces had placed land mines all throughout the hills to keep people out. Decades later, people are still unsure where those land mines are, how many are left, and if (or when) they might detonate if stepped on. Because of this, the area is clearly marked with barbed wire fencing and large yellow signs with red lettering that read *No Trespassing* in English, Hebrew, and Arabic.

I'm unsure what got into my friends and me that day, but we

thought it would be fun to scale the barbed wire fencing and run around in the mine field while one of us took a picture of the whole crazy act. I look back years later on that experience and wonder exactly what we were thinking. I shiver to think what could have happened that day had we taken one costly misstep. We could have, quite literally, lost life and limb. It was utter foolishness. When I ask God to forgive my trespasses, I have made the irrational and absurd decision to encroach on spiritual territory which is dangerously off-limits, a locale filled with mines which could detonate at any moment. I deserve to face the consequences of traversing where I clearly am not allowed to be. And I now ask my Father to forgive my foolish and rebellious offense and humbly ask for his grace.

When I pray that line and use the word *debts*, I think back to the words found in the *Book of Common Prayer*, where we ask God for forgiveness by stating, "We have left undone those things which we ought to have done; and we have done those things which we ought not to have done. The Greek word for forgiveness is *aphesis* [AH-feh-sis], which refers to the relinquishment of debt. Sin, in essence, is insurmountable indebtedness to a creditor I will never be able to pay back, no matter how long I work and no matter how hard I try. *Aphesis* also means "liberty" or "release." Forgiveness is when I am set free from debtor's prison. Sin and debt function synonymously, and thus, redemption signifies a release from slavery.[28] No more hiding from creditors, no more pulling the blinds and hoping they don't see that someone is home, and no more foreboding thoughts that we might be hunted down, harassed, and hauled off. The shackles of indebtedness have fallen off. God's emphasis is on *aphesis* because forgiveness is truly freeing.[29]

We can ask God to grant us what we need today so that we can have the strength to be congruent people. But how can we expect to receive God's forgiveness if we refrain from extending it to others? Jesus said we are to pray for our enemies (Matt. 5:44). We are not commanded to pray for those who are humbly asking for our forgiveness; if they did, these people would not be our enemies. We are acknowledging in our prayer that we will forgive others *even if they don't believe they have wronged us or that there is any reason to ask for forgiveness in the first place.*

This is a sharp stick which pokes incessantly at my hornet's nest. I can forgive quickly and easily those who ask for it with humility and contrition. But it is excruciating—and sometimes infuriating—to be asked to forgive someone who has caused emotional and relational damage and still remains oblivious, apathetic, or mean-spirited in their treatment of me. When the hurt leaves me in a state of emotional asphyxiation, the last words I want to utter are, "I forgive you." But in in my furious state, I remember that Jesus, while hanging on the cross between thieves, asked his father to forgive those who put him there because they didn't know what they were doing (Luke 23:34).

In the Lord's Prayer, Jesus says to forgive—even when our enemies know *exactly* what they are doing. Stephen, when he is being stoned, prayed for his murderous enemies when he petitioned, "Lord, do not hold this sin against them" (Acts 7:60). They were throwing those stones at him without asking for any forgiveness, yet he prayed for their release. Maybe, just maybe, I can forgive when verbal stones are hurled my way. *Love your enemies.* That one little statement—just three words—is both tenderhearted and tough-minded. *Love*, don't tolerate. *Your*, the real and specific people who possess names and stories and an address. *Enemies*, not friends or strangers, but people who have personally hurt us in some manner.

Enemies cut. They cut us off, cut us down, or cut us out of relationship. A business partner maliciously takes advantage of you, a spouse walks out on you, a boss grossly mistreats you, someone seems to purposefully pull out in front of you in traffic almost causing an accident while simultaneously causing your blood pressure to rise. But failing to forgive them while asking God to forgive us is nothing less than hypocritical. Augustine wrote that God might have a question for *us*: "Why do you ask Me to do what I had promised, when you are not doing what I commanded?"[30] This incongruence plays like a low-budget film where the audio doesn't quite sync up with the video.

Several years ago, I heard author and teacher Frederica Matthewes-Green share an ancient Eastern Orthodox practice called The Rite of Forgiveness. The practice, in which Christians have participated for over a thousand years, is held each year on the evening before Lent begins on the Orthodox calendar. All members of the congregation—people who have been putting up with each other for a full twelve months—gather together to ask and receive forgiveness from each other. They stand in two lines facing one another, seek absolution and reconciliation, and then embrace. Then, they move to the next person and repeat the practice until they have done this with everyone in the room.

This rite is challenging and incredibly intimate, a counter-formational practice which jolts us into the reality that we are not the center of the world and that our sin has polluted our lives as well as the lives of others. We experience the effects of this pollution while also contributing to it.[31] This rite reminds me of Jesus' words: "If you are offering your gift at the altar and there remember that your brother or sister has something against you, leave your gift there in front of the altar. First go and be reconciled to them; then come and offer your gift" (Matt. 5:23–24). The rite helps followers of Jesus begin the season of Lent with a clean heart. Orthodox Christians call the day after the rite is practiced Clean Monday, and in Greece, they spend the day flying kites to symbolize the joyous and buoyant feeling of being forgiven and free. Maybe we, too, need to embody the spiritual practice of flying kites, unwinding the string and feeling the breeze on our cheeks, in order to remember our own forgiven-and-free state found through forgiveness.

When one of our pastors introduced the concept of the Rite of Forgiveness to a gathered group one winter morning, twenty adults stood in the middle of a living room, facing each other in two lines, as if we were about to begin a square dance or a round of Christian speed dating. It was uncomfortable and made us squirm inside—and we hadn't even begun. We were invited to look into the eyes of the person standing across from us and say:

"Dear [name], my brother/sister in God, please forgive me for any way I have sinned against you."

The person was instructed to respond, "I forgive you."

Then the one who forgave was directed to turn and ask for their own forgiveness.

"And please forgive me for any way I have sinned against you."

"I forgive you."

As we engaged in this rite, all of us drew on our courage. Each interaction felt deeply vulnerable, yet was followed by a warm, welcomed—and welcoming—embrace. Then, we all took one step to the right, faced a different person, and engaged in the practice once more.

Please forgive me for any way I have sinned against you.

Yes, I forgive you.

We circulated around the room until each of us had spent time reconciling with everyone else in the room. By the end of that sacred experience, many of us were locked in extended embraces, some whispering "Thank you," and others grabbing tissues and wiping tears. It is deeply moving and freeing to admit we are sinners—to admit that our sin has hurt others—and to be forgiven for our wrongdoing. The Rite of Forgiveness is a slow, soul-cleansing square dance of relinquishment. Asking for forgiveness and extending forgiveness to others sets us on the path of congruent living. It also makes us want to run out and fly kites together.

We often hear the phrase, "Forgive and forget," but I find this downright impossible. I seem to have an impeccable memory when it comes to situations wherein others have wounded me. Forgiving and forgetting is naïve and foolish. Likewise, not forgiving and not forgetting is dangerous and hypocritical. Jesus asks us to forgive, though he does not expect us to forget. It is in the remembering that the act of forgiveness molds us more into the likeness of Christ. To forgive others while also not forgetting is to live into the mysterious overlap of kingdom living. This is itself a mandorla practice, where we acknowledge the reality of the hurt from our past while still believing with hope in the potential of the future.

When we are deeply hurt by others, and the repairing, reconciling conversation occurs, it is less than helpful to lessen the blow by saying, "Oh, don't worry about it; it's not that big a deal." This cheapens the act of forgiveness and the gift of grace. This it's-not-that-big-a-deal mindset is certainly not how Jesus felt on the cross. It *was* a big deal. Our sin was a world-altering, earth-scarring big deal.

When we pray the Lord's Prayer, we pray that the values of heaven would be made manifest in our community, that our inner world would match our outer words and actions, that our knowing and believing would be integrated consistently and seamlessly with our doing. If we want to learn to live differently, then we need to learn to pray differently. Allowing the Lord's Prayer to shape us doesn't mean we will be taken out of the world; instead, it places us squarely in the middle of it.[32]

When we are finished praying the Lord's Prayer, acknowledging to our good Father our desire to live a congruent life, we end by saying "Amen" with humility and confidence. *Amen* is a little word that makes a big pronouncement. It places an emphatically bold exclamation point at the end of our prayers. "This is true." "I agree with all that has just been said." "May it be so." Or, as Eugene Peterson translated in *The Message*, "Yes, yes, yes!" Whether we pronounce it with a long or short "a," *Amen* means nothing more than "May it be so." Fearing Christians might be tempted to take ourselves a bit too seriously, Dallas Willard suggested we should translate "Amen" to "Whoopee!," uttered with a high-pitched squeal.[33] (Try it tonight before dinner; it'll stir your prayer imagination).

As Paul Miller wrote, prayer is incarnation. It is God with us. It is God involved in the details of our lives.[34] When we pray, we experience the incarnation once again. We are called not to simply recite it, but more importantly, to live it congruently—*con carne*.

There's no need to wait until we take the last train to glory. Life in the kingdom starts now. Let's go fly some kites.

Whoopee!

PART 3

JOINING GOD IN THE SACRED OVERLAP

Above all, trust in the slow work of God. We are, quite naturally, impatient in everything to reach the end without delay. We should like to skip the intermediate stages. We are impatient of being on the way to something unknown, something new, and yet it is the law of all progress that it is made by passing through some stages of instability—and that it may take a very long time . . . Only God could say what this new spirit gradually forming within you will be. Give our Lord the benefit of believing that His hand is leading you, and accept the anxiety of feeling yourself in suspense and incomplete.

**—PIERRE TEILHARD DE CHARDIN, FRENCH
PHILOSOPHER AND JESUIT PRIEST**

DUAL ENGAGEMENT

Evangelism and Discipleship at the Same Time

It is the duty of every Christian to be Christ to his neighbor.

—MARTIN LUTHER

"Come, follow me."

—JESUS, MARK 1:17

If someone asked you when Peter became a Christian, what would you tell them?

Some say it happened when Jesus called him to fish for men on the rocky shoreline of the Sea of Galilee. Others offer that it was at the end of Mark 8, when Peter answered Jesus' pointed question, "Who do you say that I am?" with "You are the Christ." Others point to when Jesus restored Peter after he had denied him three times. Some are convinced that it was not until after the resurrection, when he ran to the tomb and found it empty. Still others argue it happened at Pentecost when the Holy Spirit descended.

So what's the answer? We don't know for sure. But it seems

clear that Jesus discipled his disciples long before they actually became Christians. (Additionally, the term *Christian* wasn't even used until the end of Acts 11).

Can't we have a similar discussion about getting married? When, *exactly*, does a couple officially become a married couple? Is it when they say "I do"? Or exchange rings and a kiss? Or is it when the minister officially pronounces them husband and wife? Is it when all parties sign the marriage license, or when they consummate the marriage? Or is it the entire *process* of the wedding throughout the weekend? We don't know that either; it's both an event *and* a process.

Some Christians can look back and recount a specific date on the calendar of their conversion. For me, it was August 18, 1985, when I walked down the aisle of a small Southern Baptist Church in Charlottesville, Virginia, at the ripe age of six. But other friends have shared with me that they came to trust Jesus over a period of a few years—and then looked back on their lives and realized, *I've believed this stuff for a while; my life was surrendered to and shaped by Jesus. I guess that makes me a Christian.* And maybe that's just the point. Jesus engaged in discipleship *and* evangelism at the same time with the same people. It was an event *and also* a process.

It's easy to trip and fall into a false dichotomy, believing that evangelism only occurs before conversion and discipleship only happens after it. It sounds all fine and good on the surface, but there's one problem: we don't see much evidence of that in the Gospels. It seems Jesus was discipling those who didn't yet believe *and also* evangelizing those who already did.

The top question asked by any Bible-wielding, travel-weary evangelist is, "Where would you go if you were to die tonight?" This approach seeks to persuade people to repeat a carefully-worded prayer, sign on the divine dotted line, and rest assured that our ticket to heaven has been punched. But it's not about getting our tickets punched and then riding it out until we flatline. It's about doing something of utmost importance with our lives: *following Jesus*. Instead of asking, "Where would you go if you died tonight?" Dallas Willard posed another question: "If you *don't* die tonight, what are you going to do tomorrow?"[1] A committed disciple of Jesus would most likely respond something like this: "I will wake up and live as best I can in the full trust, grace, and guidance of Christ as I submit to God's kingdom."

In our North American context, most people have preconceived notions about God and Christians, and let's be completely honest: often, these assumptions are not pretty. Author and kingdom practitioner Hugh Halter offers a great definition of evangelism, one I use frequently: Evangelism is changing people's assumptions about God and his people.[2] By Halter's definition, evangelism occurs when people begin to acknowledge, *Hey, maybe I can begin to trust this God of the Universe and maybe God's people aren't as strange/ evil/awkward/judgmental/off-based/fill-in-the-blank as I originally thought.* Evangelism, when properly understood, is the hope filled, world-changing announcement where everyone, regardless of their past or present situation, is invited to come in and join the party of kingdom living. In dying to ourselves and submitting to the King— who is a gracious and loving Father—we experience life like never before.

Let's just come out and admit it: When most of us think about evangelism, we are on the verge of breaking out in hives and feeling our tongues swell up. Maybe we've seen it done so poorly that we're embarrassed. Ask most people under the age of thirty-five, and they'll admit that evangelism makes them weak in the knees. In our postmodern culture, evangelism is tough sledding. Now, hear me out: I'm certainly not against evangelism. Not at all. It would be hard to overemphasize the importance of seeing people come to saving faith in Jesus Christ. In fact, I am not exactly sure how many people would enter into a vibrant relationship with Jesus without someone, in some form or another, communicating to them the life-altering, grace-inducing message of the Risen Christ. As Christians, we don't engage in it nearly as much as we should. But what I am advocating for is *a proper understanding and holistic approach to evangelism.*

Evangelism, as we've stated, is crucial to life in Christ. But why is it that we don't view discipleship as equally crucial? One is not more important than the other. More often than not, our

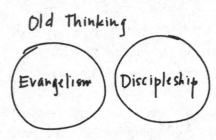

mental bowling ball ends up in one of two gutters: believing "being saved" is between me and Jesus in the present, or that it's about going to be with God in the future. What about learning to live with Christ in an ever-growing, ever-deepening, ever-expanding reality in the here and now? There are Christians who care too much about life after death, accused of being too heavenly-minded to do any earthly good. This puts us at risk of never truly experiencing life.[3] It is living with the awareness that it affects now *and* eternity. Eternity is in session.[4] If we bisect evangelism and discipleship, we miss out on the rich dimensions of life available to us in the kingdom.

Evangelism, yes. Discipleship, yes. We need both. I like the portmanteau missional stategist and practitioner Alan Hirsch created: *disciplism.* Hirsch writes, "We need to reconceive discipleship as a process that includes pre-conversion discipleship and post-conversion discipleship."[5] I've been a Christian for over three-and-a-half decades, and, truth be told, I still need others to evangelize me. I need to be told again and again about the saving message of Jesus, about my hopeless state before Christ and my hope-filled present and future with him. I need to be caught up again in the wonder of grace and the breathtaking vision of redemption and rescue. I need to be enamored again by the gospel—the good news, which is so good, I couldn't make up such a story on my own if I tried. I have friends like Brian, who surrendered his life to Christ, tripped across the threshold of the kingdom, and fell into the lap of Jesus. We celebrated his decision by hiking in the woods of Pennsylvania near a river in the Lehigh Valley, where we sat down, dangled our feet over the side of an old steel train bridge, and took Communion together. I discipled Brian every week for two years as we read through the Book of Mark over coffee before he finally pulled the trigger.

If we get our evangelism wrong, we will most certainly get our discipleship wrong, too. If evangelism is just a check-the-box insurance policy paid for with the simple verbalization of a brief prayer, then calling those same people to costly, lifelong obedience in Christ in the days ahead will be a nearly impossible task. What you win people *with* is what you win them *to*.[6] If people receive a message of spiritual comfort baptized in consumerism, they will come to expect that moving forward. Orlando Costas knew it well and said it best: if we do not communicate a gospel which expects a complete abandonment of self, we will be tempted to believe in a

conscience-soothing Jesus, with an unscandalous cross, an otherworldly kingdom, a private, inwardly limited spirit, a pocket God, a spiritualized Bible, and an escapist church. Its goal is a happy, comfortable, and successful life, obtainable through the forgiveness of an abstract sinfulness by faith in an unhistorical Christ.[7]

The first half of Jesus' message is *come and see*; the second half is *pick up your cross and follow me.*

When Jimmy Carter was president, a reporter allegedly chided him by saying he had been born again a few too

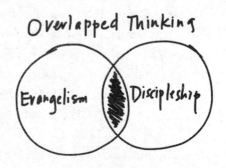

many times. Yet maybe there's more to this than we realize. Isn't that the point of maturity and discipleship, to be born again and again—*and again*? I'm in need of being converted many times over. Aren't we all?

I'm not stating that Jesus' saving work is conditional or that we need to walk the aisle during an altar call every few weeks. What I am talking about is what the Methodists refer to frequently as the process of sanctification. This was Peter's story in Acts 10–11. God used Peter to proclaim the good news to others so they might experience new life in Christ. Thousands experienced this conversion—and yet, in God's great irony, *Peter was also being converted in the process.* The messenger of conversion was experiencing his own personal conversion at the same time.[8] Maybe *that* was the moment Peter became a Christian.

Every other month for a few years, I threw on a blazer and tie and drove fifty miles on the narrow, meandering roads which led to Princeton, New Jersey to meet the venerable Dr. Darrell Guder, former professor at Princeton Theological Seminary and distinguished scholar of missional theology. I would drive past the famous Princeton gate and the beautiful stone buildings with ivy crawling slowly up their walls. Hogwarts in New Jersey. I was reminded of former US presidents, governors, Nobel Prize winners and famous scholars who were once students or faculty members there. This little town is a fortress of scholarship and a coterie of silver spoons where the majority of the world's tweed jackets reside. I would try to trick myself into believing the lie that my IQ immediately jumped twenty points each time. Darrell was always kind enough to treat me to a fancy lunch at the historic Nassau Club nestled on the edge of the university's campus, whose previous members included Albert Einstein and Woodrow Wilson. Needless to say, it was not Waffle House and I was far out of my element.

As we sat in high-backed wing chairs at tables set with white linen and fine china, I felt my insecurities rise. I fretted over which fork to use when and tried to remind myself not to crane my neck while eating my soup, all the while trying to play it cool. One afternoon, over sautéed chicken with glazed asparagus, Darrell kindly mused about church and God's mission while I furiously captured his brilliant thoughts in my little leather notebook. Each visit felt like a free seminary course in which I was the only student.

Darrell told me often that in order for us to remain faithful to God and his mission, we must submit to the work of the Holy Spirit, where we are called to be people of *yes* and people of *no* at the same time. We will experience, he told me, *a continual conversion of the church*. While rooted in Christ, it is the church's mandate to continually be renewed and reconceived. Our task in faithful witness (which is not the same thing as faithful *witnessing*, he said emphatically) is declaring that Christ is Lord, that he is risen, and that we as the church are called to live the resurrection life here and now, just as we are, in the real world. "Evangelism," Darrell reminded me, "isn't to satisfy people; instead, it is to *transform* us." If the gospel isn't transforming our lives, how can we realistically expect that it will transform the people around us? Do we even have a right to expect that?

When I teach on evangelism, more often than not someone will raise their hand and proudly share, "It's important we remember what St. Francis of Assisi said: 'Always preach the gospel; if necessary, use words.'" I allow them to finish. Then I draw one slow, full breath, clear my throat and thank them for sharing—and then tell them they're wrong. First, I tell them as politely as I can, that this quote is most often shared as an excuse to justify why we don't share (or haven't shared) our faith with others. As my friend Matt once quipped, saying this is like saying, "Feed the hungry; if necessary, use food." Second, there's no record that St. Francis actually said this, which can be unsettling for people to hear. Finally, this statement is unbiblical. I'm certainly not trying to be mean, but I *am* trying to catch this tiger by its tail, attempting to correct an erroneously attributed quote and wrongly held belief about our role in God's grand mission.

When Jesus actively shapes and forms our lives, talking about him with others becomes natural; it doesn't come out sounding like a religious sales pitch. Paul writes to Timothy, saying that we are to preach the Word, being prepared both in and out of season (2 Tim. 4:2). Peter writes that we are to set apart Christ as Lord and be prepared to gently and respectfully give an answer about the source of our hope (1 Peter 3:15). In Acts 19, during the riot of Ephesus, with tens of thousands of angry Ephesian residents filling the Great Theater and chanting for hours on end, the locals want to tear Paul's limbs apart. He begs them, not to protect him and help him escape the city, but to let him tell them about Christ, believing that even if only a few of them come to faith, it will be worth it. The Gospel needs to be told.

I'm not advocating that we stand outside Starbucks with sandwich boards and bullhorns and pass out tracts. But we're not off the hook. I'm trying to persuade all of us to officially retire the alleged St. Francis quote and tell people what Jesus means to us. Just because we've seen it done poorly doesn't mean we should abandon the whole endeavor. Salt does nothing to enhance flavor when it remains in the shaker.

What, then, is discipleship? It is the process by which we are formed in the image of Christ for the sake of others. I've heard Alan Hirsch say many times that it is *the irreplaceable and lifelong task of becoming*

like Jesus by embodying his message. To be disciples is to consistently embody the life, spirituality, and mission of our founder. Late pastor, friend, and author Eugene Peterson, on a hike around Flathead Lake near his home in Montana one June afternoon, shared truth that continues to remain with me: true disciples are people who attempt to pay attention to God and respond appropriately. Or, as the title of one of his books suggests, it is a long obedience in the same direction.

Some Christians choose to adopt a life verse. It's not required, but I have learned that in some settings it's expected. I didn't have a life verse for a long time. When people would ask me what my life verse was, I would just look at them blankly, take a breath, and mumble something vaguely spiritual, such as, "I like all the verses in the Bible." But over the past decade, 1 John 2:6, "Whoever claims to live in him must live as Jesus did," has grown on me so much, I've now given it official designation as my life verse. It's simple and to the point. It challenges me and reminds me that the purpose of the Christian life is clear: to follow Jesus obediently. This process is both who we are *and also* what we do. It is active *and also* passive. It is what God is doing in us *and also* what God does through us. It is simple *and also* a mystery.

There are two essential components necessary for someone to be a disciple of Jesus: there must be a *desire* to follow him, and there must be a *decision* to realign our lives to think and act as if Jesus were here today. Desire and commitment must go hand in hand. To be a disciple is to be an apprentice, a hands-on learner who doesn't simply want information, but is passionately committed to becoming like the master teacher. In ancient Greece, the word *mathetes* was used to describe a disciple, a learner–apprentice. Apprentices were purposefully engaged in instruction in various fields such as dancing, wrestling, music, astronomy, writing, hunting, and medicine. They were committed to imitation through proximity, time, and experience in order to become like their masters. Certain professions today, such as electricians, mechanics, bricklayers, and carpenters require apprenticeships with hands-on training. To be a disciple of Jesus is to sign up for apprenticeship in kingdom living, not simply to read the manual and successfully pass a comprehensive multiple-choice exam. Instead, we cooperatively interact with God in order to have our character transformed to be like Jesus in our everyday experiences. We are participants in the life of Jesus, not just by accepting him as Lord and Savior, but also by seeing him as our master teacher for right living.

Canadian teaching pastor Bruxy Cavey taught that there are five main elements of apprenticeship in the life and way of Jesus. First, a disciple *submits to a teacher* who teaches him or her how to follow Jesus. Second, a disciple *learns the words of Jesus.* Third, a disciple *learns the way of ministry of Jesus.* Fourth, a disciple *imitates the life and character of Jesus.* And fifth, a disciple *finds and teaches other disciples who will also follow Jesus.* Most ministries and churches, Bruxy says, contain three of the five components—specifically numbers two, three, and four. But discipleship is accepting Jesus' challenge to follow him *in all five areas.*[9]

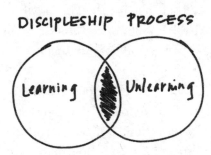

DISCIPLESHIP PROCESS

Learning   Unlearning

We tend to believe that discipleship is primarily what we learn, a classroom-centric cognitive view of following Jesus. But what if becoming a disciple of Jesus was as much about *unlearning* inaccurate or unhelpful views of God and his story as it is about learning new things?[10]

There are several common misconceptions about discipleship.

It's not simply Christian education.

It's not a Bible study or an accountability group or class or program where you automatically become like Jesus upon completion.

It's not a feel-good support group.

It's not Oprah with a little bit of Jesus sprinkled in.

Discipleship is costly. We must be careful not to simply embrace an American cultural Christianity that sees religion as a shiny hood ornament on our spiritual car. If our approach to discipleship leads us to greater comfort, safety, and predictability in all areas of our lives, we can be sure we've missed the boat. If our Christianity is doughy, passive, consumeristic, capitalistic, Republican (or Democratic), and soft, we're following something, but it's certainly not Jesus. It was author Marianne Williamson who said that when you invite God into your life, you think he's going to walk around your spiritual house, look around, and recommend you need new furniture and maybe a little tidying up around the place. But after a while, you look out the window and, to your horror, you notice there's a wrecking ball outside. It seems God thinks your whole foundation is crumbling, and he wants to knock the whole thing down and start over.[11]

Discipleship is not about models or religious programs intended to make us try harder, look better, or sound holier.

It's not a bunch of rules and regulations.

It's not a moral checklist.

Additionally, we can't fall into the temptation of believing that simply showing up for a Sunday morning service each week will form us to be like Jesus. As Dallas Willard wrote, "One of the greatest current barriers to meaningful spiritual formation into Christ-likeness is overconfidence in the spiritual efficacy of regular church services. They are vital, but they aren't enough. It is that simple."[12] We need more. We need a robust, life-giving, hope-infused plan that engages the Monday-through-Saturday life, too.

Perhaps the most damning of all misconceptions about discipleship is the belief that it is optional. Somehow we've created a spiritual partition between being a Christian and being a disciple.

This dualistic approach to the Christian life is anemic and inaccurate. The truth is that to be a Christian is to be a fully devoted, committed, obedient disciple, seeking to imitate the life and teachings of Jesus. Discipleship in the way of Jesus requires obedience. There's no other way around it. We are not called to know all *about* Jesus. We are not called to be enthusiastic admirers or fans of him. As pastor Kyle Idleman wrote in his book *Not a Fan*, many of us want to cohabitate with Jesus without actually committing to him.[13] Nowhere in Scripture will we find it's plausible to be a Christian without ever becoming a disciple.

Nobody drifts into a committed, growing relationship with Christ. Nobody wakes up one day and says, "I'm not sure how it happened, but without any effort or thought, I've become a lot like Jesus in every area of my life." To be a disciple of Jesus means a purposeful and intentional engagement with and commitment to follow Jesus and his ways. This takes practice. People who are actively engaged in discipleship are committed to seeing individuals who are far from God grow into deeply devoted followers of Jesus, where they long for every person to believe God's purposes in life are the best path forward. Neil Cole pulls no punches:

> Ultimately, each church will be evaluated by only one thing—its disciples. Your church is only as good as her disciples. It does not matter how good your praise, preaching, programs or property are; if your disciples are passive, needy, consumeristic, and not radically obedient, your church is not good.[14]

In the Gospel of Matthew, Jesus says the following:

> "Come to me, all you who are weary and burdened, and I will give you rest. Take my yoke upon you and learn from me, for I am gentle and humble in heart, and you will find rest for your souls. For my yoke is easy and my burden is light." (Matt. 11:28–30)

And yet, the Gospel of John tells us that Jesus' followers felt his teaching was demanding.

> On hearing it, many of his disciples said, "This is a hard teaching. Who can accept it?" Aware that his disciples were grumbling about this, Jesus said to them, "Does this offend you? Then what if you see the Son of Man ascend to where he was before! The Spirit gives life; the flesh counts for nothing. The words I have spoken to you—they are full of the Spirit and life. Yet there are some of you who do not believe." (John 6:60–64)

Several of Jesus' followers found this teaching to be so difficult that they turned back and no longer followed him (v. 66). As a result, Jesus had an intense interaction with the disciples:

> "You do not want to leave too, do you?" Jesus asked the Twelve. Simon Peter answered him, "Lord, to whom shall we go? You have the words of eternal life. We have come to believe and to know that you are the Holy One of God." (John 6:67–69)

Jesus told them that if they couldn't stand the heat, they needed to get out of the discipleship kitchen. But wait a minute. Which is it, an easy yoke and a light burden or such a difficult teaching we're tempted to walk away? It's both. How wonderful. And how scary.

We could summarize Jesus' invitational posture found in the gospel in three parts: (1) *Come and see*, (2) *come and die*, and (3) *go and do*. Look at the way Jesus called his first disciples in John 1:

> The next day John was there again with two of his disciples. When he saw Jesus passing by, he said, "Look, the Lamb of God!"
> When the two disciples heard him say this, they followed Jesus. Turning around, Jesus saw them following and asked, "What do you want?"

They said, "Rabbi" (which means "Teacher"), "where are you staying?"

"Come," he replied, "and you will see."

So they went and saw where he was staying, and they spent that day with him (John 1:35–39).

Jesus' first engagement with these future followers was a question: "What do you want?" They responded with a question of their own: "Where are you staying?" His response: "Come and you will see." Can't you just imagine Jesus, with a slight grin on his face and a twinkle in his soft eyes, confidently but peacefully saying, "Come"?

In the Gospels, we not only see Jesus exhibiting an invitational posture; we also see people who are deeply impacted by Jesus' gracious approach who turn to others and extend the same invitational posture. A few verses later, Jesus continues in this posture:

The next day Jesus decided to leave for Galilee. Finding Philip, he said to him, "Follow me."

Philip, like Andrew and Peter, was from the town of Bethsaida. Philip found Nathanael and told him, "We have found the one Moses wrote about in the Law, and about whom the prophets also wrote—Jesus of Nazareth, the son of Joseph."

"Nazareth! Can anything good come from there?" Nathanael asked.

"Come and see," said Philip. (John 1:43–46)

Jesus asks Philip to follow him. *Come and see* is always an invitation to the truest form of learning. Philip was convinced that Jesus was the One his people had been waiting for. His first response was to locate his friend Nathanael and persuade him to pursue Jesus also. But Nathanael isn't so sure. Nazareth? That forgettable, on-the-way-to-nothing little town—*seriously?* Instead of offering data, a thorough and logical rationale, or key theological details to explain and defend his conviction about Jesus, Philip responds in the best way possible, with three little words: *Come and see*.

And how about the woman at the well in John 4? She experienced Jesus' invitation when he asked her a question: "Will you give me a drink?" (John 4:7). Their conversation resonated so significantly that she left her jar at the well, ran back into town, and said to the locals, "Come, see a man who told me everything I ever did. Could this be the Messiah?" (John 4:29). It sounds like she might have had doubts of her own. She invited and yet still questioned. Yet her question seemed to be an appeal for others to see Jesus, too. *Come, see.* Even in her uncertainty, she became a conduit for the spreading of the news about Jesus.

Almost always before people come and see Jesus, they need to *know someone else who knows Jesus*. This is where we come in. People who know Jesus and want other people to know Jesus need to be the bridge, the introducer—just like Philip was to Nathanael and the estranged woman was to the Samaritan village. There are exceptions, of course. When my dad was in college, he put his trust in Christ late one night in a hotel room. He pulled open the drawer of the nightstand, cracked open a Gideon Bible, read about the compassion of God, and surrendered his life right there on the bed. He thought he was the only person who had ever become a Christian. It wasn't an arrogant belief; he was simply ignorant of the truth, unaware of the vast community of Jesus followers around the globe. No one had ever explained God's hope-filled rescue plan to him before, and he thought he had found an answer nobody else knew. But for the vast majority of us who are followers of Jesus, we can most likely trace the beginning of our faith story to a moment when someone said to us the equivalent of *come and see*. At the beginning of almost everyone's faith story is someone who introduced them to Jesus. People have to trust you to *come and see* Jesus before they trust him for themselves.

In Acts 17, we see Paul's embodied posture of invitation when he hung out in Athens. He was asked to explain Christianity in clear and compelling ways to Stoic and Epicurean philosophers, two groups with massive worldview differences. When he opened his mouth to speak, Paul sought to find common ground, so he offered a compliment: "People of Athens! I see that in every way you are very religious" (17:22). Paul met them on *their* terms, quoted *their* poets, and built bridges of trust and commonality. But he didn't stop there: he went on to call them ignorant. He continued sharing with them about a God who is not unknown; this God not only has a name, but is also accessible and nearby. Paul was soft *and* hard with them. He didn't simply arrive on the scene and condemn their culture, but neither did he accommodate and endorse it wholeheartedly.

With this overlap of evangelism and discipleship, how do we help people *come and see* in order to eventually follow? Several years ago, I was driving in my car listening to a talk by Erwin McManus. He shared that every one of us has three significant longings: a longing for *destiny*, a longing for *community* and a longing for *significance*. All three of these longings were placed in us by the God of the universe when we were created. It's what the author of Ecclesiastes meant when he wrote that God has "set eternity in the human heart" (Eccl. 3:11).

When we long for *destiny*, we want to know we are going somewhere. It's why questions about the afterlife have dominated the minds of people for generations. We are wired to ask such significant questions. They're stamped upon our souls. When we long for *community*, we want to know and be known. We are wired to long for love, to be cared for, to be touched and embraced. And when we long for *significance*, we are asking questions about purpose. *Why am I here? Is the whole purpose of my life to get up, go to work, make money, come home, go to bed and get up and do it all over again tomorrow for the next forty years? Is this all there is?*

Destiny addresses where we are going. Thus, we can explore our future and how it impacts the ways we invest our days right now.

Community addresses who we are and being known as we truly are. This allows us to explore our loneliness, worth, and identity.

Significance addresses meaning. This also allows us to explore our purpose and reason for living.

Sadly, we've all seen how people try to fill these longings with all sorts of substitutes, many of them destructive. The drive to fulfill these longings is so strong that we will still pursue them *even if we have the full knowledge and awareness that what we are trying to fulfill them with is harmful and destructive.* Isn't this the nature of idols: they seem so promising and yet leave us unfulfilled in the end? All addictions can be traced back to a desire which ultimately seeks to satisfy at least one of these three longings of the human heart. They may satisfy us for a short time, but we will always be left disappointed and dissatisfied. To challenge people to *come and see* is to help people get a fuller glimpse of Jesus as the only one who can fill all three longings of the human heart.

McManus' words were insightful. I began to think about the ways in which I could work naturally, patiently, and compassionately to connect the dots in conversations with my friends, coworkers, and neighbors. When a friend told me he was afraid to die because he didn't know what would happen next, I looked for ways to connect the dot of his longing for destiny to Jesus. When someone in the neighborhood admitted to me that he felt like he was wasting his life by making lots of money but absolutely hating his job (and ultimately making his life miserable), I sought out appropriate opportunities to converse with him about his longing for significance. When a dad at my kids' school vulnerably shared one afternoon how lonely he was and how awful loneliness felt, I leaned into the conversation, asking questions to connect the dot of community in his life. All three of these people opened up to me—and it opened the door for me to talk about Jesus.

These three longings give me a clear paradigm for engaging in conversations with people about Jesus in ways that are natural and meaningful. When I connect those dots to Jesus, I am amazed by the kinds of conversations I have with others. If God has placed these longings in every person we will ever meet, it shouldn't surprise us if we find ourselves engaging in meaningful conversation about God, faith, Jesus, eternity, and the kingdom, about destiny, community, and significance.

When was the last time you told people what Jesus means to you? Michael Greene, a British historian of evangelism, posed this question at a gathering several years ago. Among those in the audience was Martin Copenhaver, pastor of a congregation in Burlington, Vermont. This question remained in Copenhaver's mind as he stood to preach the last sermon of his nine years of service to his congregation. He spent the bulk of that sermon sharing his devotion to Christ. Copenhaver concluded with the following words:

> As I am about to leave, there is something I want to tell you. I want to tell you what Jesus means to me. I want to share my belief that everything depends upon him. I want to urge you to learn from him. I want to assure you that you can lean on him in times of trouble. I want to ask you to listen to his words of challenge. I want to tell you that I believe that you can entrust your life to him. I want to affirm that he is Lord of this church and that in his name, you are freed to love one another and empowered to share that love with a hurting world. I want to profess that, though once people could not look at the face of God and live, now we are invited to look at the face of God in him, in

Jesus, and live as we have never lived before. He is Emmanuel, God with us, God with us all, whether we are together or apart. That's what it's all about.

That's all I know. Amen.

At the end of the service, Copenhaver positioned himself at the back door of the church and shook the hands of people as they left. One woman, a longtime member, was so emotional when she reached him that she could not speak. She retreated to the back of the receiving line to collect herself and try again. Copenhaver assumed she was saddened by his departure and was having difficulty saying goodbye. When she arrived at the front of the line again, she shook the pastor's hand, leaned in, and asked a question which has haunted Copenhaver ever since. With tears in her eyes, in a cracked voice she asked, "Why didn't you tell us this before?"[15]

Evangelism is, as N. T. Wright says, to discover forgiveness for the past, an astonishing destiny in God's future, and a vocation in the present.[16] And discipleship is the process by which I am converted again and again and again. Many years ago, John Bright said it winsomely:

We can't preach the ethics of Jesus and leave behind his mission and personhood. Nor can we sneer at the approach for not preaching a full gospel and then when we urge people to saving faith in Christ, not confront the systemic issues and demands of righteousness of the kingdom. We do not have two gospels, social and personal, which vie for the limelight. We have one gospel, the gospel of the kingdom of God, and it is both. We have simply nothing else to preach.[17]

Discipling the lost and evangelizing the found: an overlapped vision for the overlapped life.

CHAPTER 10

PRACTICING RESURRECTION TOGETHER

Peculiar Practices of the Overlapped Life

Practice resurrection.

—WENDELL BERRY

The obviously well-kept secret of the "ordinary" is that it is made to be a receptacle of the divine, a place where the life of God flows.

—DALLAS WILLARD

I was a four-year starter on my high school varsity basketball team. As a shooting guard, I wasn't tall, extraordinarily fast or overwhelmingly strong. My game could be described as well below the rim. I was a solid shooter and what people call a cerebral player (a coach on the floor, as my coach described me). I prided myself on being consistent from the free throw line. I practiced free throws for hours at a time in an empty gym—before school, at lunch, during practice, and again after practice was over. *Toe the line, three dribbles, ball spin, knees bent, ball up. Swish.* I live by the bone-deep conviction that every high-caliber basketball player, from high school on up, should be excellent at free throws. Just you and the ball at the same place on the floor, and the rim, the same distance away. That's why it's called a *free throw.* Invest enough intentional time and focused practice, and just about anybody can be great at it.

Hundreds of hours, thousands of repetitions. *Three dribbles, ball spin, knees bent, ball up. Swish.* Sometimes I wouldn't stop until I had made twenty-five in a row. The hard work paid off as I finished second in the state of Virginia two years in a row in the Hoop Shoot contest sponsored by the Elks Club. At points during each season, my free throw percentage reached into the low-to-mid-nineties. When I broke my ankle in an AAU state tournament game my junior year, I couldn't practice or play, but I would still hobble to the free throw line, drop my crutches, and sink free throws for an hour. What I did in the early mornings before school in an empty gym felt the same as on a Friday night in a packed gym with the game on the line. At that point, it was just muscle memory. Practice.

It was the great poet and essayist Wendell Berry who first used the phrase "practice resurrection." But what exactly does it mean to *practice* resurrection? How do I practice resurrection on an ordinary morning when I'm trying to get the boys to brush their teeth and get out the door to school on time without fighting with each other? How do I practice resurrection on an evening when Megan and I are draped across the couch, exhausted and indecisive about what movie to watch? Practicing resurrection, I've come to learn, is a way of life which leads me down the path toward God-oriented maturity.

Practice, I've learned, has less to do with free throws than I thought. It's more in line with attorneys who practice law or doctors who practice medicine or nuns who enter into the practice of prayer.

It's what they devote their lives to, their vocational callings. It's a purposeful process that brings our bodies, minds, and souls into alignment around a common purpose—an engagement in some sort of ritual. A dedicated, daily exercise of commitment.[1] We read in the Gospels that Jesus grew in maturity in his younger years. He "grew in wisdom and stature, and in favor with God and man" (Luke 2:52). What a fascinating thought: *Jesus had to grow in maturity.*[2] I wonder what it must have been like for Mary and Joseph to see this happening before their eyes.

Practicing resurrection means we grow in our maturity as well. Eugene Peterson surmised that birth receives far more attention in the American church than growth. Birth is quick and easy (at least to fathers and children), and marked by a specific event. Growth is endless and complex, full of fatigue and pain and uncertainty. Growth happens gradually over a long period of time.[3]

Take a moment and think carefully about the tasks you participate in on a typical Tuesday. You may think of staring at a screen doing data entry in a cubicle or driving a truck or doing the dishes or picking up shirts from the dry cleaner or sitting through another mind-numbing experience of death-by-meeting. Maybe you feel stuck in a dead-end job which excites you about as much as a colonoscopy. The weeks have turned to months, which have turned to years. Now what? To practice resurrection is to be fully aware that we are Christians-in-the-making, to live an unhurried life of becoming reconciled with God and others.[4] It is where "we will grow up healthy in God, robust in love" (Eph. 4:16 MSG).

To practice resurrection seems peculiar. Truth be told, it *is* peculiar. In fact, we are underestimating our peculiarity.[5] As we yield our lives to a peculiar God, we must also engage in practices of resurrection peculiarity. *All this is good and well,* you may think, *but how do we do this? What practices can we engage in to ensure that we live into the ethos of this posture?*

We'll dive into the practical in a bit, but first, some context. While

I'm going to offer practical steps forward, I would never want anyone to interpret what I am saying as a formula to follow, making life overly simplistic or depersonalizing our relationships. I want to provide a form without a formula and an intention without an equation. Since this kind of life is not a mechanical, cut-and-dried approach, this chapter won't be, either. I won't provide you with six easy steps or instructions to add water and stir. But it can be helpful to have rails to run on, especially while exploring a new way of thinking and living. I want to help you find the tension point between purposeful preparation *and also* holy anticipation of interruptions that can arrive unannounced on your doorstep. Faith is both planning *and* trusting. Too loose and nothing gets done; too controlling and only *our* plans might be accomplished. Read these practical opportunities the way you would enjoy seafood: eat the fish and throw away the bones. The best part: you get to decide what is meat and what are bones.

Practicing free throws can be done in isolation, but practicing resurrection by pressing into our God-initiated peculiarity must be done in the context of community. The Christian story, faithfully embodied and practiced with others, leads to a more variegated experience with Jesus. This happens in many ways, but I submit these specific practices for your discernment.

Peculiar Practice One: Participating in Communion Regularly

The late journalist and filmmaker Nora Ephron said that a family is a group of people who eat the same thing for dinner. Ordinary meals form us. Tables shape us. Tables create cultures. And families. Few things express our identity as brothers and sisters more tangibly than sharing bread and wine together in shared remembrance of Jesus. Interestingly, it was Jesus' table manners that often got him in trouble and ultimately got him killed. Theologian Robert

Karris wrote, "Jesus was killed because of the way he ate."[6] Leonard Sweet said we could sum up the Gospels this way: Jesus ate good food with bad people.[7] Growing up, I went to a lot of church potlucks where I ate bad food with good people, God bless 'em. But Jesus chose to do the opposite.

John 21 records Jesus, bodily resurrected, standing on the shore of the Sea of Galilee while his disciples are out in the boat fishing. He calls out to them, knowing they haven't caught a thing. The disciples recognize the stranger's voice: it is the Risen Christ in flesh-and-blood form. In all their hysteria and excitement, they get to shore and learn that Jesus has cooked breakfast for them. Out of Jesus' mouth comes one of the most comforting and welcoming lines we might ever hear: "Breakfast is ready" (John 21:12 MSG).

There is nothing more ordinary and routine than eating a meal with others. We are formed in the routines of meals, even as we twirl spaghetti around a fork or ask, "Could you pass the butter, please?" Eating is a necessity for our own nourishment, but also for our enjoyment and connection with others. This is the nature of the Communion meal. There is nothing more ordinary and also nothing more extraordinary than remembering Jesus' body and blood. "O taste and see that the Lord is good," wrote the psalmist (Psalm 34:8 NASB). I relish the fact that this verse begins with "O," an expression of utter delight, the way we start a sentence when we are enjoying a meal which is downright delicious. Our senses—including our spiritual senses—are heightened and engaged when we eat.

Communion, Holy Communion, the Lord's Table, the Lord's Supper, or the Eucharist—call it what you may—is powerfully formative. The Communion table created a society of subversive love and inclusive redemption. It's where we are reminded that there is no hierarchy of spiritual importance. At this meal, Jesus is host, and we are guests. As nineteenth-century philosopher Ludwig Feuerbach famously stated, "Man is what he eats." It is this table that shapes every other table at which we sit and eat.

While our church doesn't call it by the more formal name, the Eucharist, I love that that original word, *eucharistia*, means "thanksgiving." Communion is a weekly Thanksgiving meal with members of God's family. Former archbishop of Canterbury, theologian and author Rowan Williams, wrote,

> We take Holy Communion not because we are doing well, but because we are doing badly. Not because we have arrived, but because we are traveling. Not because we are right, but because we are confused and wrong. Not because we are divine, but because we are human. Not because we are full, but because we are hungry.[8]

This is plenty of reason to be thankful as needy guests at God's plentiful table. If I cannot have a thankful heart when I come to the table, then I am not fit to come. And if I do not come with a repentant heart when I come, I am also unfit to come. Communion is repentance *and also* praise. Its implications are personal *and also* communal. If baptism is where we are handed our green cards, reminding us of our resident alien status, it is the Communion table which reminds us of our true identity as loved, saved, rescued, redeemed, and commissioned children of God.

Adam and Eve's grave mistake wasn't that they touched the fruit or smelled the fruit or looked at the fruit. It wasn't even that they held it in their hands. The damning effect of humanity is that they *ate* it. They swallowed sin. It became a part of them because they ingested it.[9] We are regularly reminded that our ancestors ingested death, which took place in a garden. We, too, need to regularly and frequently ingest life which took place on a bloodied cross and in an empty tomb. That life ingestion takes place around the Lord's Table. The first Adam ingested death; the second Adam—Jesus—made the way possible for us to ingest life.[10] Communion is not a mid-service snack; it is the sustenance of the sacred overlap.

I grew up in a church context which contracted a severe case of *Eucharistophobia*, the condition of being afraid to partake in Communion too frequently for fear it might become stale, rote, or passé, thus losing its meaning and power. What resulted was partaking in Communion once or twice (maybe three times, if we were fortunate) each year, despite the fact that much of the early church partook in Communion every single day. When we planted our church several years ago, I had similar concerns. But I realized over time that the Communion table, as amazing and sacred and rich as it is, at times *does* feel ordinary—and that's okay. We began celebrating it more regularly; first, once a month, and we now celebrate every time we gather. We have grown to realize that this is central to all we do. After the message, we quietly rise and shuffle up the two side aisles to the Communion table, a weathered and stained round table placed inside the blue circle of center court in the gym where our church gathers, a detail I've found to be both spatially and theologically important.

For each of our gatherings, someone in our community brings freshly baked bread. We want the personal nature of this time to be evident at the table, even in how the bread looks and tastes. It's not the tasteless, white circular wafers with a perfectly embossed cross—we want a full-bodied experience with our senses fully engaged. On the rare occasion that someone forgets to bake the Communion bread, a good soul will make an emergency run to the grocery store to pick up the second-best thing: King's Hawaiian rolls, which are sometimes referred to in our church as "Sweet Baby Jesus."

When the Communion leader for the morning finishes explaining what we are about to partake in and why we do it, there is always a slightly awkward but noticeable moment of struggle. Putting down the microphone, the leader holds up the bread and, with a slight sense of nervousness and a subtle look of intensity, uses all of his or her strength to rip the loaf in two, much like trying to open a new bag of potato chips without splitting open the entire bag. Eventually the bread tears with a slight but noticeable jolt, and the halves are placed on two plates to be distributed to all of us. These certainly are not empty calories we are about to partake of; they are our sustenance, the Bread of Life. The ripping, the struggle, the awkwardness, the jolt—all help us understand the sacrifice of Jesus.

Sometimes, before I am given the elements, the server embraces me with a hug, then holds out the elements, looks me in the eye, and addresses me by name:

"J.R., this is Christ's body broken for you."

"J.R., this is Christ's blood poured out for you."

When I receive each element, I always say, "Thanks be to God" in something slightly louder than a whisper. This is about grace—wildly undeserved grace—which should evoke deep gratitude in us. Contrary to popular belief, nobody owes us anything. The Great Thanksgiving deserves at least a simple *Thank you*. Author and professor A. J. Swoboda wrote that "if you don't come to the table as broken as the bread and as dark as the wine, then you don't deserve to partake . . . At the body and blood of Christ in the bread and wine, we are confronted with a God big enough to save us from our sins and yet tiny enough to get stuck between your teeth."[11]

Some join the Communion line with walkers and knee braces while others, usually children, come bounding, dancing, and twirling in anticipation. I love it when the kids approach the table with their parents. Children have not yet gained the social sensibilities of making sure there is enough for everyone to partake. They are eager and excited to have freshly baked bread handed to them, as they should be. When the Communion server bends low and offers the plate of bread, uttering a few words to remind them that Jesus loves them, their eyes grow large, and with their grubby little fingers, they rip off the largest piece they can get away with. Sometimes mom and dad limit the size of their piece, but they are not always quick enough to catch them in time. Also, kids don't dip the bread in the cup; they *baptize* it. Full immersion. The entire piece of bread (and sometimes all of their fingers) go right into the chalice of juice. As they bring their soaked and limp bread to their little mouths, the juice runs down their arms, onto their shirts and drips all over the floor. I love watching the whole ordeal. I usually look down on the floor to see the crumbs and the drips. Kids like Isaac and Mercy and Teddy teach me how I should approach the table—when I am willing to let them be my teachers. They show me the eagerness with which I can come to the table as someone dependent, someone needing grace. It's not selfishness to want a large piece; it is a clear awareness that I need more of Jesus in my life. I need to be reminded that without him, I will be hungry and thirsty—and I should not be afraid to show my need.

Sharon is an older single woman in our congregation, quiet but thoughtful. I met her several years ago when her neighbor, Beth, called me in a panic, saying Sharon was in her living room clutching a bottle of pills and threatening to take her own life. Loneliness and hopelessness were, quite literally, on the verge of killing her. I dropped everything and drove as fast as my car would take me to Beth's house to listen to Sharon, share words of comfort, pray, and convince her to seek professional treatment, which she did.

Throughout the following weeks, Sharon came to our church. She joined one of our house churches (what we call our smaller gatherings of community within our larger church). Her house church smothered her with love. Children hugged her when she walked in the door. Others welcomed her into their homes for dinner during the week. Her house church found out it was her birthday and surprised her with a cake. After singing and blowing out the candles, Sharon spoke softly, telling her spiritual family that this was the first birthday cake anyone had made for her in over forty years. Saved on my computer is a grainy picture of Sharon staring at her cake just before blowing out the candles, with parents and children from the house church standing next to her. For me, it's a visual reminder of practiced resurrection.

Over the next few years, Sharon came to faith in Christ, and I had the privilege of baptizing her in a backyard pool one July afternoon with the entire church gathered around watching. Everyone went nuts when she came up out of the water. Her whole life has turned around. She's an entirely different person than when I first met her. After Sharon's baptism, the church presented her with a framed picture of her big moment, soaking wet and smiling from ear to ear. She recently told me it still hangs in her bedroom, where she looks at it every day—a reminder of how much she's changed and how much she's loved.

Sharon is on the rotation to serve Communion. When I approach the table and she offers me the elements, I get emotional. When Sharon reminds me with a smile that this is Christ's love represented in front of me, I get all choked up. I need people like Sharon in this spunky little Jesus community to remind me that while I am a resident alien, while I don't fully belong in this world, I *do* fully belong in God's family and in this community of brothers and sisters. And Sharon is sometimes the one doing the reminding. Once on the brink of death herself, Sharon now hands the rest of us the symbols of Jesus' death in order to remind us of the availability of new and real life.

Baptism and Communion make a wonderful pair. They serve as tangible reminders of *heaven-right-here-on-earth* reality, where we are washed in the waters of baptism and edified and nourished at the table. One reminds me that I don't completely belong to this world; the other reminds me that I belong to Christ completely. Participating in Communion by receiving the elements is where we come to acknowledge that we are both saints *and* sinners, where we are called to repent *and* believe, where we come with our mixture of faith *and* doubt to receive grace. The good news of Jesus is that the table is level; no one side is higher than another. The gospel is the great leveler. And Jesus says, *Come, let's eat. Breakfast is ready.* So are lunch and dinner—and there are even leftovers.

Peculiar Practice Two: Engaging in the Season of Advent

Outside of a family Advent calendar, the church I grew up in didn't participate in the season of Advent. Advent means "arrival." It's during this season, the handful of weeks leading up to Christmas Day, that Christians around the world enter into active waiting for the arrival of the Christ child. In my childhood church, there was a covert understanding that Advent was somewhat Catholic in nature. But Episcopalians, Moravians, and Lutherans, among others, have a rich and long tradition of celebrating Advent, too. A growing number of denominations and churches in the past few decades are seeing its richness and jumping into the refreshing stream of tradition, including ours.

Relatively speaking, Advent is a late addition to the church calendar. It didn't become a part of the Christian tradition until 490 A.D.[12] As an adult, I've come to see how rich the season is and how much I had missed out on its annual formational activity. I now love Advent. Advent ushers us into a time of waiting, anticipating, and preparing. It is one of the clearest examples of how Christians can enter into training for the almond-shaped life. Advent is the time each year to purposefully follow the star, just like the Magi, so that it may lead us to Christ and the joy of his arrival. We experience the tension of celebrating the arrival of Christ's birth while we wait for his return. Fleming Rutledge, an Episcopal priest and theologian, wrote a fantastically helpful book on Advent. In it, she describes Advent as the place where the Christian community lives at all times, because the season finds the healthy point of tension between living in the now and in the not-yet.[13] It's like the prophet Isaiah who wrote, "The watchman replies, 'Morning is coming, but also the night'" (Isa 21:12). During Advent it is morning *and also* night—the spiritual season of dawn. It was Karl Barth who asked rhetorically, "What other time or season can or will the Church ever have but that of Advent?"[14]

Advent is filled with suffering and hope, expectation and longing. In its mandorla posture, it prepares us for the coming of the Christ-child and also prepares us in real time for the Second Coming of Christ, for which we need to be ready at a moment's notice. Cyril of Jerusalem, a theologian of the fourth century, called it a hidden coming.[15] Advent is both a celebration of the past and a dress rehearsal for the future.

I participated in an event in New York City during the first weekend in December, a two-hour train ride from where I live. After the event, I was riding the uptown subway line from Lower Manhattan back to Penn Station and, like almost everyone else around me, I had my earbuds in. As it was the first week of December, I happened to be listening to "O Holy Night." The subway car was packed with riders—bubbly tourists; blue-collar workers slumped over in their seat and nodding off after a long day on their feet; a young couple dressed up for a fun night out in the city; an exhausted young mother trying to remain patient with a wily preschooler who couldn't stay put; and a homeless man 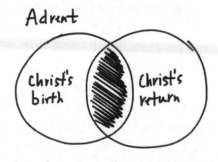 with gentle yet desperate eyes, asking for coins as he extended his worn McDonald's cup in each rider's direction with a slow nod. As I looked around at this diverse mass of humanity, I caught the line in my earbuds: "A thrill of hope, the weary world rejoices." We know Christ has been born. But we are weary. We need him to come again—and come again soon. But it's not just hope of the kind baseball fans feel in their bones on Opening Day. It's more than that; during Advent, we need *defiant* hope.

This season is when we practice living what the late South African missiologist David Bosch called creative tension.[16] It is the tension of the beautiful and gracious work God did when he entered space and time to save his people and inaugurate his kingdom on earth. The world is yet to be set right; we are still waiting for the renewal of all things. Our church purposefully practices several different tensions during Advent. We lament *and also* we praise. We offer up petitions *and also* extend gratitude. We cry in sorrow *and also* cry out in our rejoicing. Our church often prays together aloud, and we're encouraged to voice our prayers in two ways. First, we begin by offering prayers beginning with, "Lord, thank you for . . ." Individuals have shared their gratitude for the blessing of their family or a good report from the doctor or for their dog or for a friend who has encouraged them through an exhausting struggle with depression. When each has been voiced, we all exclaim in unison, "Thanks be to God!" Then we transition to offering up prayers of petition which begin with, "Lord, would you . . ." After someone's short prayer is shared aloud, all together we respond, "Lord, hear our prayer." This simple *thank you/would you* structure to our prayers helps us all—kids as well as grownups—look back with gratitude and forward with expectation and anticipation, humbly yet confidently asking our heavenly Father to intervene in our world. Lighting candles, reading Old Testament prophecies, singing Advent hymns—this participation in Advent each December is significant because it teaches us to practice Advent the other eleven months of the year.

Peculiar Practice Three: Entering into Lent

For two millennia, Christians around the world have celebrated the culmination of our faith on Resurrection Sunday. It is the day when we laud the miracle of miracles, Christ raised from the dead, as we sing alleluias and respond aloud with, "Christ is Risen indeed!" It is the high-water mark of our hope, the day Jesus turned the world upside down by planting a vacancy sign outside the tomb.

It is when hope surprised the world in person by coming forward from the future into the present.[17] The Risen Christ, alive again. The foundation of our hope.

But because of the outlandishly exuberant implications of Easter, we can't just jump into it that glorious morning. It requires preparation. We've got to back up the truck a bit, because such a dramatic, significant, life-bending, history-altering experience shouldn't just pop up and surprise us. It was Dorothy Sayers who wrote, "To make the Easter story into something that neither startles, shocks, terrifies, nor excites is to crucify the son of God afresh."[18] Our souls need to enter into a season of preparation, because a glorious interruption to life by the horrific reality of crucifixion can help us usher in the terrific news of an empty tomb.

This is why, for hundreds of years, the church has entered into the season of Lent. In 325 A.D., bishops from all over the world gathered in Nicaea (in present-day Turkey) to discuss and agree on important elements of Christian doctrine. It was here that church leaders decided it would be a good idea for the broader Church to practice Lent for a period of forty days.[19]

Lent is a somber season of reflection which begins on Ash Wednesday and continues for forty days (excluding Sundays). No, Lent isn't in the Bible. But the spirit behind Lent and the practices encouraged in this season are found throughout its pages. Why forty days in all? It rained for forty days in Noah's day (Gen. 7), Moses fasted for forty days on Mount Sinai (Ex. 34:28), Elijah fasted for forty days when he met God at Mt. Horeb (1 Kings 19:8), and Jesus fasted for forty days in the wilderness in order to prepare for his public ministry (Matt. 4:1–11). It only makes sense that Lent, a time of devotion as we encounter God, would last as long.

Lent is traditionally associated with repentance, fasting, prayer, reflection, and giving to those in need. Quite literally, Lent means "springtime," a purposeful time where we seek to join with Jesus for forty days of preparation. Just as Jesus was in the wilderness, in essence, Lent is where God is calling his people into the wilderness. It is the season where, as Joan Chittister writes, we learn to abstain from "worshipping at the shrine of the self."[20] It was in the wilderness that Israel encountered God and learned not only that their salvation was not earned, but what it meant to be saved.[21]

Our church holds an Ash Wednesday evening service to officially start the Lenten season, but some years, during my lunch hour, I walk to the large Lutheran church across the street from my house and slip into one of the back pews during their noon service. Near the end of the service, I stand in line with others waiting for the imposition of ashes, slowly shuffling forward to where a minister stands at the front with a bowl of ashes—burnt palm branches from last year's Palm Sunday service. He places his index finger across my forehead in the form of a cross. Nothing brings you as quickly to the place of humility and vulnerability than to have someone impose ashes on your forehead, look you in the eye, and tell you somberly, "Remember you are dust, and to dust you shall return."

Admittedly, I become self-conscious walking around the rest of the day with black smudge marks on my forehead. People around town stare at me. On occasion, a polite and well-meaning stranger will offer me assistance: "Excuse me, sir. I am not sure if you are aware, but you have something on your forehead . . ." I can feel a bit foolish—and that's just the point. Lent is the beginning of a season of emptying myself, of giving up my pride and my desire to look good to others.

I did not come from a tradition that practiced Lent. Like Advent, it was brushed aside for being "too Catholic" (as if the Catholics have gotten everything wrong throughout their history). Many Protestant denominations have practiced Lent through the centuries— Anglicans, Episcopalians, Lutherans, Methodists, Presbyterians, Anabaptists, and a growing number of evangelical nondenominational churches as well. In essence, Lent is to Easter what Advent is to Christmas. It prepares us in a way nothing else could. It arranges my soul for the good news that is on the way. Sometimes the best way to prepare for that good news is to quiet myself, to reflect on some of the messes and rough edges of my life. Such a posture leads me to confession and repentance. The themes of Lent usually include the temptation of Christ (the first Sunday after Ash Wednesday), the call to deny sin (the second Sunday), the call of repentance (the third Sunday), healing and conversion (the fourth Sunday), a foretaste of Easter (the Sunday before Palm Sunday) and, of course, Palm Sunday (the week before Resurrection Sunday).

Lent is a forty-day intentional process of giving up comfortable elements in my life in order to rid myself of pride and of my misinformed thoughts that I need certain attachments without which I cannot survive. Sometimes this involves giving up activities or pleasures for a season. I've known people who have given up chocolate or beer or fast food during Lent (traditionally, people gave up meat on Fridays, and many still do). I know someone who gave up complaining for Lent. A friend of mine gave up grabbing meals at drive-thru fast food joints as a way to slow down, casting off his, "I want it, and I want it now" attitude.

For a few years, I tried some of these practices, giving up chocolate or meat or beer—some were more difficult to eschew than others. Sometimes I give up social media during these six weeks. But a few years ago, I committed, above all else, to just giving up. Not giving up on life, but giving up on trying to control my life and the lives of those around me. It was—and still is—both excruciatingly difficult and tremendously freeing. This is prime time for Christians to let go of excuses for our failings and shortcomings, a time to stop hanging on to whatever shreds of goodness we perceive in ourselves, to ask God to show us, as scary as it may seem, what we *really* look like.[22] We are called to something more than just abstaining from chocolate or Twitter or meat on Fridays; we are called to *die with Christ*. This giving up is the process of cutting off the attachments that entangle me and entice me to believe that life is best lived in self-reliance. Lent is like a pair of scissors which cuts the ropes of my miscalculated desires and skewed attachments.

Lent is still an anomaly for some people. "Why would I intentionally put myself in a bad mood?" a friend asked me a few years ago. "Isn't there enough bad news going on in the world today? And if we know Jesus will be raised from the dead, why do we have to mope around for a few weeks leading up to it?" Moping around is not the purpose of Lent, but in some ways, I see what he means. It's what I felt when I first learned about Lent. Jesus made his way to Jerusalem, knowing suffering and death awaited him, and through Lent, we can join him in that journey. We accompany Jesus, not simply allow him to cross our path.[23]

This mandorla practice of Lent puts me in a strange and sometimes awkward place: I find great hope, even when it feels like gloom on the outside. Lent helps me see where I've been getting in my own way and where I cut off Jesus from certain areas of my life. For me, Lent is like what John the Baptist said: "He must become greater; I must become less," (John 3:30). When the Lenten season is difficult for me, it is usually because I'm considering how many other important and more life-giving things I could be doing with my time, but then I recollect the words of German theologian Meister Eckhart, who wrote almost eight hundred years ago that those who have the hardest time with Lent are "the good people" who feel that all of this is a waste of time and energy. This puts me squarely in position for further repentance.

I need the constant reminder that Lent is an embrace of both pain *and also* promise. It is where we discover "the scarred God, crucified, bloody, and dying on a cross, even in the world of the alluring gods of the feel-good age."[24] When approached properly, it brings up all sorts of mandorla–ish feelings: are we supposed to be feeling joy? Isn't hope the central focus of our faith? Yes, it is. But joy and hope can only be experienced when we first ponder our faults, our limitations, our sin, and even our own death. Despite our repentance and fasting, it cannot supersede, eclipse, or outdo the good news that Jesus Christ conquered sin. Repentance is where we abdicate our thrones and relinquish our lives, only to be reminded on resurrection morning that this is how we receive true life.

What I misunderstood in my younger years was that Lent is not a legalistic requirement that has bearing on my eternal destiny; instead, it is an invitation every year for me to join Jesus on the journey toward the cross and the tomb and, ultimately, real life. We read in the Gospels about the triumphal entry of Jesus into Jerusalem, where people cast palm branches and clothes on the road for Jesus to walk on. Lent has become for me the time to fling myself under his feet as he walks by. Without Lent, my eyelids may become heavy, and I might fall asleep while Jesus suffers in prayer as he sweats drops of blood in the garden. Lent is that important mandorla practice which keeps me awake. All of this leads us naturally right into the final week of Lent, Holy Week.

Peculiar Practice Four: Enter into the Richness of Holy Week

Good Friday gives us space to reflect on the death of Jesus on the cross. This day is the dissonant space between the apparent failure of the crucifixion and the joyous victory of the empty tomb. We often want to rush quickly to the good stuff, but our spiritual impatience can take the depth and power out of Easter glory. We can't truly celebrate the greatness and hope of the resurrection if we don't first understand a bloodied cross and an occupied tomb. Good Friday is the darkest day of the church calendar. But it's also a discipleship day, when we give serious thought to the question: *Am I willing to journey with Jesus all the way to the bloodied cross?*

During my twenties, I served on the pastoral staff of a large nondenominational church. I had been exploring the richness of the church calendar in my own personal journey and suggested to the programming team that we think more purposefully about holding a Good Friday service. Subsequently, I was asked to preach at the service, a space intended to carry a somber, reflective feel. Due to the hectic nature of the week leading up to Easter, I had failed to connect with the worship leader to coordinate the preaching and the worship. Lent was somewhat new to our worship leader, so his grasp of the tone and posture of a Good Friday service was limited.

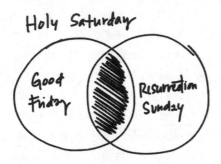

After I finished preaching a short sermon, laced with a tone of solemn contemplation, touching on our need for deep repentance, the worship leader excitedly asked the congregation to stand and sing "Up from the Grave He Arose" and "In Christ Alone." I was horrified. Everything in me wanted to rush up on stage, run to the piano and say, "No, this is not what today is about! We'll get there on Sunday—but not tonight!"

But it was too late. I cringed my way through the songs. As Christians, we must first feel the weighty pain of Friday, as it makes the joy of Sunday all the sweeter. Good Friday. How can the death of the savior of the world be *good*? The name itself is a bit of a linguistic mandorla: it only makes sense if we view Friday retrospectively, if we see it through the lens of Sunday and work backward.

Good Friday gives way to Holy Saturday. Catholics and Episcopalians know not only how to engage in Good Friday, but also how to enter into Holy Saturday (also called Silent Saturday), the day Jesus lay in the grave. It can be easy to miss the beauty and the horror of Holy Saturday. The day is not meant for us to busy ourselves by preparing tomorrow's ham, baking hot cross buns or filling Easter eggs with chocolate for the kids. Those who engage with Holy

Saturday have admitted to me that they aren't exactly sure what to do or feel. Most liturgical churches don't hold a Holy Saturday service. It's set aside to rest, to fast and to prepare our hearts, not tomorrow's dinner. It can be a bit disorienting—and that's the point. The Christian life can feel disorienting. Fleming Rutledge noted that the Christian life is lived somewhere between, "My God, My God, why have you forsaken me?" and "Into your hands I commit my spirit."[25] Holy Saturday reminds us of our identity as Easter people who continue to live in a world of Good Friday. Holy Saturday is the truest and purest expression of the sacred overlap.

The experience of Jesus' gruesome Friday death, fresh in our minds from yesterday, is juxtaposed with the celebration of the resurrection of Jesus to come tomorrow. Our thoughts and emotions—even our futures—are caught in the middle. The Psalmist captured this well in the arrangement of Psalms 22 through 24. Psalm 22 is to be read on Good Friday ("My God, my God, why have you forsaken me?"), Psalm 23 on Holy Saturday ("Even though I walk through the valley of the shadow of death . . .") and Psalm 24 ("Who is this King of glory? The Lord strong and mighty . . .") on Easter Sunday.

A Quaker friend of mine engages her family members in the unique practice of remaining silent on Holy Saturday, refusing to utter a single word the entire day. Holy Saturday is when the church feels the weight and the tension of the cross like no other day on the calendar. It is a space where, as Tish Harrison Warren writes, "We live between D-Day and V-Day. The victory is secured, but the war continues a little longer."[26] If we rush too quickly into Sunday, whizzing past the rich, yet weighty embrace of Friday and Saturday, we miss experiencing the fullness and the depth of the resurrection on Sunday.

But what about Easter *Monday*? Nobody seems to talk much about this day (except for pastors, who want to do nothing but sleep all day due to exhaustion from the week). The Eastern Orthodox

Church commemorates this day on the calendar. They call it "Bright Monday" or "Renewal Monday." I'm never quite sure what to think on Easter Monday. Now we have significant work to do: to bring the reality of heaven into earthly reality.[27] But interestingly, despite the magnitude of Jesus' resurrection, we only have a single day on the calendar to celebrate

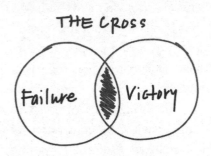

it. I like what N. T. Wright suggests: we should enter into a week-long festival, where we serve champagne after morning prayer, or even before, with lots of celebration, alleluias, and extra hymns and spectacular anthems.[28] I like this idea of a week-long resurrection party, especially the part about champagne before and after morning prayers. Good Friday, Holy Saturday, Resurrection Sunday, and Celebration Monday push us further into holy tension. When Easter morning eventually comes, I find that Lent, Good Friday, and Holy Saturday work together to make Resurrection Sunday much more spiritually meaningful and rich. In a season of self-reflection and giving up control and pondering Christ's sufferings, I find myself getting quite emotional on Easter mornings. I wake up ready to dance.

Peculiar Practice Five: Immersing in Scripture

To many of us, reading our Bibles is like flossing. We are all fully aware of its benefits, but we don't do it as often as we feel like we should. One Bible, comprised of two testaments, is full of rich diversity as well as rich, overarching unity. The Old Testament resounds with a hopeful future tense ("behold the days are coming") met with the New Testament's emphatic present ("the kingdom of God is at hand"). If we only read the Old Testament, it is a building without a roof, but if we only dwell in the New Testament, we will have a roof without a building.[29] In order to understand the depth and richness of God's great story, we need both in order to construct a house.

The union of heaven and earth is what the story of the Bible is all about. Once fully united in all completeness, then driven apart by sin, God's divine rescue plan is about bringing them back together once again.[30] When we talk about the Book of Revelation, we tend to think of tribulations and horses and blood and swords and confusing predictions about the future (and the weird people with sandwich boards who make them). But the bringing-heaven-and-earth-together-again future reality is what Revelation is all about. One could summarize the entire strange and often complex book of Revelation in two words: *Jesus wins*.

But often, this is not how we were taught to read our Bibles. Instead of seeing the Bible as an entirely connected narrative, we often view it as something between a daily inspirational calendar, a car manual, and a Waffle House menu. But its primary purpose is invitation, not merely information. When we realize the depth and fullness of the story, interconnected and unified, we begin to see the beauty and the challenge of living in the in-between. The Old Testament, referred to by some as the First Testament, includes foreshadowing, hinting, and prophesying about the coming of the Messiah. The New Testament, which some refer to as the Second Testament, recounts, references, reminds us of, and fulfills much of the First Testament. We are told that all Scripture—all of it—is inspired and useful for training in righteousness (2 Tim. 3:16–17). When we bifurcate the Bible, we suffocate the story.

The Bible, a collection of books written over thousands of years—history, poetry, prophecy, wisdom, firsthand accounts, and letters—is a unified story of a new creation and resurrection. Each of the four Gospels ends with the resurrection of Jesus, not in heaven, but *right here on earth*. Then, Revelation concludes with the new heaven and the new earth filled with the people of God who have also risen from the dead. We shouldn't be surprised to learn that this is something we can begin to live into right now, not just at the end of time.

One of the most helpful metaphors for understanding the arc and scope of the Bible is N. T. Wright's description of a five-act play.[31] This play of the grand story of God is structured as *Creation* (Act I), *the Fall* (Act II), *Israel* (Act III), *Jesus* (Act IV) and *the Church* (Act V). The Book of Acts and the rest of the New Testament comprise Act V, with the final scene of the play being the Book of Revelation, describing the new heaven and the new earth. Today, we're living in the middle of Act V. We see what has happened in the play thus far, and we know how it will turn out in the end. Based on the historical past and the hopeful future, we live in the present but improvise in our part here and now.[32] We don't do whatever we wish; we simply continue from what we've learned, by the guidance of the Holy Spirit, and point toward the impending future. The way we best know how to improvise is to be committed lifelong students of Scripture, where we're all encouraged to break a leg in God's grand story.

But the Bible wasn't written merely to inform us of the story. God is too loving to just tell us a story. He wants us smack-dab in the middle of the story with him. He invites us to participate in it, and he enfolds us right into the narrative, equipping us for the tasks necessary to see his mission fulfilled.[33]

Peculiar Practice Six: Pondering the Mystery of Marriage

Earlier we touched on the wildly incomplete Christian objective of *going to heaven*. This might shake your drawers a bit: *there is not even one passage in the Bible that talks about going to heaven after you die*. The phrase "go to heaven" doesn't even appear anywhere in either the Old or New Testaments in relation to death—*not once*.

The Bible certainly has some things to say about what happens to God's people after they die, but "going to heaven" wasn't part of the mindset of the biblical authors. Instead, they believed our hope was about being *with Jesus*.[34]

As we touched on with the Lord's Prayer, the Christian hope of "going to heaven" when we die is not about waiting for our opportunity to lounge around on puffy clouds, strumming tunes on our celestial harps. This kind of salvation story leans out and away from the world.[35] In the beginning of time, the Garden of Eden was the location where the perfect overlap between God and humans existed. *Shalom* was the beginning of God's story, but let's pause to ponder the end of the story. It's important that we look at another fancy hundred-dollar theology word: *eschatology*. Eschatology is nothing more than how Jesus will bring everything to full completion and redemption in the end, to re-*shalom* the world. Pondering eternity is anticipating and longing for the re-*shaloming* process to come to fruition.

Pondering eternity can at times seem too overwhelming. We need something more concrete and relatable for our finite minds to grasp. This is why pondering the mystery of marriage is a peculiar practice for peculiar people. The English Standard Version of the Christmas story retains the archaic word used to describe Mary and Joseph's relationship status: *betrothed*. Betrothal went even further and was more serious than our cultural understanding of engagement, involving just about everything except the enjoyment of sex. To break off a betrothal was not about

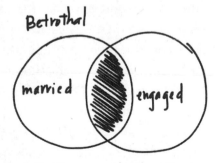

losing the deposit on the reception facility or writing to all your guests to say you've broken it off, please hold off on sending that blender. In the first-century Jewish context, it would be considered divorce. This is why Luke records that Joseph originally intended to *divorce* Mary quietly. Jesus was in utero in the midst of this betrothal—an awkward and tenuous situation in the first century if there ever was one.

Engagement is a mandorla space—it's more than dating, yet not marriage. When my wife, Megan, and I were engaged, we were well past the infatuation stage of our relationship. We'd seen each other on our worst days, and yet we were still madly in love, though we had not fully committed to one another at the altar before family and friends. Engagement was better than singleness, but certainly not as good as being married.

When we are married, we live out our days in sacred overlap. We have our own personal identities, and yet as separate people, we are united and become one. We lose some of our identity, but not all of it, in order to be changed into a new identity together. It's me, but it's *also* we. It is meant to be an additive and synergistic union. While we lose a part of our lives in marriage, we gain much more—this is one of many profound mysteries within marriage. I can be quite selfish. I can get flustered when Megan gets back from a meeting later than she told me she would or roll my eyes and sigh when she asks me to fold the laundry after a long and stressful day or retort with a snide or sarcastic remark when I'm put on the defensive (she puts up with a lot, I tell you). But when we live into our marriage healthily, we operate in the midst of a mandorla relationship, honoring each other for our individuality *and also* respecting each other *and also* attempting to live as teammates. It's why we refer to ourselves as Team Briggs. Each of us attempts to die to our own *me* so that *we* may live. Especially in marriage, couples are invited to practice resurrection together.

At the end of the Bible, in Revelation 21 and 22, we see the image of marriage: the New Jerusalem comes down out of heaven like a bride dressed for her husband. Heaven and earth are not poles apart, needing to be separated forever when all the children of heaven have been rescued and protected from the wickedness of earth. Nor are they just different ways of looking at the same thing. They are strikingly different, while at the same time, being made for each other, much like how we think about men and women. When heaven and earth are finally fully united, it will bring about the same experience of joy we experience at a wedding. Maybe the Book of Revelation is just one long wedding invitation, where we're encouraged to persevere because we'll all be welcome guests on the big day.

When I officiate a wedding, as the bride walks down the aisle while everyone stands so elegantly, I always keep my eyes locked on the groom. The bride, to be sure, is radiant and beautiful, attracting most of the attention. But in that moment, I am more interested in seeing the joy of the groom as I stand just a few feet away. His joy is ineffable, unable to be captured, not even by the most skilled photographer. It is a joy so palpable it has to be experienced firsthand. It is this kind of joy that we will experience one day, at the end of the age, when the new heaven and the new earth will join hands, kiss, and be called one. Differences within creation—whether heaven and earth or men and women—are made for union, not competition.[36]

Within marriage is another form of union, a sacred and powerful gift that God graciously gives to us: sex. It's an undeniably sacred and mysterious mandorla. I give myself away, and I receive at the same time; the result is pleasure for Megan and also for me. It's so powerful, in fact, that when we steward it faithfully, this physical act expressing mysterious union is unbelievable. But when handled carelessly, the consequences wreak incredible havoc, causing deep pain and wrenching wounds.

There's an apocryphal quote attributed to Martin Luther: If I believe the world were to end tomorrow, I would still plant an apple tree today. Maybe this is marriage, too: willing to invest in a future we are unsure of, together we plant trees. And fold laundry. And make dinner. And put the cap back on the tube of toothpaste. And pray. And enjoy the God-given gift of sex. Pondering the mystery of marriage helps us ponder our role in God's great story.

Some of these peculiar practices occur on Sundays, and others throughout the week. Our Monday-through-Saturday lives are significant, too. As Christians, we believe our occupation is what we *do*; it should not define us. It is not who we are. Sunday practices remind us of our true identities as beloved children of God.

One of my favorite parts of our gatherings is the benediction. Benediction—two Latin words, *bene* (from which we get the word "beneficial") and *dictus* (from which we get the word "dictionary")—are squished together and given holy meaning: "the good word," or "the good saying." Before we leave our gathering space, scattering into the week ahead, we receive in the benediction—a challenge, a blessing, and a charge to live out our true identities, not defined by our annual income or job title (or lack thereof), but given to us graciously by our heavenly Father. We are sent back into our everyday lives, our Monday-through-Saturday, as missionaries cleverly disguised as good neighbors, friends, and employees.

Communion, Advent, Lent, Holy Week, reading Scripture, and the mystery of marriage—all practices for building muscle memory in the mandorla life.

CHAPTER 11

SACRED CELEBRATION

EMBRACING JOY AMIDST A WORLD RIDDLED WITH PAIN

> Some of you say, "Joy is greater than sorrow," and others say, "Nay, sorrow is the greater." But I say unto you, they are inseparable.
>
> **—POET KAHLIL GIBRAN**

> Joy is the infallible sign of the presence of God.
>
> **—PIERRE TEILHARD DE CHARDIN**

Outside of the realms of the Christmas season or wedding days, Americans don't often talk about or experience joy in our culture. Journalist David Brooks wrote, "Our society has become a conspiracy against joy."[1] We seem to live with the assumption that joy is something that *happens to* us. But we can actually cultivate and practice it.

One Sunday morning during Advent, our little Jesus community explored the topic of joy together. Ben, one of our pastors, who is thoughtful and reserved, preached the hell out of joy—and I mean this in the most theological sense of the word. He didn't just preach

177

it—he *embodied it*. Right in the middle of his sermon, he did a few cartwheels and front-roll somersaults, sending his lapel mic flying. Those of us who know Ben's stoic demeanor were utterly shocked. But Ben was right: simply *talking about* joy just wasn't enough. Our church gathers in the gym of a drafty Boys & Girls Club at the center of our little community of Lansdale, Pennsylvania. At the end of his sermon, Ben requested that all of us stand up and push our folding chairs against the walls of the gym. With the space cleared, we could do what joy necessitates: have a dance party. As the worship band played, grinning grownups high-fived, linked arms, and jumped up and down. Children grabbed the hands of others and twirled in circles as we sang songs of praise to our God and Father. Halfway through the second song, I shed my zip-up fleece because I was sweating through my shirt. As people received the Communion elements, they called out, *Thank you, Jesus!* Then, during the final song, we heard the loud pops of confetti cannons exploding. As we felt the confetti descending upon our heads like colorful dry snow, I turned to my dance partners and said, "Now, *this* is joy!"

The sacred feasts of the Old Testament were, in a sense, dress rehearsals for what was to come. In some ways, our gatherings should be the same: dress rehearsals for the wedding feast of the lamb.

The whole ordeal, I assure you, was entirely appropriate. Holy jocularity. These were not over-the-top ecclesial theatrics meant to wow or sensational effects designed to impress. It was simply the most natural and sensible overflow of what joy looked like that morning. We were convinced that joy—true, relentless, hope-filled joy—*necessitates* this kind of reaction when we're written into a story as great as the one God has penned. Joy, as Ben shared that morning. After the dance party, my friends Rick and Becky bent down, scooped up handfuls of confetti off the gym floor and stuffed their pockets. They, along with their two young sons, created a

Christmas ornament by placing the tiny shreds of colorful paper inside a clear plastic bulb. They wrote the date on it and hung it on their tree. They wanted to remember for years to come that God's people should be about uninhibited and energetic joy. Maybe we all should have stuffed our pockets full of confetti and created ornaments to remind us that deep and wild expressions of joy are legit.

Ben shared with me later that there is a spot in the gym which makes him smile. One small portion of the gym floor was wet on the morning of our dance party. When some of the colored confetti landed on the wet spot, the color bled onto the floor and remains there to this day. I want abounding joy to leave a mark on my life that same way, where I smile whenever I see it. Joy: the tattoo of heaven.

"Seriousness is not a virtue," wrote G. K. Chesterton in his classic book, *Orthodoxy*.[2] In addition to prayer, the Word, and the Holy Spirit, joy was one of the defining characteristics of the early church as recorded in the Book of Acts.[3] Read Acts, and you can't miss it. There was joy in the midst of miracles, healings, good news, baptisms—even in the midst of suffering. Joy is the aroma of God's kingdom. Paul wrote about this in Romans: "For the kingdom of God is not a matter of eating and drinking, but of righteousness, peace and joy in the Holy Spirit" (14:17). It's one of the fruits (evidence) of the Spirit at work in God's people (Gal. 5:22–23). I find it interesting that one of the primary criteria the Roman Catholic Church uses to determine canonization for sainthood is whether the person produced joy in others.

These kinds of joyful outbursts are not out of the norm for our church. We practice another form of joy each summer with our baptism celebrations. At baptisms, we strictly adhere to one (and only one) rule: *no polite golf claps allowed*. As people acknowledge their public faith and trust in Christ and come up out of the water soaking wet, the angels of heaven do backflips. We can't just clap politely like we're standing along the fairway at Pebble Beach;

we've gotta go nuts. And so we do. We beat the snot out of drums and djembes; blow air horns, whistles, and vuvuzelas until we feel light-headed; and roar with shouts of joy until we're on the verge of losing our voices. But we're all convinced it's worth it, because joy needs to be uncorked when the spiritual stakes are this high. (Tell me, what's more significant than these kinds of public declarations?) All of it—the dance party, the confetti cannons, the air horns blasting at baptisms—helps our little community cultivate and embody uninhibited joy. If baptism is the bold announcement over the public address system about one's crossing of the Rubicon, then an authentically incandescent response seems reasonable.

My friend Jared Mackey loves Jesus, and he loves the city of Denver, where he pastors a beautiful church. He also loves making cocktails for people. His business card reads *Concierge, Cocktails & Clergy.* When we were talking about joy, he shared that he believes a well-crafted cocktail is one of life's great gifts to share. Spirits lift the head and bring levity to the heart. All of this is ironic, mind you, as Jared comes from a faith tradition of teetotalers. He was twenty-two when he had his first drink—a Jack Daniels with two other pastors. We raise a glass for consolation or celebration. If we get the opportunity to choose what we do for eternity, where all is made new, where nothing is broken and there are no tears or sadness, Jared has plans. "If this is the case," he told me, "then I'll choose to be a bartender." As he sees it, in heaven all drinks will be raised in everlasting joy and the eternal celebration of life. One day, when I've gone to be with Jesus, I'm going to belly up to the bar and have Jared make me a Moscow Mule.

You may be reading this and thinking, *We don't shoot off confetti cannons during worship at my church, nor do we blow air horns during baptisms—and quite frankly, we don't plan on starting any time soon.* If you think our church is half-crazed, well, I won't try to convince you otherwise. To each his own, I guess, but you need not roll your eyes. Hold my drink while I throw my hands up in celebration and dance with others—and then I'll tell you straight up: you're missing out on a really big thing, because joy is one of the primary colors in God's kingdom. We take joy seriously because we're playing for keeps. We pop the corks and go nuts for the things that matter most. If the *perichoresis*, the divine dance, is used to describe the Triune God, then I think we can confidently assume he's out there on the dance floor—and we might as well join him.

As Augustine wrote, a Christian should be an alleluia from head to foot. In Luke 15, we read a trio of stories Jesus tells about a lost sheep, a lost coin, and a lost son. All three of these stories end with a party, entire communities coming together to go nuts over something—or someone—worthy of being celebrated. Jesus tells these party stories to get our attention in order to say loudly and clearly: *This is who the Father is. Now, go and party like this in my name.* Joyful celebration is at the center of the heart of God.

Maybe you've heard people say, "Don't let the devil steal your joy." Sometimes I wonder if there's even any joy at all to be stolen from some Christians. There is a direct connection between our joy and our freedom. Episcopal priest Robert Farrar Capon, in his book *Between Noon and Three*, wrote:

> The church, by and large, has had a poor record of encouraging freedom. She has spent so much time inculcating in us the fear of making mistakes that she has made us like ill-taught piano students; we play our songs, but we never really hear them, because our main concern is not to make music, but to avoid some flub that will get us in trouble . . . [The church] has been so afraid we will lose sight of the need to do it right that it has made us care more about how we look than about who Jesus is.[4]

Yes, sometimes joy is a feeling or experience. But dig a little deeper, and we find that it can actually show us our desires, what our soul ultimately longs for deep down. And if we refuse to practice joy, we cut off an important indicator of what we truly yearn for. We become a mirror-image of the older brother Jesus talked about in the story of the prodigal son. All that belonged to the Father belonged to him—yet still, he was without joy. Since the word *prodigal* means "extreme squanderer," it prompts the question: which brother squandered more—and thus, who was the actual prodigal in the story?

We want to live with such freedom and joy, as Steve Brown quipped, that uptight Christians begin to doubt our salvation.[5] Living with joy should compel those who are not yet convinced to consider joining Jesus' party because of it. Our church has made the decision that when it comes to Jesus, we've given up on decaf Christianity; we're drinking the strong stuff, baby. This kind of practice of joy shouldn't be something we just talk about; it should be something we participate in with *a full-bodied, all-caps YES*. I'm convinced that a church's vitality is directly related to its level of joy. It's why, as C. S. Lewis wrote, "joy is the serious business of heaven."[6]

I recently read a piece written by Josh Noem on why he collects images of walk-off home run hitters rounding third base.[7] He does this, he said, because they are a visceral portrayal of heaven. I was so moved when I read about this practice, I've now begun collecting and storing them in a file on my computer. Sometimes I even make them the wallpaper on my home screen. My favorite is Chicago Cubs pinch hitter David Bote's improbable walk-off grand slam on August 12, 2018 at Wrigley Field to beat the Washington Nationals 4–3. In the picture, his teammates ecstatically and impatiently wait for him at home plate to share their joy and celebrate together. When Bote arrived at home plate, his teammates were so excited they ripped his jersey right off his back.

I slowly and carefully study each one of these images, noticing the expressions on the faces of players and fans alike. With raised arms and broad smiles, hitters often receive a Gatorade bath. I look beyond the field and into the stands and see spectators with arms extended heavenward and exuberant fans hugging complete strangers. In moments like these, we are reminded that we can't simply keep joy to ourselves; our joy *must* be shared. Reflecting on these walk-off home run images, Noem asked three poignant questions, "Why do moments like this ricochet around in our hearts? Could it be that we are made for such glory—that reunion is strung through our DNA and restoration lives in our bones? Won't that be what heaven feels like—coming home?" [8] All of this shows us, of course, that baseball is God's game.

I've preached a few times at my friend Mike's church, which meets in a community center about an hour away. Hanging from the center of the room where the church gathers is a disco ball. When I stand to preach, before I even open my mouth, I look up at the dozens of square, mirrored tiles in that ball and consider its spiritual implication. On occasion, my kids will ask, "Hey Dad, when we are going back to that church with the disco ball?" I sometimes imagine what it might be like if every church had a disco ball hanging from the center of its worship space.[9] How might this stir our kingdom imagination about the role of joy and celebration as the people of God?

The morning Ben taught on joy at our church, before the cart-wheels and the dance party and the confetti, he shared that humans are neurologically hardwired for joy. There is a part of the brain dubbed the "joy center." This region regulates emotions, controls pain, and even controls your immune system. It's the only part of the brain capable of overriding the main drive centers, such as anger, food, and sexual impulses. And catch this: *it's the only part of the brain that doesn't lose its capacity to grow throughout our lifetimes.*[10] Joy is, quite literally, what we were designed to do.

It's startling to realize there were times in Scripture when God *commanded* his people to be joyful. Steve Brown said that if there's no joy and freedom, it is not a church; it's just a crowd of serious and gloomy people basking in religious neurosis. If you've ever had the opportunity to worship with Christian sisters and brothers in certain parts of Africa, you know what a holy dance party is like. That, my friends, is *church*—one of the clearest pictures of heaven on earth. Walk-off home runs every single Sunday. How easy it is for Christians in the West to forget that we serve a God who doesn't just invite us to get out on the dance floor and party; he actually commands it.

But joy doesn't just happen to us. We have to intentionally, purposefully choose it. And I admit it's messy. (You don't want to know how long it took to clean up all that confetti off the gym floor.) But it's worth it.

Cultivating joy means we must also cultivate gratitude. In fact, gratitude must precede joy. Benedictine monk David Steindl-Rast stated that it is not joy that makes us grateful; it is gratitude that makes us joyful.[11] Name a time when you were truly joyful and not also grateful. (Hint: you can't.)

Part of this practice is reflecting on the source of our joy. Somehow. many of us have forgotten that God is the God of joy. *He takes delight in you with gladness . . . He will rejoice over you with joyful songs* (Zeph. 3:17 NLT). One hundred years ago, the cheeky writer G. K. Chesterton wrote about the joy God must experience when he creates:

> Because children have abounding vitality, because they are in spirit fierce and free, therefore they want things repeated and unchanged. They always say, "Do it again"; and the grown-up person does it again until he is nearly dead. For grown-up people are not strong enough to exult in monotony. But perhaps God is strong enough to exult in monotony. It is possible that God says every morning, "Do it again" to the sun; and every evening, "Do it

again" to the moon. It may not be automatic necessity that makes all daisies alike; it may be that God makes every daisy separately, but has never got tired of making them. It may be that He has the eternal appetite of infancy; for we have sinned and grown old, and our Father is younger than we.[12]

All this sounds great, you may be thinking, *but do you know the suffering that exists in the world? Do you know the pain and suffering and isolation and heartache and sin and death in the world?* Just turning on the evening news is enough to send us over the edge some nights. I'm deeply challenged by the joy of people like Paul in his letter to the Philippian church, written while he was in prison, chained to a Roman guard. I also think of people like Joni Eareckson Tada. As a teenager, she dove into the shallow water of Chesapeake Bay and broke her neck in several places, which instantly paralyzed her from the shoulders down. Since that fateful accident, she has been confined to a wheelchair. She uses that terrible incident and her limiting situation not to complain or live in despair, but instead to joyfully talk about Jesus and serve as a tireless advocate and encourager to countless individuals with disabilities around the world. She speaks in front of thousands, hosts a radio program, writes books, and creates beautiful paintings (by holding the paintbrush in her mouth)—and she does all of it with joy oozing out of every pore. Joni is *peculiar* in the best sense of the word. Those outside the hope of Christ shake their heads in disbelief at how someone like her can live out joy so authentically and courageously each and every day. Her body may have significant limitations, but there is no limit to her joy.

We may never experience paralysis—or start an organization or write books or create amazing works of art with a paintbrush between our teeth—but we can still choose joy when we've lost our job or when our spouse leaves us or when our kids are making destructive choices. We can choose joy when our boss seems unfair and the money and bills don't match up at the end of the month. Yes, joy. It's crazy, right? But joy—*defiant joy*—is available to us, even in the midst of our sorrow. If we try to generate ongoing joy based on the circumstances of our days, we're toast. Life is just too difficult—even downright painful—for us to achieve authentic, lasting joy by reading another self-help book or watching another TED Talk. But when our source is rooted in the person of Jesus, joy is available.

Joy is rooted in gratitude, and gratitude is rooted in hope. It *has* to be, or there would be no reason for joy in the first place. In the overarching narrative we find in Scripture, life is lived between two trees. Life isn't lived under the shady branches of Eden's tree of life that we read about in Genesis 3, nor is it lived beneath the healing leaves found in Revelation 22. We live in a world caught between those two trees, where the reality is that *life is hard*. But the church has been entrusted with the message of hope. We can be honest enough to admit that life really *is* hard, and yet we can also proclaim a message bold enough that while we live between these two trees, there really *is* hope. The reason we have hope is because there was a redemptive tree that was planted and flourishes between the other two: the true tree of life—the bloodied cross of Calvary.[13] Between the two trees, we cling to the only one capable of rescuing, saving, and redeeming: Jesus. He is our hope.

Because joy is so peculiar, living between the extremes of inauthentic, annoyingly cheery happiness and chronic Eeyore gloom is one of the ways we live as mandorla people. I take great joy in the words of the author of Hebrews:

> And let us run with perseverance the race marked out for us, fixing our eyes on Jesus, the pioneer and perfecter of faith. For the joy set before him he endured the cross, scorning its shame, and sat down at the right hand of the throne of God. (Heb. 12:1–2)

We only know how to do this joy thing correctly when we've got a model who shows us how to do it. Jesus was willing to endure death—even death by crucifixion—because he knew the joy that would eventually be found in it. It's not a *rah-rah* Christian pep rally kind of joy, as sturdy as cardboard in a rainstorm. It's the kind of joy that can make us jump around with our hands in the air and smiles on our faces, even when there are tears streaming down our cheeks. Sorrow *and also* joy. Hope-filled joy is the mortar that fills in the cracks between the bricks of the difficult present and the victorious future.

All this talk of joy prompts several questions in me.

What blocks our joy?

What is it, exactly, that keeps us from experiencing joy?

What holds us back?

What if joy was the tangible expression that made following Jesus so darn attractive to outsiders?

What if people, when asked how they came to faith in Christ, said that the primary reason was because of the effusive joy they saw in Jesus' followers?

We must, as Ralph Waldo Emerson wrote, be people who scatter joy.

CHAPTER 12

MANDORLA MISSION

LIVING OUT FRESH EXPRESSIONS OF CHURCH

You are not a human being in search of a spiritual experience. You are a spiritual being immersed in a human experience.

—PIERRE TEILHARD DE CHARDIN

The Church is the one institution that exists for those outside it.

—WILLIAM TEMPLE

If you want to know who God is, look at Jesus. If you want to know what it means to be human, look at Jesus. If you want to know what love is, look at Jesus. If you want to know what grief is, look at Jesus, and go on looking until you're not just a spectator, but you're actually part of the drama which has him as the central character.

—N. T. WRIGHT

I have a lot of pastor friends named Mike, and recently, one of them shared a meal with the Sons of Satan. Not the actual *sons* of the actual *Satan*, but close. Several years ago, Mike's church began thinking compassionately and creatively about starting a fresh expression of the kingdom out of their church for members of motorcycle gangs in his neck of the woods near Reading, Pennsylvania.[1] His church isn't full of biker gang members, although there are those in his congregation who love riding motorcycles. Mike possesses a heart that beats hard for others, believing that no one is outside of the realm and reach of Christ's love. Mike invited the bikers in his church to live a life that goes deeper than simply dreaming about a weekend ride. He and a team of bikers worked patiently and deliberately to cultivate relationships with bike clubs in the area over a long period of time.

The church ultimately decided to throw a party for the clubs. They rented out the basement of a VFW hall, served great food, and enjoyed hanging out. Black leather gloves, chains hanging from jeans, handlebar mustaches, and people with names like "Bull," "Bones," and "Slasher" showed up—and that was just the women. Thirty minutes into the event, a family from the church got up to leave. Mike was surprised. The family told Mike they felt uncomfortable because a biker had a patch on his vest emblazoned with the words "Sons of Satan."

When Mike told me this story, he said he was disappointed by this family's choice to leave, yet he also felt affirmed. He told me that following Jesus means you're going to end up sharing meals with others who might make us uncomfortable. As poet Gerard Manley Hopkins wrote, "Christ plays in ten thousand places."[2] One of those places happens to be the basement of a VFW hall where the children of God and the Sons of Satan hang out and eat potato salad together.

In chapter 10, we explored the peculiar practices in which resurrection people are invited to participate together. You might have noticed that most, though not all, of these practices occur naturally within the realm of those who are already believers in Jesus

(Mark Scandrette's yellow space idea). But it is crucial to explore practices and postures we can participate in within the realm of the world, around those not yet believers in Jesus (blue space). Again, the goal isn't to separate our lives, but to brush on several coats of yellow and blue paint so they eventually mix, creating a strong and pleasing green hue.[3]

Living the mandorla life as an individual is a great start, but the adventure gets even more real when we join with other members of God's family on God's mission to bless the world. By this, I'm not referring to attending another church Bible study or potluck, good as those may be. But I'm not exclusively talking about traveling across the Atlantic to do

missions overseas, either. Our greatest mission field may not be halfway around the world, but halfway down the block. God is a missionary God. It's not what God *does*; it's who he *is*. Because God is a missionary God. He sends his people out to be a missionary people—no matter our theological training, what day of the week it is, or what neighborhood we live in. It's been said that there are seven channels of cultural influence:

media, business, arts & entertainment, education, government, the social sector, and the church.[4] We have the opportunity to live, serve, lead, and embody Christ in these seven channels for kingdom influence. Wise and effective missionaries know the delicate tension between truth and context. Truth without context leads to absolutism. Context without truth takes us on a ride down the slippery slope of relativism. But truth and context together are an effective missionary posture and approach.

We all sense it in our bones: something is amiss with the North American church these days. Churches don't seem to be as appealing as they once were. Many are shrinking and closing their doors. Two churches in my community have sold their buildings. One is now an architectural firm, and the other will be developed into apartments. Other buildings across the country that used to be places of worship have been converted into swanky pubs, work spaces, and nightclubs. Church attendance in North America is on the decline. It's no secret: the church is not the driving cultural force it once was. What are we to do about the millions of Americans who are genuinely curious about Jesus, who might be open to the movement of God in their lives, but who would never set foot inside a church, no matter how amazing the music may sound, how state-of-the-art the building may look, or how rich the organic, fair-trade coffee may taste? What about *them?* If they won't ever stumble into a local church, how will they ever stumble into a real, direct encounter with Jesus?

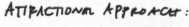
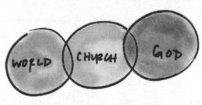

Sometimes we can live the overlapped life, but it's not the overlap Jesus intended. Sometimes it looks like this:[5]

This assumes that those who are far from God are capable of connecting with God only if they attend church. So we ramp up our resolve, raise large amounts of money, and double down on our efforts to attract them to a high-quality Sunday morning experience. Hear me: I'm not against church. I believe in the church; it's Christ's bride. Church is Jesus' idea, and I like Jesus' ideas a great deal. The church is his instrument to bring redemption and healing to the entire world. And it is important for the church to know

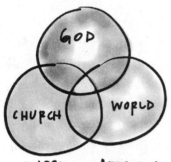

MISSIONAL APPROACH

its history and tradition well—the story of the men and women whose shoulders we stand on—which can offer us the courage and vision to dream boldly about the future. We must know our past in order to run faithfully in our future.

A faithful future is where God, the church, and the world overlap, intersecting with and bumping into all sorts of people in all sorts of unique situations.[6] Where there's mission, there are going to be messes.

Few movements over the last few decades have embodied a more exciting and robust philosophy of mission for the overlapped life better than Fresh Expressions, which started in the U.K. and has spread to various continents. Fresh Expressions is a movement igniting God's people to join with God's mission through fresh expressions of the kingdom of God; they are living out the values of the kingdom of God in various places and with various groups, all for the sake of seeing the gospel transform people's lives. There are new and creative Jesus-oriented kingdom initiatives emerging where not-so-religious people are already hanging out: dog parks, skate parks, running trails, tattoo parlors, bars, coffee shops, Mexican restaurants, and community centers. I'm fortunate to serve on the Fresh Expressions U.S. team. When people ask me what I enjoy most about serving with this organization, I tell them I'm in it for the stories—for the life change, the transformation, the hope.[7]

These are the places in which hope-filled freedom meets people where they are. It's where the real, life-altering stuff with Jesus actually happens. Joining God's mission means we intentionally seek ways for the church Jesus loves to rub elbows with the people Jesus loves. It means creating safe spaces for people to explore the dangerous message of Jesus. It's our "mandorla mandate."[8]

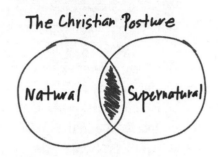

What excites me about Fresh Expressions (FX) is its strategic intentionality to allow relationships to form in naturally supernatural ways. FX refuses to follow a step-by-step formula to God's mission. It's full of intention, but free from an equation. It's purposeful without being mechanical. It meets people on *their* turf, not ours. It seeks to train people to think and pray and live like missionaries in their ordinary, everyday experiences.

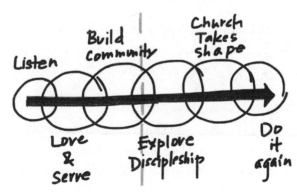

One of the most helpful elements of Fresh Expressions is the process established to help people connect and engage. When we lead trainings, we unpack this diagram of six circles. As we share in our trainings, the lightbulbs often turn on.

The process starts where all healthy relationships start—with listening. Listening requires a great deal of asking questions. As we ask, we also listen to the Spirit.

Where is God already at work in our midst?

Who has yet to be exposed to the dynamic and life-altering message of Christ?

Who is in my constellation of relationships and sphere of influence?

What am I passionate about, and where has God already placed me in the midst of existing relationships with those far from Christ?

It also involves listening to others in a particular context:

What are they passionate about?

What are their hopes and dreams, fears and insecurities?

What keeps them up at night?

Where do they find meaning, purpose, and significance?

Finally, we develop a team of people who seek God and his kingdom and want to join with others in a unique and fresh expression of church:

For whom are we burdened?

Where are there already existing relationships?

What do we sense the Lord wants to do in and through us?

Who would we love to see experience a firsthand encounter with Christ?

This process, mind you, is no microwavable dinner. It's slow cooker time, requiring plenty of patience and faith. You can't rush listening with fresh expressions of church, just as you can't rush listening to a good friend. But over time, as intentional listening leads to trust through conversations, meals, or a bottle of wine, we can move to the second circle—loving and serving. This is when the trust is deep enough that we can love and serve *together*, side by side, with those we're trying to connect with, where we can join together in a purpose greater than simply hanging out.

And all the listening and the loving and the serving, the trust that begins to be established, together yields a true sense of community. Trust gives us the space and the opportunity to encourage people to explore Jesus with us: *Who is he? What was he about? And why do we care so much about Jesus that we surrender our lives to him?* This process, like all processes, requires wisdom, tact, courage, and, most of all, a pure motive of love. It's a clear appeal to examine further who Jesus is and how his life might intersect with theirs. As people explore discipleship, we're finding that they're coming to faith—often in unique and creative ways. Sometimes it feels like trying to build a house in the middle of a hurricane, but it can be a beautifully formative process. One friend showed me a picture of his buddy, the owner of the tattoo parlor where one of their fresh expressions meets. In the photo was a man, arms covered in inky patterns, large gauges in his ears, dipping bread into a chalice as he received Communion for the first time. Rising above the persistent zapping sound of needles penetrating skin, a voice uttered, "This is my body, broken for you." New ink and new life under the same roof.

Wherever there is new life in Christ, we see church taking shape. It's a different kind of shape than most Christians are used to; this is not only okay, it's absolutely necessary when you're thinking like a missionary. The kinds of people who come out of darkness and into an encounter with Jesus most likely aren't going to want to dress up, sit in pews beneath stained glass windows, and sing songs out of a hymnal. There's nothing wrong with pews, stained glass, or hymnals, of course, but demanding that those who are unfamiliar with Jesus align with our cultural religious norms in worship most certainly is. Church can happen anywhere, but sometimes it takes purposeful and contextualized ministry for people to experience God passionately and directly.

Over time, the contours of church begin to emerge. Whether rabbits, tomatoes, humans, or churches, healthy things reproduce. Where there is a healthy fresh expression, where church is taking shape, it equips and sends out others to extend God's mission in other spaces and to other people in other contexts who have not yet experienced the love and grace of Jesus Christ. The process starts all over again—the kingdom-oriented, God-initiated, self-perpetuating organism of heaven-on-earth.

There are a bunch of mandorlas in the six circles diagram—you noticed it, didn't you? Of course, Christ is present throughout the entire process of the formation of a fresh expression of church. But we've found that Christ's presence is most needed and most evident in the overlaps. As God's people, we need to be present in each of these spaces, too.

Over the past few years, the Fresh Expressions team has begun to notice a significant trend. Through all the conversations, coaching calls, training events, and national and regional gatherings we've hosted, we've discovered that a significant number of people feel stuck when they're trying to move from the space of building community to exploring discipleship. When we ask groups of pioneering leaders if this is a point of tension in the ministry context, there is almost universal agreement. Some have said with exasperation, "I *know* I need to move from just hanging out and building trust to something deeper. I *want* to talk about Jesus with others. I *desire* for people to have natural and safe spaces to engage with God's kingdom through what we are doing and what we sense God is calling us to do with people. But I don't know how to move forward. *How in the world do I get unstuck?*"

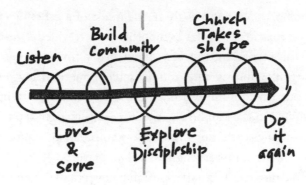

It's as though there is an invisible force field running right through the spaces of building community and exploring discipleship, keeping them from moving forward. It seems that more fresh expressions stall or fall apart in this particular space than during any other part of the process.

Why? Well, first, I think many of us genuinely don't know what to do. We need guidance, coaching, encouragement, prayer, and training in this pioneering work, something the team is working to provide. And second, while I'm not one to go looking for the devil hiding under every rock or behind every email, I believe the Evil One would love for well-intentioned followers of Christ, seeking to pioneer new and creative initiatives in order for people to come to know Jesus, to become discouraged and disillusioned. Satan would love nothing more than to see kingdom pioneers remain stuck in this crucial space, lose hope, and throw in the towel.

In 2015, the AA minor league baseball team, the Biloxi Shuckers, affiliate of the Milwaukee Brewers, were forced to participate in an unprecedented experience: a beautiful new baseball stadium was under construction in Biloxi, Mississippi, but construction crews were unable to complete the project until late spring. As a result, the team was forced to participate in a fifty-four-game road trip to start the season. (For perspective, many professional baseball players complain when they are in the midst of a grueling eight- or nine-game road trip.) For two months, they traveled 2,800 miles through the south, hitting just about every town except Biloxi. They slept in countless hotel rooms, schlepping their luggage from hotel to bus to stadium and back to bus, teammates giving each other haircuts in the clubhouse, the bus making nightly pit stops at out-of-the-way gas stations for a bathroom break at 3 a.m. Ah, the glamorous life of a minor league baseball player.

North American Christians are in a new era: we, too, no longer enjoy the benefits of a home-field advantage. In this cultural moment, we are always the away team, no longer privy to the comforts and luxuries enjoyed by previous generations of Christians in North America. This means we have to think like bilingual missionaries in our particular contexts, especially when we feel stuck between building community and helping people explore discipleship. Culture, to put it succinctly, is what people do—the rhythms, values, patterns, symbols, taboos, priorities, and characteristics of the way a particular people group operates. Our missionary role is to celebrate and affirm the good elements and speak into and call out the bad elements— and those bad elements always involve idols, which speak both to our hearts as individuals and to our cultural norms.

As we explore moving from simply hanging out to helping people connect with Jesus, here are several suggestions to see naturally supernatural movement occur in our relationships with others.

Practice: Engaging in the serious business of humor

As seriously as we take following Jesus, we can't take ourselves too seriously. As American film director Billy Wilder said, "If you're going to tell people the truth, be funny or they'll kill you." It reminds me of something the Apostle Paul wrote to the church in Colossae: "Act wisely with outsiders, making the best of the present time. Always talk pleasantly and with a flavor of wit but be sensitive to the kind of answer each one requires" (Col. 4:5–6, NJB). We've got to lighten up and be willing to poke fun at ourselves from time to time. The goal isn't to make fun of ourselves as Christians (although sometimes it's quite tempting), but utilizing wit and humor helps grease the gears, acknowledging that Christians haven't always gotten things right. "Laughter," as Anne Lamott writes, "is carbonated holiness."[9] When I beat people to the punch with my humor, I acknowledge an awareness that sometimes Christians can come across as weird. It breaks the ice a bit and, in a counter-intuitive way, builds trust and credibility.

I keep a handful of tongue-in-cheek statements in my back pocket and use them whenever I sense people are uneasy talking about faith, religion, Christianity, or church:

> You don't have to worry, man. We're not a weird cult. We stopped sacrificing cats months ago.
> Come check it out: but if you come, you must be aware your attendance is required every Sunday for the next thirty years—and we will issue you a location-tracking device for your ankle when you walk in the door.
> When our church gathers together, we usually only talk about three things: sex, the end times, and that there will be sex in the end times.

When I invited a couple with no church experience to attend our weekend gathering, they agreed and asked what they should wear. I was tempted to give the standard response: "We're pretty casual. Wear whatever you want, whatever makes you feel comfortable." But instead, I decided to take a different route. With a serious look on my face, I responded, "Well, we have a strict dress code policy to which everyone must adhere." Their eyes got big, and they inched forward. I continued, "Everyone is required to wear clothes. We don't take naked people seriously at our church. *Do not come without clothes.*" They hesitated, looked askance at me for a moment, and then we all burst into laughter. And when the wife snorted between laughs, it made us all laugh even harder.

A few years ago, a sixty-eight-year-old former neighbor told me he was going to be visiting our church that upcoming Sunday morning and asked what time we started. He wanted to come, but he admitted he was apprehensive. Other than attending a wedding or a funeral, he said he hadn't been to church since before the Vietnam War. I thought he was kidding. Nope. He was clearly a bit nervous and expressed his apprehension; he asked me to help him because he didn't know the rules of church—when he was supposed to stand or sit or kneel or sing or pray. Sensing his apprehension, I used one of my favorite lines: "Don't worry. We only have one rule at our church: no perfect people allowed." He clearly felt a rush of relief and excitedly blurted out, "Well, shit. I guess I belong then!" His eyes grew big as he realized he'd just cursed in the presence of a member of the clergy. He apologized quickly and profusely. I smiled and offered a rejoinder: "Hey, you're imperfect—great! That means you can come tomorrow!" We laughed so hard we were close to seizures. This small interaction helped take some of the pressure off. Every time I saw him over the next year or so, he'd remind me about our interaction, and we'd double over in laughter once again.

These one-liners may not work for you or your context—and that's fine. But if you can get people to move from laughing *at* Christians to laughing *with* them, that's a pretty good start. I try to put people at ease and build trust and credibility by not taking myself, our church, or Christians too seriously. I am seeking to express enough awareness that talking about spiritual matters makes many people extremely uncomfortable. If I beat people to the punch regarding some of their reservations, it can lower their anxiety level and begin to soften their hearts. Our humor can be a conversation starter, working to catalyze and contribute to our peculiarity in the best way. If people think we're normal, well, maybe we need to use humor to change this perception. If people think we're a bit too weird, we can utilize humor to help them see we're more normal than they might have originally imagined.

Practice: Invite people to explore discipleship in groups

Several years ago, I came to a startling realization: Jesus hardly ever discipled people one-on-one. I know of people and organizations who disciple others one-on-one, which is well and good. I've discipled others individually, and I've benefitted from people discipling me that way, too. Jesus engaged in spiritual conversations with Nicodemus (John 3) and with the woman at the well (John 4). But I can't help noticing the communal discipleship settings Jesus cultivated. Most of the time,

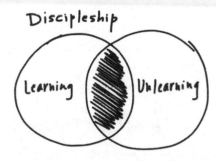

Jesus discipled all twelve of his traveling companions together. Other times he pulled in the inner circle—Peter, James, and John—to join him on a ministry venture, to have them witness one of his miracles firsthand, or to discuss a certain topic.

I've found that when the topic of discussion is faith-related, it can feel safer for individuals if they are in a group setting. Several years ago, I invited a twentysomething to a group discussion where we were exploring Jesus together with others who were not followers of Jesus. After a few months of building a context of trust, he opened up and admitted to me that if I had invited just him to the conversation, he never would have agreed; meeting one-on-one, he told me, would have made him think I *was* the leader of a cult. Because it was a group setting, though, it put him at ease. It wasn't going to have the feel of, as he called it, "a religious timeshare pitch."

Additionally, there are often more entry points to talk about Jesus in group settings. For example, when someone shares a thought, opinion, or question it may be appropriate to say, "Thanks for sharing. Does anybody else feel the same way?" or "That's a good point. Has anybody else in the group experienced this?" These become points of shared reference, which build safety. They allow people to be more open and vulnerable about their own spiritual exploration. Group settings can be a lot more fun, too. If you've already worked hard to build trust in the midst of community, chances are pretty good you'll have fun and find significance when you aren't just hanging out together, but when you've got real purpose and focus to what you are doing. The most practical pointer I can offer is this: start by thinking about discipleship in groups first and then move to thinking about one-on-one discipleship—not the other way around.

Practice: Throw purposeful parties

Rowan Williams wrote that "When reading the Gospels you sometimes get the impression that if anywhere in ancient Galilee you heard a loud noise and a lot of laughter and talking and singing, you could be reasonably sure that Jesus of Nazareth was around somewhere nearby."[10] One of the most strategic and fruitful ways to live in the midst of the overlap of the building community and exploring Jesus spaces is to throw parties with purpose. Hosting parties can cultivate fun, connection, celebration, engagement, and a meaningful shared experience. (In fact, they *should* include these.

Without them, your parties will most definitely be lame.) All of these elements are beneficial. But if you stop here, they remain in the building community circle. We still need to look for ways to move the ball down the field.

Throwing parties with purpose can be a wonderful naturally supernatural way to connect with people who don't have much history with Jesus, but who might be interested in exploring who he is. Jesus loved parties. Many of his kingdom parables were about parties. His first miracle happened at a party—and it involved alcohol. Jesus had a knack for showing up at the best parties. Some have referred to these kinds of spaces as Matthew parties, taken from the story found in Luke 5. Jesus called a Jewish tax collector (who was understood to be a traitor who worked for the Roman government and was compensated sufficiently) to follow him. Levi, who was also called Matthew, in turn hosted a party at his house which included other ill-reputed tax collectors, religious experts, and Jesus' own disciples on the guest list (Luke 5:27–32). You could hardly have found a more diverse group of people in all of Palestine to attend the same party. Jesus loved parties, and he saw the potential of this kind of party: his mission of love colliding with a diverse crowd. Levi's life was changed because of it. This shouldn't surprise us; the Gospel writer Mark tells us Levi was the son of Alphaeus (Mark 2:14). And I love this little detail: in the original language, *Alphaeus* means "changing."

When a group of kingdom pioneers who've worked hard to build trust with spiritual explorers throws parties and anticipates the presence of the Spirit, it's not surprising we get into all sorts of good kingdom mischief. Several years ago, I encountered a group of kingdom-minded party hosts who meet with the intention of seeing God show up in the midst of meaningful connection. They realized that many of their friends were wine connoisseurs who were also curious about the Bible and hungry to have their spiritual questions answered. They gave it the curiously peculiar name *Bible Tasting*

& *Wine Readings*. They created a safe environment for social connection to occur over a shared interest while also giving purpose to the gathering.

In the fall of 2007, I attended a gathering at a Catholic retreat center in the mountains of New Mexico with a group of unique Christian leaders who were thinking creatively about new forms of church. I heard kingdom entrepreneur Andrew Jones share about neighborhood pizza parties he hosts on Friday nights in his home. While eating out is often a fun way to connect with people, Andrew is passionate about challenging Jesus-followers to host parties in their own homes, places where Jesus purposefully spent time with people.

Andrew's family provides the dough and sauce, but he encourages everyone to bring their favorite toppings. The guests knead the dough together and make pizzas to their liking. While the pizzas are baking, Andrew calls the guests into the living room and facilitates conversation around what can be learned from the pizza-making process. He shares one of Jesus' parables: The kingdom of God is like a woman who took a little bit of yeast and it worked all through the dough (Matt. 13:33). Even though the kingdom is invisible, it reveals itself and its effects in the world.

He also shares that Jesus talked about another form of yeast, the yeast of the Pharisees. Yeast can either give itself away (good) or keep everything for itself (bad). The yeast of the kingdom gives itself away continually. If you were to look under a microscope, he continues, you'd find the yeast continually looking for ways to give itself away. This process is called bud emergence. Andrew tells his friends this is the nature of what it means to be in relationship with Jesus. Jesus desires for us to give ourselves away to his Father and to others, just as he gave himself away to the world. This is *agape* love. Once the pizzas have finished baking, everyone gathers in the kitchen to enjoy the food family-style, while conversation continues and people ask about the nature of Jesus and his kingdom. At the end of the night, Andrew invites people back the following week for more pizza and conversation around another Jesus story. People always come back. Andrew has started several churches—many of them can be traced back to a pizza party in his home.[11] Thin crust, tomato sauce, a church plant.

Practice: Speak with creativity to cultivate curiosity

When people ask me what I do, I don't tell them I am a pastor. Because of the jaundiced perspective many people hold regarding Christians and Christian leaders, I used to say I'm an author or a leadership coach or that I started an organization to help hungry leaders improve—all of which are true. But I noticed that most people didn't find that interesting. So instead, I started telling them I am a practical and educational theologist. It's not a real job title; I made it up. But it works. It piques curiosity and regularly leads to spiritual conversations. And because of the increasing politicized nature of the word, lately I am describing myself less as a "Christian" and more as a follower committed to the Way of Jesus. I am not ashamed of following Jesus—not at all. I simply want to remove barriers people may have in understanding God and his people. This is not mere nuance; what we say matters—and how we say things matters, too. We must watch our language.

Consider this for a moment: How could you be creative with language in a way that makes you peculiar and urges curious people further into conversation? Think about words used frequently by Christians: *Church. Bible. Prayer. Discipleship. The gospel. Worship.* These are good words, important words, but could there be creative, compelling, contextual ways to communicate the same thing? Instead of church, could we say a Jesus community? Could we describe prayer as talking with Jesus about the things we're going to do together? Or how about discipleship as following the Way of Jesus? Or how about describing baptism as a sacred pool party? The goal of thinking about language differently isn't an attempt to be manipulative, deceptive, or cute. It is neither an attempt to ignore nor to discard traditional words. The goal instead is to help us read our contexts in order to best love and serve others in a particular place and to describe our wonderfully gracious God and his loving mission of redemption in colorful, clear, creative, compelling, and curiosity-inducing ways.

Part of watching our language means developing and collecting purposeful, engaging phrases. For me, the tipping point of deeper spiritual relationships has often started with one of these questions/ statements:

- I want you to consider a new opportunity, a new initiative I am starting. This might be different for you, but I want to encourage you to try something different. Will you trust me?
- Hey man, there's something I want you to think about. I want to challenge you to engage with me further . . .
- I wonder if you would be interested in joining me in something that means a lot to me.
- I've enjoyed hanging out with you all. But I'm wondering if there might be something more here. What if we hung out with a greater purpose in mind? Can I share what I mean?
- Here's what I'm thinking. . . . What do you think?

One of my favorites is from Canadian pastor Bruxy Cavey. He finds himself regularly saying, "That reminds me of something Jesus said . . ." or "Oh, when you say that I think about how Jesus was in a similar situation . . ." These aren't infomercials for Jesus; it's about dropping a line into the conversation to see if anyone is curious enough to nibble. It may go without saying, but in order to do so, we need to be disciples who truly know what Jesus told us to say and do.

Our language can even reinforce and reveal our deeply held assumptions of dualistic spirituality. When we talk about the world *out there*, while we remain *in here*, we see the church as being in an *either/or* existence when God wants us to see opportunities for the kingdom to flourish in all situations, times, and locations. "Our interior faith must meaningfully reflect our exterior practices."[12] We're not always going to get it right—and that's okay. But it's still important to ask, to scatter the conversational seed and see if it lands on good soil. Take the risk. If the phrases listed above won't work effectively in your context, brainstorm with friends or other leaders what phrases could be effective and natural with spiritual explorers in your own life.

Consider this fun exercise: write down on a whiteboard, flip chart, or piece of paper all the potentially overused insider Christian language—words, phrases, and euphemisms—you can think of (what is referred to as "Christianese"). Once you've identified which phrases are unhelpful and shouldn't be used regularly, make a commitment to refrain from using them when you are together. While there may be creative ways to speak of common concepts about God and his mission, we should work hard to avoid insider phrases altogether when in settings where people are exploring who Jesus is.

Practice: Grow to ask incisive questions

One of the most relationally engaging ways you can live is to ask thoughtful, meaningful, and caring questions of others. It's all too rare today to have someone who is willing to look us in the eye and listen. When it happens, we've been given a gift. This gift carries the potential of opening up wonderful and significant spiritual conversations.

I want to suggest a few ways to cultivate this question-asking skill, as well as provide several questions which can be used easily as tools in everyday conversations—or to begin new ones.[13]

- When you think of a great question, write it down and save it for later. Write it down on an index card, add it to a file on your computer, or create a note on your smartphone.
- When you hear someone else asking great questions—in person, in class, at work, on television, in a book, in a coffee shop, etc.—jot them down.
- Reflect on the great questions others have asked you. Ask yourself why *those* questions were so important to you. Consider asking others to share with you the best two or three questions they've ever been asked.
- Skip the generic and bland questions (*How are you?*, *What's up?*, *How's your day?*) and replace them with better ones (*If you could describe how you are feeling in two words today, what would those words be?*, *What are you looking forward to the most this week?* or *What part of your day gave you the most joy—or gave you pause—or both?*) Ask questions about people's passions. Adding just a little more thought and intention can turn an ordinary conversation into a deeper connection. When meeting with someone you don't know well, ask them to tell you their story. While it's not technically a question, it retains the same posture of humility and understanding that questions provide.

A few spiritually oriented questions I like to ask:

- When you hear the word "Jesus," what comes to mind? When you hear "Christian," what comes to mind? Why do you think there is a difference?
- What questions do you have for Christians but have been too nervous to ask?

- If you could ask God two questions, what would you want to ask him? Why these questions?
- What are two questions you'd like to ask people who go to church?
- What do you think about church? What has been your experience? Was it positive or negative? What do your friends think about church?
- If you were in charge of a church, what would you do to make it more engaging, relevant, and significant for you?

A few weeks ago, I was with a group of people who couldn't understand why anyone would want to give up a good weekend morning's sleep to go to church. So I asked them, "What are two questions you'd like to ask people who go to church regularly? If you were in charge of a church, what would you do to make it more engaging, relevant, and significant for you?" They loved the conversation and didn't want it to end. Neither did I.

When we're training kingdom leaders who long to live in the overlap, we teach them to read a passage of Scripture and ask five specific questions to increase the bandwidth of accessibility. It works for all sorts of people, from those who are trained seminarians to those who have never picked up a Bible before.

1. What is going on in the passage/story?
2. What do I like—or what encourages me—in this passage?
3. What disturbs, jolts, or startles me in this passage?
4. What do we learn about the nature of God or the character of Jesus?
5. What will I do with this in the next seven days? (What implication does this have on my week ahead?)

If you wonder what passages of Scripture might be good to start with, start with stories. Print off a parable of Jesus and allow people to enter into a story, like Andrew Jones and his pizza parties. Some good questions to ask when reading parables together would be:

- Who do you relate to most in the story? Why that particular person?
- As you read/heard this story, what were you feeling? Did anything surprise you or confuse you? Why?
- Why do you think Jesus told this story? What do you think he wanted us to learn from it?
- If you were to retell the story in your own words for our culture today, how would you retell it?
- Does this remind you of any other story—a novel, a movie, a play, or a real-life occurrence?
- Is there anything for us to do with this story beyond our discussion here?

Of course, don't ask all of these. Just pick a few that might work in your context. Try them out in the next week and see what happens.

Practice: Offering prayer to others

A few years ago, I coached a leader of a fresh expression in Kentucky who gathered a team together to play volleyball at a local bar every week. The bar built several sand volleyball courts and hosted sand volleyball leagues and tournaments during the warmer months. The leader wanted to see her love of volleyball and her passion for seeing Jesus work in unexpected places overlap. Her vision was to start a volleyball team in order to naturally connect with people far from God.

Her husband, however, was not all that into volleyball. He supported her vision and wanted to participate in this Fresh Expression in some capacity, but he wondered where he might fit. While the team played every Tuesday night, he would simply walk around the bar, introduce himself to other people, and let them know he would be glad to pray for any need they might have. For the first several weeks, people politely declined. But over time, he began to build rapport, and people began to open up. The regulars would text, call, and email him with requests. The bartender started asking for prayer. During a break in the volleyball game, this leader told me she looked over to the bar area and noticed her husband, with his arm around the shoulders of the bartender, both of their heads bowed in prayer.

Our community of Lansdale, Pennsylvania, a borough in the greater Philadelphia area, hosts town-wide celebrations called First Friday on the first Friday evening of every month during the warmer months of the year. The downtown area is filled with live music, performing entertainers, artists, vendors, and other businesses offering their wares. Hundreds of people come out to eat, connect, and enjoy the beginning of the weekend. A handful of years ago, a group of leaders in our church suggested we might do something entirely different: offer free prayer. Initially, I was skeptical, not because I felt prayer was unimportant, but because I wondered if it might turn people off or make things awkward for the community. Reluctantly, I agreed. The team gathered together in homes before the beginning of the First Friday season. One of our elders trained the group on how to offer prayer, how to pray, and how to follow up with people later—even where to stand around the prayer tent, in order to be natural and strategic and to avoid making others think we were a cult. The team bought a large vendor tent and small furniture items from IKEA in order to make the tent warm and welcoming. They asked a professional designer in our church to create a large banner to put over the tent which read, "Free Prayer . . . No Strings Attached."

During the first few Fridays, visits to the tent were scarce. But those who did visit found it to be natural and welcoming, even surprising. Some expressed their appreciation for the kind gesture. Some shared that they had grown up Catholic but hadn't been to church in years. Some had no faith background whatsoever. Others opened up and shared that they had been hurt by church, vowing never to return again. But as people began to see the consistency and regular presence of the team each month, they began to feel more open. Those who were at a distance began to wander over. A few admitted they had watched the group from afar and finally felt comfortable enough to come over and ask for prayer. The team wrote down their name, their request, and their contact information, following up a week or two later to see how they were doing and asking if they could pray about anything else. The team began to report back, sharing stories from the people they were praying for. Some asked for prayer regarding their health or a broken relationship with a family member or an estranged spouse. Others came back every First Friday to say hello and to receive a hug from someone on the prayer team. Initially, I was skeptical. But I'm glad I was wrong.

What's the worst someone can say if you offer prayer? "No." Can you handle that? I imagine so. There are times I've found myself praying for people's dogs to be healed. Parents have asked me to pray for their kids to do well in their Saturday morning soccer games. On a few occasions, I've felt a bit silly praying for certain things, but if it meant connecting with people who, deep down, have a longing to connect with God (whether they knew it yet or not), I was willing to do it. I'd ask them if they wanted me to pray later on my own time or if they actually wanted me to pause right then and there to pray for them. Many times I've been surprised by people's willingness to be open and vulnerable with me regarding prayer, right on the spot, even though I had just met them. Offering prayer can be a practical way to lean in. It all starts with a simple ask.

Thomas Rusert, a Lutheran pastor, decided to offer free prayer in a Starbucks in Doylestown, Pennsylvania, about thirty minutes from where I live. He created a simple sign made from card stock that said, "Free Prayer" with a quote from Martin Luther: "Pray and let God worry." Thomas would set up his sign, sip his coffee, and see what the Spirit might be up to. He showed up consistently each week over a period of time, and people eventually began to wander over to talk and ask for prayer. All this cost Thomas was a cup of coffee, a piece of card stock, and some purposefully invested time.[14]

My sense is that you might be surprised at how few people will actually turn you down. But if they do, don't take it as personal rejection. Always keep the offer for prayer open. When people decline, I smile and say, "No problem. If you change your mind or something comes up, just let me know. I'd be glad to pray at any time in the future." I've had people circle back around months later and say they'd like to take me up on my offer.

Practice: Cultivate a deep and ongoing dependence on prayer

In his book, *Out of the House of Bread*, Preston Yancey likens different spiritual practices to baking bread. He suggests prayer is like kneading bread dough. He writes, "Kneading is an essential process not because without it we have no bread, but because without it our bread does not have good texture, form, or stability."[15] I like this image. I get my hands dirty, my forearms and fingers grow tired. It is repetitive, and yet it creates that texture, form, and stability. Offering prayer is one thing; believing prayer is central to faithfully embodying Christ's mission is quite another. I could pontificate about the importance of prayer, but I sense that if you're reading this, you know it already. Admittedly, prayer is comforting and perplexing at the same time. It is often simple, yet at times it can be excruciatingly difficult. Most of us are educated well beyond our level of obedience. We know what to do; we just think up a thousand reasons not to do it. I'll say it as simply as I can: *If we believe in prayer, we will pray.* If we are to take prayer seriously in the overlapped life, there are three specific areas where we can aim our blowtorch.

First, pray that the fear and acceptance of others would not be an idol in your life. It's amazing how powerful the fear of others' opinions can be in our lives. These opinions can impede potential spiritual conversation because we fear rejection, awkwardness, or being ostracized. There may currently be areas in our hearts and minds which keep us from immersing ourselves in vulnerability with others because we fear we might rock the boat in a certain relationship. In Acts 4, we read about Peter and John being in hot water with the members of the Jewish Council for talking about the resurrection of Jesus. They were threatened and told not to talk about Jesus again. What was their response? They did not immediately seek to smooth things over, offer an apology, or backtrack. They did not complain, whine, or sulk. They responded boldly, "Do you think God wants us to obey you rather than him? We cannot stop telling about everything we have seen and heard" (Acts 4:19–20 NLT). The council threatened them further. And what was the response when they returned to the believers to tell them what had happened? The believers didn't pray that the threats would stop; they prayed that Peter and John's courage would grow (v. 29). They prayed that God would do a miraculous thing—and he did. May we commit to regular prayer so that we would be full of boldness and courage as we speak, not giving in to opinions at the expense of pleasing God.

Second, pray for people of peace. In Luke 10:1–7, Jesus offers his missionary strategy. It's not extremely complex, but it is revolutionary. He tells us to pray for people of peace so that others will receive our message with favor and want to know more. People of peace are not yet followers of Jesus, but they are open to your message, though they may not know why. They smell the aroma of Christ on you, even though they haven't yet identified it's him. And, should they come to faith in Christ, they are gatekeepers for other groups and door-openers to circles of influence into which we would never be welcomed on our own.

Our church believes in this so strongly that there have been several times when we've asked people to pull out their phones right in the middle of our gatherings and encouraged them to set their alarms for 10:02 a.m. We encourage them, wherever they may be when their alarm goes off each morning, to stop and pray Luke 10:2: "The harvest is plentiful, but the workers are few. Ask the Lord of the harvest, therefore, to send out workers into his harvest field." It is a wonderful thing to know that at 10:02 a.m on any given day, there are people scattered all over the northern area of the greater Philadelphia region pausing to pray for God to work mightily in the region and the world. Try it yourself—and encourage others to join with you in praying just after ten each morning.

Third, pray for wisdom. Earlier, I mentioned James 1:5: "If any of you lacks wisdom, you should ask God, who gives generously to all without finding fault, and it will be given to you." Pray specifically for wisdom to know when to courageously engage further and when to patiently slow down. Pray for the wisdom to know who to connect with, what to say, and where to invest.

One final practical point: having and setting appropriate expectations is vitally important to the process. It has been said that frustration is the difference between expectation and reality. Sometimes, when we are doing God's work, we can hold onto misconstrued expectations, believing we have to boil the ocean by Friday. But when it comes to thinking about fresh expressions and living in the sacred Venn diagram of invitation, we should not expect everybody to be wildly enthusiastic about what we're doing.

Sure, there have been times when I've been told to take my efforts and stick them in anatomical places I am not able to describe specifically in this book. But I can't take this as a rejection of my efforts, and neither should you. We must trust the work of the Spirit in people's lives. Conversely, I've also learned not to expect everyone to reject the opportunity to explore and discover Jesus. God works in various ways to bring people to himself. When people see others who are motivated by love, rooted in faith, and buoyed by hope, it's attractive.

One of the beautifully enticing elements of the character of the Holy Spirit is surprise. The Spirit startles, lures, and creates anew. Because of this, we can cultivate a posture of holy anticipation and pray into this posture regularly. Jesus described the Spirit as being like the wind, blowing in whatever direction it desires. It seems the role of the Spirit is to interrupt business as usual. The Spirit is the anti-status-quo member of the Trinity. Aren't you glad that while God is the same in the past, present, and future, he is uninterested in simply making things safe and predictable in order to maintain the status quo?

Who knows—he may even seat you across the table from a guy named Mad Dog who happens to be wearing a Sons of Satan patch on his vest.

FAITHFUL POSTURE

Convicted Civility

Civil discourse isn't the answer to everything, but
uncivil discourse isn't the answer to anything.

—N. T. WRIGHT

A gentle answer deflects anger,
But harsh words make tempers flare.

—PROVERBS 15:1 NLT

Chances are good that at this very moment one of your friends
is yelling at their political enemies on Facebook—and maybe
the person they're yelling at is you. Or maybe you're the one doing
the yelling. Just recently I read someone's comment on the site:

> I just nitpicked on a friend's status because he was being an idiot.
> Then people yelled at me. Then I yelled back. They stopped
> yelling. I think I won?

If winning means yelling the loudest so that everyone pipes
down, then yeah, you won a gold medal, my friend.

I mentioned that my family and I live in the greater Philadelphia area. We love living in the Northeast for countless reasons. When people think of our great city, they often think of soft pretzels, cheesesteaks, the Liberty Bell, and the Eagles. The people here are loyal, passionate, and proud, but you may have heard that Philadelphia is not known for its politeness. The people are seen as direct, gruff, and at times, even downright rude, especially when the Eagles lose. Many people here will tell you what they are thinking, whether you want to hear it or not. It may hurt to hear the truth, but there's no doubt you'll receive it anyway. Here the car horn is commonly used in conjunction with the middle finger. The comedian Jim Gaffigan quipped, "Philadelphia, the City of Brotherly Love. And if you've been there, you know they mean that sarcastically." It's why some people have even dubbed it Negadelphia and the City of Brotherly Shove.

At times, I'm asked to speak at events in the Deep South. With each visit, I find myself greeted with full-on hugs of warm hospitality while I'm handed a tea sweet enough to choke a horse. The kindness is palpable. I'm genuinely surprised to learn that people in the South are so kind and polite they wave at you using *all* of their fingers. But I've since realized, despite the kindness and near endless *bless-your-hearts*, they aren't always telling me the truth, at least not as fully as I'd like. Afraid to offend or upset the apple cart, these Southern folks, at times, choose to lie politely. While my passionate (and at times, acerbic) neighbors here in Philly major in truth and minor in kindness, my warm-hearted friends in the South often major in kindness and minor in truth-telling.

Civility is a topic we don't spend much time pondering or discussing, but we should. The Institute for Civility and Government defines it as "the claiming and caring for one's identity, needs, and beliefs without degrading someone else's in the process." Simply put, it is "human commonness."[1] Writing five hundred years ago, the Dutch Christian humanist and scholar Erasmus of Rotterdam addressed European culture, which was deeply hedonistic, vulgar, and violent. During this period of European history, people killed or permanently injured one another over the smallest of disagreements and miniscule unpaid debts (owning a credit card must have been lethal). Erasmus was certainly not the first to write on the topic, but he may have been the clearest and most compelling. He warned that unless people learned to become self-controlled, their unchecked desires would make them no better than animals. "Self-discipline was the mark of civilization; anything less was barbaric."[2]

Erasmus helped to popularize the idea of *civilité*, from which we derive our English word "civility." It can also be translated as "politeness," but it means something more. It suggests an approach to life, a way of carrying ourselves and relating to others in which we honor each other and society. The idea of *civilité* arose at a period in European culture when a society marked by chivalry and the unity of the Catholic Church were falling apart; in the midst of the chaos and uncertainty, Europe was seeking guidance on how to avoid killing each other over the smallest of offenses.[3] It reminds me of how people are killed in Philly fighting over parking spots.[4]

According to Erasmus, *civilité* is what enables us to live together. It's where we get the words *civilized* and *civilization*, whose original meaning was "a member of a household." To be civilized people means seeing ourselves as living in a household within a society. Author Stephen Carter points out that if we are to be moral and kind and good, "it means we understand that our relationship to others is like being in the same house—with family members—and that our freedoms are limited for the common good."[5]

Religion scholar Martin Marty stated, "One of the real problems in modern life is that people who are good at being civil lack strong convictions and people who have strong convictions lack civility."[6] I like the phrase "convicted civility," because it captures so well what is needed in our present age. When I read about Facebook feuds, hear politicians dehumanizing other people in their speeches, or learn of parents brawling on the sidelines of their kids' soccer games, I sometimes wonder if maybe we're flirting with the extinction of civility. Even the global pandemic led to bitter political division and blaming at the very moment when our country needed unity. At our most vulnerable time, in the midst of so much uncertainty in the early stages, there was evidence of acrid disagreements and taking of sides. To put a spin on Marty's assertion, some people major in conviction and minor in civility; others major in civility and minor in conviction. But as Christians who understand our call and place in culture, we must choose to double-major. We need strong conviction united with graceful humility.

Daryl Davis is an accomplished jazz and blues musician with a unique hobby I deeply respect: for the past thirty years, he has met with and befriended members of the Ku Klux Klan. What makes his hobby radical is that Daryl is African American. Many of the KKK members he meets with admit that they have never met or interacted with a black man before meeting Daryl. When he meets with Klansmen, he asks one direct, penetrating, and provocative question: "Why do you hate me when you know nothing about me?" This one question cracks open doors, making a way for truth-filled conversation. Daryl is steely and unflinching as he listens to and loves these Klan members, even when they say terrible and feckless things about people of color.

As Daryl proactively and compassionately pursues friendship with them one at a time, he has helped many of them leave the KKK altogether. In *Accidental Courtesy*, the gripping documentary featuring his life, Davis goes to his closet and holds up many of the robes and hoods given to him by his friends as they've left the KKK.[7] In fact, he has been given 200 Ku Klux Klan robes over the years.[8] One day, he plans to open a museum where he will put them all on display. Daryl Davis is a living example of how convicted civility is not only capable of tearing down walls of hostility, but also moving mountains by faith. And forcing you to get a bigger closet. This kind of courtesy doesn't sound accidental at all.

Living as agents of the kingdom, we are called to double-major in truth *and* kindness, Philly *and* the Deep South. Paul wrote when we are "speaking the truth in love, we will grow to become in every respect the mature body of him who is the head, that is, Christ" (Eph. 4:15). When grace and truth are absent, it leads to bitterness and rage. When we major in both grace and truth, there is an empowered freedom which flows into our relationships.

Yes, you might think, *but what does double-majoring actually look like?* First, we must live by our convictions. As we explored earlier with Daniel and his exiled friends,

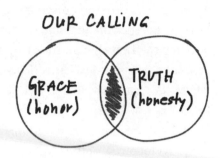

they never saw themselves as victims. They were bold while at the same time remaining faithful. We're not called to be doormats. We are called to stand for something. We stand for what is right as we believe it to be true through the Scriptures, through our interaction with the Spirit and with other wise followers of Jesus.

Certainly, there is no surefire, foolproof manual for handling all issues, decisions, and situations. Yes, we have the inspired Scriptures and the guidance of the Spirit, but they are not a quick-reference guide to everyday decisions. The author of Hebrews wrote, *"Make every effort* to live in peace with everyone and to be holy" (Heb. 12:14). Other translations use the word *strive*. When I strive for something, I find it takes a lot out of me, draining my emotional, mental, and physical tanks. No doubt convicted civility requires significant effort. It also requires patience as we wait for God's future involvement to overcome evil. Remaining calm and humble isn't merely a way to wait it out until the end of time; it actually builds our spiritual muscles here and now.[9]

I have the privilege of speaking on college campuses around the country. As I meet with students, I've noticed their underlying fear of being perceived by their classmates as judgmental. For the students I meet, it's the worst possible accusation they could receive: a scarlet J on their chests. Often, students don't say much of anything if speaking will put them out on a limb, and if they do, they often hedge their bets and begin with common prefaces, such as, "Well, I am not one to judge, but . . ." or "There are a lot of ways to look at it, but I feel . . ." In their discourses, *I believe* has fallen prey to *I feel*. We're concerned about being wrong or unpopular or in the minority or firing the first shot and starting World War III.

But this is not just on college campuses; it's practically everywhere. We must speak and live with the conviction to honor and be faithful to Christ, all the while knowing that on occasion, our stance will be unpopular. What we're after is not popularity, but truth. As followers of the One who claimed to *be* the truth, we must stand by, with, and for the truth.

While we need to speak with truth, we must be kind and respectful in doing so. As one young twentysomething shared, "I don't have to be right to feel loved. I have to be dignified in our disagreement." We can have all the right theology, but if we don't have the right posture, it won't matter. To live in the sacred overlap is to live with the willful conviction that we must work shoulder to shoulder with people, even if we don't see eye to eye. In Galatians 5, the apostle Paul lists the fruit of the Spirit, the evidence and byproduct of the Spirit's work in our lives. This evidence, he wrote, is exhibited through kindness and self-control. Chuck Colson wrote, "The obligation to show respect for others does not come from a soft sentimentalism but is rooted in the theological truth that we are all created in the image of God."[10] Scholars have used the Latin phrase *imago dei*—the image of God— which is stamped upon the hearts of every human. C. S. Lewis wrote, "Next to the Blessed Sacrament itself, your neighbor is the holiest object presented to your senses."[11] People have immense value.

As I type these words, millions of Americans are going to the polls for the midterm elections. A few hours ago, I returned from my sons' elementary school, our local polling location. I sauntered into the gym, stepped behind a cordoned-off booth with gray curtains, and pulled the lever. Now I'm sporting my nifty *I Voted* sticker on the pocket of my button-down dress shirt to prove it. I expect it to fall off some time before lunch, and I'll probably find it tomorrow, stuck to the bathroom floor or crumpled up on the floormat of my car.

After settling back in at my desk, I clicked on Facebook—a big mistake. Disgusted by what I read, I logged out after just a moment or two, but the next hour was ruined for me. I was kicking myself for logging on, because I've held the strong conviction that the days around each national election should be dubbed National Stay Off Social Media Week. It seems apparent: as Americans, we love to hate. We have a strong tendency to demonize The Other. As Pope Francis tweeted, distance creates distortion, especially in a time when what is needed most is a culture of encounter, not confrontation.

E pluribus unum, the motto of America, printed on all our currency, means "Out of many, one." But as the late historian Arthur Schlesinger, Jr. is credited with saying, it seems we are quickly becoming a place with too much *pluribus* and very little *unum*.[12] "Instead of talking *with* people, we talk *over* or *at* or *about* or *behind* or *through* them instead. Our prepositions are messed up. God is always building unity among his children, yet we seem to be working against him with greater intensity."[13]

To be clear, *unity* is not the same as *uniformity*. Unity is finding commonality in the midst of our differences. It's striving to find some overlap, which may be difficult, but it's there somewhere. In the biblical context, there were Jews and Gentiles, Greeks and

Romans, men and women, slaves and slave-owners. It continues to amaze me how much time Jesus spent with his enemies, which included religious leaders and *even one of his own disciples*. Then he told us to not just tolerate our enemies, but to love them—and to go out of our way to do so (Matt. 5:43–48). "The diversity of the early church was staggering, and this kind of unity was and is only possible because of unity around the person of Jesus."[14] The compassionate, category-busting unity of Jesus was rooted in his Father.

In his book *Uncommon Decency*, Richard Mouw writes that we live in a culture which shouts to us that the way the world works is *us versus them*. We are in an intense era in American politics—in all of American life, really—wherein people are trying to convince us to join the side of the donkey or the elephant. William Sloane Coffin, Jr. says this can lead us to become either uncritical lovers of country or loveless critics of country—but neither one is what we're after.[15] As Christians, our calling is to follow the Lamb wherever he goes. It's not about red states and blue states; for Christians it's about purple, the color of royalty. Jen Pollock Michel writes, "When God's people stand, they sing not 'Hail to the Chief' but hallelujah."[16]

I know I must be careful here. It's not always as simple as what I shared in the previous section. In fact, to live in the overlap means we can't ignore politics entirely. It is not an option to live as ostriches sticking our heads in spiritual sand. Tim Keller, author and founding pastor of Redeemer Presbyterian Church in New York City, wrote an opinion piece in the *New York Times* titled "How Do Christians Fit into the Two-Party System? They Don't."[17] He stated, "Christians cannot pretend they can transcend politics and simply 'preach the gospel.' Those who avoid all political discussions and engagement are essentially casting a vote for the social status quo." To be silent on certain issues is to support those issues. To not be political, Keller says, is to be political. In the Old Testament, figures like Joseph and Daniel had important roles in government and found it impossible to be apolitical.

While Christians can (and should) be involved in political issues, we must be careful not to officially identify the church with either political party. In thinking consistent with this book, Keller states that the two main options are (1) to withdraw and attempt to be apolitical, and (2) to assimilate and swallow the offerings of one of the political party options in one giant gulp. Neither option is wise. Michael Wear is the chief strategist for the AND Campaign, a Venn-postured organization which describes itself as "biblical Christians spreading the gospel through civic and cultural engagement and as being committed to biblical values and social justice." Wear said something which has splintered my brain: "The crisis for Christians is not that we are politically homeless. The crisis is that we ever thought we could make our home in politics at all . . . Our home is with him who has made his home in us, and our hope is with the kingdom that is right at hand. If we find ourselves in Babylon, let's make sure we don't become Babylonians."[18] As kingdom people, we should never feel completely at home in one party or the other. It is part of our prophetic witness. "It is time," as Wear says, "for Christians to stop looking to politics for hope, and to start carrying kingdom hope into politics with them out of love of God and for the good of their neighbors."[19] Their organization challenges people with this practical piece of advice: vote in a way that best loves your neighbor.

We do not belong to our politics; mandorla Christians refuse to find identity and ultimate meaning there. "Jesus," as pastor Tony Evans wrote, "did not come to take sides. He came to take over."[20]

So, what to do? How are we to choose? It's complicated, for sure. We must be people who are committed to praying diligently, discerning carefully, and engaging humbly. In our current political climate, there are no simple solutions or approaches. Every election year, I dig up the best voting advice I've ever come across and read it as a reminder of what is before me:

> I met those of our society who had votes in the ensuing election, and advised them (1) to vote, without fee or reward, for the person they judged most worthy, (2) to speak no evil of the person they voted against, and (3) to take care their spirits were not sharpened against those that voted on the other side.

This is sage and timely advice. What amazes me is that this was not written by a wise American politician or a popular author or blogger. It was penned by Methodist Church founder John Wesley in his journal on October 6, 1774—almost 250 years ago. Yes, go to the polls. Vote with all the wisdom and conviction you can possibly possess. But we should never look to our candidates as saviors or models of morality. Politicians are vehicles of potential change, but they are not rescuers. Sure, they can help, but they cannot ultimately fix the sin-marred world we live in.

We pledge allegiance to a king and a kingdom, and because of this, we don't need to be afraid. Yes, there are important issues at hand—war, poverty, immigration, human trafficking, taxes, drugs, racism, sexism, and other complex social, economic, and political issues that require attention, concern, and care. But we do not have to be afraid. The command is one of the most repeated in Scripture: do not fear. We live in a culture that preys on people's fears. The political machine is designed to thrive on making people angry, scared, or both. And when we are fearful and feel unsafe, we become unkind. But the call of Jesus is this: *do not be afraid.*

Peter spoke to Christians who lived as religious minorities by challenging them with this:

> But in your hearts revere Christ as Lord. Always be prepared to give an answer to everyone who asks you to give the reason for the hope that you have. But do this with gentleness and respect,

keeping a clear conscience, so that those who speak maliciously against your good behavior in Christ may be ashamed of their slander. For it is better, if it is God's will, to suffer for doing good than for doing evil. (1 Pet. 3:15–17)

The *what*—the conviction and reason for our hope—is met with the *how*—civility, living with gentleness and respect. Many people have wondered how such a pervasive breakdown of civility has occurred in our society in such a short amount of time. Author Stephen Carter writes that civility is held up and held together by three primary institutions: the home, school, and our places of worship. Borrowing from the well-worn metaphor of a three-legged stool, Carter states that when one or two—or all three—legs fail, the stool of civility topples over.[21] I think we'd all agree that we've felt the loose and wobbly reality of all three of those institutional legs over the past few decades.

But ultimately, when we talk about convicted civility, our sacred call is to be *more than civil*. To describe God as simply being nice or remaining civil leaves us with a shallow, inaccurate, and anemic view of the Creator. God is a God marked by category-defying love. Jesus' aim was never to be tolerant; his approach was remarkable compassion. Can you imagine John 3:16 beginning with the words, "For God so *tolerated* the world that he gave his one and only Son"? Niceness and love are two different things. It's not how we treat those who are just like us; Jesus said that's easy to do. It's how we treat others who aren't like us at all. We are not to strive for tolerance, no matter how attractive the culture makes it sound. Nobody wants to be just tolerated. Tolerance is woefully insufficient compared to the compassionate vision Jesus offers the world.

In the political climate in which we find ourselves, one of the most countercultural ways followers of Jesus can live is to humanize those who are different from us. How do we do that? We can begin by concentrating on *our own sinfulness* and *other people's humanness*. It's so easy to do the opposite of that, isn't it? But doing so brings humility and dignity back to our conversation with others. We can love each other with both our mouths *and also* our ears.

In times of conflict, psychologists tell us that our human nature will respond in one of three ways: fight, flight, or freeze. We resort to silence or violence. But what if there is another way, a way that honors the *imago dei* rooted in each one of us? We need to be both honest and also honoring. It is the way of remaining in without bailing. It means being respectful without resorting to attack as well as remaining confident without being a pushover. This third way is sometimes referred to as yielding—yielding to God, to his kingdom, and to others. I've found that this kind of submission takes the most faith.

Jesus commanded us to love our neighbors. John adds that if we say we love God but don't love others, we are liars (1 John 4:20). If we take this seriously, then we must ask the important question: Who are my neighbors, and practically, what is my responsibility to them?[22]

Sociologists tell us that we all live in five different neighborhoods. We live in a *geographic* neighborhood, where we've traditionally understood neighbors as being those who live in our physical neighborhood: Jim and Cathy across the street, Mrs. Davidson next door, and Jeff, Jill, and their girls just down the alley. We also live in a *familial* neighborhood, an extended family of social networks including grandparents, aunts, nephews, and second cousins. Yes, this even includes your crazy Uncle Willy (every family's got at least one crazy uncle, right?). We live in a *relational* neighborhood comprised of our friends and companions. We live in a *psychographic* neighborhood with those who think or behave similar to us. We all have these pockets of shared identity, even if we don't know people personally: Mac owners, vegans, dog lovers, runners, and those who are really into CrossFit (even if they do talk about it all the time).

And finally, we live in a *digital* neighborhood, our online presence of social media and email and texting. Lord knows we need help in this neighborhood, maybe more than in the others. *How* matters—and in our digital neighborhoods, *how we type* matters.[23] I've only unfriended a small handful of people on Facebook. The act of unfriending wasn't because of something they said, their opinion about a matter, or their political affiliation. The unfriending was prompted by a consistent pattern they exhibited: the way they said things—their tone and their posture—which constantly undermined the *imago dei* in others. We can only participate in the *missio dei* if we are committed to honoring the *imago dei* in every human being with whom we come in contact.

As I attempt to live as an almond-shaped follower of Jesus, I try to run each thought through a digital neighborhood filter:

What is my motive?
Will this matter in a month?
Is this wise?
Is it worth it?
Am I encouraging conversation or shutting it down?
Am I making the world a better place by sharing this?
Am I inflating the truth, even just slightly, in what I am writing?
Is what I am about to share both honest and honoring?

This last one is a difficult line to walk. It seems sarcasm has suddenly become a virtue in the minds of many. But sarcasm is not a fruit of the Spirit. Yes, we can be filled with joyful hilarity, but not with a critical, cynical, skeptical spirit behind it. What the world needs is more hope and less cynicism.

As we seek to live between these emotional extremes, embodying *civilité*, we would be wise to live by this principle: *when you disagree, don't disengage.* Running is easy. Running is cowardly. Over the long haul, running away dishonors people.[24] Pastor and author

Rick Warren said wisely, "Our culture has accepted two huge lies: the first is that if you disagree with someone's lifestyle, you must fear or hate them. The second is that to love someone means you agree with everything they believe or do. Both are nonsense. You don't have to compromise convictions to be compassionate."[25] As Christians, we can't succumb to these two lies. Doing so pushes us toward damaging forms of tribalism—petri dishes which rapidly spawn the bacteria of *us vs. them*. We must commit to *disagreement without disengagement*. Biblical community is not the absence of conflict; it's the presence of Jesus in the midst of it. Take the high road, even when others refuse to do so. We will never regret it. Mandorla people double-major in being honest and honoring, being full of both grace and truth.

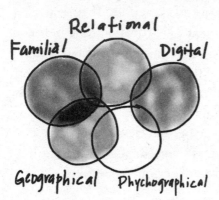

Civilité. We are members of the household of God and society, where we learn to live as family members. Even on Facebook.

A FINAL THOUGHT

The Ampersand God

"I am the Alpha and the Omega," says the Lord
God, "who is, and who was, and who is to come,
the Almighty."

—REVELATION 1:8

One of my favorite symbols is the ampersand—that little squiggly notation &. Originally I considered *Ampersand* as a potential working title for this book, but later thought it would be an even better band name instead. (Ironically, I later learned there's already a band by that name.)

Faithfully pursuing Jesus requires *attention, intention,* and *tension.* Our attention must be squarely on Jesus and his kingdom. Our intention is to seek, submit to, and bring the kingdom to earth as we live. And our tension is found when we live with that rubber band mentality, stretched but not to the point of snapping. This should make the church more confident and more humble at the same time. We must feel the tension. A tension-less church is a mission-less church.

The gospel story even reminds us of the ampersand of God. This way of life finds comfort in Christ's presence and yet pushes us to new levels of discomfort. It finds the center of God's will to be both the safest and the most terrifying place to be. But we can live here because Jesus modeled that way for us and promises to never leave us. When we screw it up, grace is close by. We are sinners *and also* saints. The gospel is both bad *and also* good news. We are so sinful that we have no right to be puffed up when we do right. But we are beloved sinners in Christ—"so loved that we don't have to despair when we do wrong."[1] "We are "more flawed and sinful than you'd ever dare believe and yet more loved and accepted than you'd ever dare hope."[2] We are between two worlds. And yet, we are also in *both* worlds.

As you've read this book, I hope you've found these words to be comforting *and also* provoking. I hope I've clarified the mission of Jesus *and also* provided some healthy cognitive dissonance. I hope I've given you a larger, more glorious picture of God and his kingdom *and also* a more inspiring and robust vision of Christ's church and our role in it.

Abraham met the God who needed nothing and also asked for everything.

Moses met the God who was far away and yet was so close.

Job met the God who was active and also inactive.

Habakkuk met the God who was consistent and also unpredictable.

Jonah met the God who was indiscriminate and also selective.

Esther met the God who spoke and also remained silent.

The cross reveals the God who won even as he lost.[3]

With the God who is powerful and also gentle,

With the God who is transcendent and also imminent,

With the God who demands faithfulness and also freely forgives,

May we be the kind of people who embrace the Ampersand God and who also embody the way of the sacred overlap.

We've now reached the end. And also we've just begun.

A NOTE FROM
THE AUTHOR

If you've enjoyed the concepts in this book,
have further questions, or want to interact
with me directly, I invite you to email me
at jrbriggs@kairospartnerships.org

I'd love to hear from you.

ACKNOWLEDGMENTS

It was James K. A. Smith who wrote, "You want to be a writer? In our day and age, it's easy to 'get published.' Set higher goals: hope to be edited." I'm deeply grateful for the confidence of the team at Zondervan to not only publish this work, but also edit it. Thank you to Ryan Pazdur, whose job title is editor, but who also served unofficially as my therapist through the nurturing process. And thank you to Seedbed for your graciousness and belief in this project.

Thanks to my team of readers, who experienced a form of torture by being subjected to this inchoate writer's early editions of the book: Caleb Mangum, Dave Bielecki, Lindsay Smith, Ben Pitzen, A. J. Gretz, Luke Edwards, Rita Platt, Adam Gustine, Alan Briggs, Matt Lake, Josh Meyer, and Bob Hyatt. They tirelessly invested in this project by helping me process these ideas and concepts in their prenatal form, helping me bring this project to full term, and giving me the courage to deliver this baby and snip the umbilical cord. Thank you for your investment.

A special thanks to Steve Taylor and Scott Jones, who carefully reviewed the theological points and biblical references throughout. Their brilliance honed my thinking and my theology and encouraged me through the process. Any biblical or linguistic inaccuracies found in the book are entirely mine, not theirs.

Thank you to Denise Baum, former director of interlibrary loans at Missio Seminary, who worked tirelessly to track down and secure dozens of books and articles throughout the research and writing process.

Thank you to Chris Backert for his original vision for this project.

Thank you to the Fresh Expressions U.S. training team for not only teaching the concepts of this book, but also living them.

Thank you to The Renew Community, where many of these experiences, ideas, and stories were hatched and embodied throughout the years. I love being a part of this peculiar portion of God's family.

Thank you to Megan, Carter, and Bennett for your ongoing love and unending support. I'm grateful to be in your family.

And thank you to Jesus Christ, who through the incarnation modeled what it meant to live the sacred overlap and invites us to join him in that reality every day.

All is grace.

NOTES

Introduction: A Simple Shape, an Italian Word, a Way of Life

1. Leonard Sweet shared this in a phone conversation with the author on January 10, 2019.
2. Leonard Sweet and Frank Viola, *Jesus: A Theography* (Nashville, TN: Thomas Nelson, 2012), 22.
3. See the chapter by this name in Eduard Schweizer's *Jesus*, translated by David Green (Richmond, VA: John Knox, 1971), 13.
4. David E. Fitch, *The Church of Us vs. Them* (Grand Rapids, MI: Brazos Press, 2019), ix.
5. Fitch, 10.
6. Rich Villodas (@richvillodas), Twitter, February 21, 2019, https://twitter.com/richvillodas/status/1098710693644242945.
7. Leonard Sweet, *Carpe Mañana: Is Your Church Ready to Seize Tomorrow?* (Grand Rapids, MI: Zondervan, 2001), 134.
8. Phone conversation with Leonard Sweet, January 10, 2019.
9. A.W. Tozer, *Knowledge of the Holy: The Attributes of God: Their Meaning in the Christian Life* (San Francisco: HarperCollins, 1961), 6.
10. "The Crack Up," *Esquire*. February 1936.
11. Jim Collins, *Built to Last: Successful Habits of Visionary Companies 3rd Edition* (New York: Harper Business, 2004), 44.
12. Aristotle, *Nicomachean Ethics*, 4.5.3.
13. The surround sound and harmony metaphors come from Leonard Sweet, who shared these in a phone call with the author on January 10, 2019.

Chapter 1: Overlapping Worlds: When God Moved into the Neighborhood

1. Anthony William Fairbank Edwards,*Cogwheels of the Mind: The Story of Venn Diagrams* (Baltimore: Johns Hopkins University Press, 2004), 3.
2. Edwards, V.
3. More complex and intricate Venn diagrams using multiple case are called Edwards-Venn diagrams, but for the scope of this book, we will deal with Venn's simplest expressions.
4. Karen Swallow Prior, "Saints Against Slavery: A World-changing Set of Friendships," *Christian History Magazine*, no 132 (2019): 33.
5. Gregory the Theologian, *Oration*, 29.20.
6. Fr. Maximos Constas, *The Art of Seeing: Paradox and Perception in Orthodox Iconography*(Alhambra, CA: Sebastian Press, 2014), 10.
7. Constas, 51.
8. Leonid Ouspensky and Vladimir Lossky, *The Meaning of Icons* (Crestwood, NY: St. Vladimir's Seminary Press, 1982), 68.
9. Sweet and Viola, *Jesus: A Theography*, 87.
10. Leonard Sweet shared this in a phone conversation with the author on January 10, 2019.
11. Sweet and Viola, *Jesus: A Theography*, 57.
12. See chapter 1 of Jen Pollock Michel's book *Surprised by Paradox* (Downers Grove, IL: InterVarsity Press, 2019).
13. William H. Willimon, *This We Believe: The Core of Wesleyan Faith and Practice* (Nashville, TN: Abingdon Press, 2010), 31.
14. Ignatius, *Documents of the Christian Church* (Oxford, New York: Oxford University Press, 1999), 32.
15. Paul W. Chilcote, *Recapturing the Wesleys' Vision: An Introduction to the Faith of John and Charles Wesley* (Downers Grove, IL: InterVarsity Press, 2003), 12.
16. Sweet, *Jesus: A Theography*, 69.
17. Ken Wytsma and A.J. Swoboda, *Redeeming How We Talk: Discover How Communication Fuels Our Growth, Shapes Our Relationships, and Changes Our Lives* (Chicago: Moody Publishers, 2018), 103.
18. Few people have written more clearly on the overlap of the

incarnation than St. Athanasius. Athanasius, a bishop in the third century, argued that Jesus had to be fully human in order to pay for the sin of humanity and that he also had to be fully God in order to be powerful enough to save humanity. Athanasius' relatively small (and easily accessible) book *On the Incarnation* is one I highly recommend.

19. C.S. Lewis, *Mere Christianity* (San Francisco: HarperOne; Revised edition, 2015), 179.

20. Edmund Hill (trans.), *The Works of St. Augustine: A Translation for the 21st Century.* Sermons 184–229Z (Vol. III/6. (Hyde Park, NY: New City Press, 1993), 191.1

21. Watch this wonderfully engaging and brilliantly explained video by The Bible Project: https://www.youtube.com/watch?v=Zy2AQlK6C5k&t=4s.

22. See The Bible Project for a brilliant explanation of the overlapped role Jesus played in the incarnation and in salvation. Read https://thebibleproject.com/explore/heaven-earth/ and https://d1bsmz3sdihplr.cloudfront.net/media/Study%20Notes/heworkbookfinaldigitaldownload.pdf.

23. The Bible Project, YouTube: https://www.youtube.com/watch?v=Zy2AQlK6C5k

24. Tertullian, *Against Praxeas*, chapter 9 (New York, Macmillan, 1920).

25. A.W.F. Edwards, *Cogwheels of the Mind*, 17.

Chapter 2: Scandalous Misfit: Hanging with Saints and Sinners

1. For more on shame, failure, and rejection see my book *Fail: Finding Hope and Grace in the Midst of Ministry Failure* (Downers Grove, IL: InterVarsity Press, 2014). Though it's written primarily for pastors, many of the concepts apply to all people.

2. Howard Thurman, *Jesus and the Disinherited* (Boston: Beacon Hill, 1971), 18.

3. Brant Hansen, *Blessed are the Misfits: Great News for Believers Who Are Introverts, Spiritual Strugglers, or Just Feel Like They're Missing Something* (Nashville: Thomas Nelson, 2017), 2.

4. Ann Voskamp, *Unwrapping the Greatest Gift: A Family Celebration of Christmas* (Carol Stream, IL: Tyndale, 2014), 21.

5. Sister Columba Guare, "O Eve!" Sisters of the Mississippi Abbey, 2005.

6. Dallas Willard, *The Divine Conspiracy: Rediscovering Our Hidden Life In God* (New York: HarperCollins, 1998), 123-125.

Chapter 3: Double-Major Jesus: Embracing Justice and Embracing Grace

1. Scot McKnight, *The Jesus Creed* (Brewster, MA: Paraclete Press, 2004), 145.

2. Adam Gustine, *Becoming a Just Church: Cultivating Communities of God's Shalom* (Downers Grove, IL: InterVarsity Press, 2019), 110.

3. For a deeper explanation of the Jewish context around this passage and why Jesus' listeners were so incensed, read Joe Amaral's book, *Understanding Jesus: Cultural Insights into the Words and Deeds of Christ*, (New York: FaithWords, 2001), 33–35.

4. Anne Lamott, "12 Truths I Learned from Life and Writing," 15:46, TED Talk, April 2017, https://www.ted.com/talks/anne_lamott_12_truths_i_learned_from_life_and_writing

5. I first read this wonderful phrase in Tim Keller's book *Preaching* (New York: Viking, 2015), 52.

6. Richard J. Foster, *Streams of Living Water: Celebrating the Great Traditions of Christian Faith* (HarperSanFrancisco, 1998), 166–172.

7. I first learned of this practice from author and seminary professor Dr. Scot McKnight, who has engaged in this practice with his classes for the past several years. He also writes about it in his book *The Jesus Creed*.

8. Scot McKnight, *The Jesus Creed: Loving God, Loving Others* (Brewster, MA: Paraclete Press, 2004), 141.

9. While not likely part of the original manuscripts of the Gospel of John (quite possibly added later) the account is left in our Bibles for us to read and study nonetheless—thus making it a *mandorla* story in and of itself.

10. Howard Thurman, *Jesus and the Disinherited* (Boston: Beacon Press, 1971), 106.

11. For an example of a *remez*, see the story of the triumphal entry in Matthew 21. When the religious experts became angry that children were shouting "Hosannah!" Jesus quotes Psalm 8:2. On the surface, this does not make much sense. But since the religious leaders memorized Psalm 8, they were aware of the next line in verse 3, which talks about the enemies of God. Jesus' *remez* of Psalm 8:2 hints that Jesus was implying the religious leaders were God's enemies, which is why they became so angry.

12. For more on this, read Bob Wilkin's article, "'The Finger of God' Refers to His Power," Grace Evangelical Society (GES), May 1, 2016, https://faithalone.org/grace-in-focus-articles/the -finger-of-god/.

13. Scot McKnight, *The Jesus Creed: Loving God, Loving Others* (Brewster, MA: Paraclete Press, 2004), 144.

14. N. T. Wright, *Surprised by Hope* (New York: HarperCollins, 2008), 144.

15. Wright, *Surprised by Hope*, 218.

16. See N. T. Wright, *Surprised by Hope*, 215–216.

17. Howard Snyder, *Liberating the Church* (Downers Grove, IL: Intervarsity Press, 1983), 11.

18. Dallas Willard, *Renovation of the Heart* (Colorado Springs, CO: NavPress, 2002), 15–16.

19. N. T. Wright, *Surprised by Hope*, 216.

20. Adam Gustine, *Becoming a Just Church: Cultivating Communities of God's Shalom* (Downers Grove, IL: InterVarsity Press, 2019), 21.

21. Gustine, 64.

22. Rodney Stark, *The Rise of Christianity: How the Obscure, Marginal Jesus Movement Became the Dominant Religious Force in the Western World in a Few Centuries* (HarperSanFrancisco, 1997), 161.

23. For a further explanation of the peculiarity and radical love of the early Christians and the impact it made on the world, read Alan Kreider's *The Patient Ferment of the Early Church: The Improbable Rise of Christianity in the Roman Empire* (Grand Rapids, MI: Baker Academic, 2016).

24. Wright, *Surprised by Hope*, 215.

25. This line is also the title of a wonderful book by Stanley Hauerwas and Jean Vanier.

Chapter 4: Orthoparadoxy: Right Believing and Right Living

1. Although the earliest records do not list his attendance at the council, one account mentions a bishop by the name of St. Nicholas. As Arius shared his views—that Jesus was not divine—allegedly St. Nicholas became enraged by what he was hearing, walked across the room, and slapped the heretic in the face. The bishops at the council motioned to strip Nicholas of his staff and bishop's hat and arrest him. Yes, that's right: it is purported that St. Nicholas (yep, *that* St. Nick), assaulted a bishop at one of the most important gatherings on Christian orthodoxy in history, a fun bit of trivia you can throw into the conversation at your next Christmas party.
2. Skye Jethani, *What if Jesus Was Serious? A Visual Guide to the Teachings of Jesus We Love to Ignore,* (Chicago: Moody Publishers, 2020), 150.
3. C. S. Lewis, *Mere Christianity* (New York: HarperCollins, 2001), 148.
4. A phrase I first heard from Dwight Friesen.
5. Alan Hirsch and Mark Nelson, *Reframation: Seeing God, People, and Mission Through Reenchanted Frames,* (100 Movements Publishing, 2019), 137.
6. Hirsch and Nelson, 136.
7. Krish Kandiah, *Paradoxology: Why Christianity Was Never Meant to Be Simple* (London: Hodder & Stoughton, 2014), 4–5.
8. Phone conversation with Leonard Sweet, January 10, 2019.

Chapter 5: Resident Aliens: Too Christian, Too Pagan

1. Stanley Hauerwas and William Willimon, *Resident Aliens: Life in the Christian Colony* (Nashville: Abingdon Press, 2014), 12.
2. See chapter 5 of Adam Gustine, *Becoming a Just Church: Cultivating Communities of God's Shalom* (Downers Grove, IL: InterVarsity Press, 2019).

3. C. S. Lewis, *Mere Christianity* (New York: HarperOne, 2006), 135.

4. Adam Gustine, *Becoming a Just Church: Cultivating Communities of God's Shalom* (Downers Grove, IL: InterVarsity Press, 2019), 43–44.

5. Stanly Hauerwas and William Willimon, *Resident Aliens: Life in the Christian Colony,* Expanded 25th Anniversary Edition (Nashville: Abingdon Press, 2014), 49.

6. Hauerwas and Willimon, 52.

7. You can learn more about ReImagine at www.reimagine.org. Also, Mark's book on this topic, *Practicing the Way of Jesus: Life Together in the Kingdom of Love* (Downers Grove, IL: IVP Books, 2011), is fantastic. I highly recommend it.

8. Michael Frost and Alan Hirsch, *The Shaping of Things to Come: Innovation and Mission for the 21st-Century Church* (Peabody, MA: Hendrickson, 2003), 27–28.

9. Dick Staub, *Too Christian, Too Pagan: How To Love the World Without Falling For It* (Grand Rapids, MI: Zondervan, 2000), p. 15–16.

10. Staub, *Too Christian, Too Pagan*, 32.

11. John R. Stott, *The Message of Ephesians*, The Bible Speaks Today Series (Downers Grove, IL: InterVarsity Press, 1979), 23.

12. Staub, 14.

13. Staub, p. 74.

14. Hauerwas and Willimon, *Resident Aliens*, p. 38.

15. Annie Dillard, *Teaching a Stone to Talk* (New York: HarperCollins, 1982), 52.

Chapter 6: Being Peculiar: Inhabiting the Space between Normal and Weird

1. I've learned a great deal from Mike's teachings and writings, and I am grateful for the occasional opportunities we've had to interact. He's had a significant impact on my life and ministry, for which I am deeply grateful.

2. This is the title of chapter 2 of Martin Luther King Jr's book *Strength to Love* (Fortress Press, 2010).

3. Richard Rohr, "Liminal Space," July 7, 2016. Center for Action and Contemplation: https://cac.org/liminal-space-2016-07-07/.

4. *Frost,*150.
5. See chapter 5 of Richard Beck's book, *The Slavery of Death* for more on this concept.
6. Richard Beck, "Eccentric Christianity: Part 1, A Peculiar People," August 13, 2014. Experimental Theology: http://experimentaltheology.blogspot.com/2014/08/eccentric-christianity-part-1-peculiar.html.
7. Michael Frost, *Surprise the World: The Five Habits of Highly Missional People* (Colorado Springs, CO: NavPress, 2016), 10.
8. *Keep Christianity Weird,* 11.
9. *Keep Christianity Weird,* 59.
10. Quoted in Jon Tyson and Heather Grizzle's book, *A Creative Minority: Influencing Culture Through Redemptive Participation* (New York City: Heather Grizzle, 2016), 33–34.
11. *Hauerwas and Willimon,* 93.
12. Martin Luther King Jr., *Strength to Love* (Philadelphia: Fortress Press, 1963), 14.
13. *Resident Aliens,* 52.
14. Emmanuel Katongole, *Mirror to the Church: Resurrecting Faith After Genocide in Rwanda* (Grand Rapids, MI: Zondervan, 2009), 170.
15. "Mehrabian's 7-38-55 Communication Model," *World of Work Project,* https://worldofwork.io/2019/07/mehrabians-7-38-55-communication-model/.
16. Howard Thurman, *Jesus and the Disinherited* (Lees Summit, MO: Beacon Press, 1996), 49–50.
17. Thurman, 50.
18. Nordling shared this idea at the Young, Wrestling, and Always Reforming conference in Philadelphia, PA in May 2016.

Chapter 7: Faithful Witness: Living the Right Preposition

1. Over the past several years, the phrase "radical middle" has taken on certain political connotations within the church, an ideology of living in the middle between the conservative right and the progressive left. Certain pockets within the church in North America have rallied around specific hot-button issues in order to

make their case with the radical middle. To be clear, there is no desire for this book to make political pontifications in this manner. I want this book to highlight the radical middle, not the political middle.

2. Bill Jackson, *The Quest for the Radical Middle* (Sugar Land, TX: Vineyard International Publishing, 1999), 21.

3. Dallas Willard, *The Great Omission: Reclaiming Jesus' Essential Teachings on Discipleship* (San Francisco, HarperOne, 2006), 61.

4. One popular element of dualism that existed in the first century was Gnosticism. Scholars believe John's letters—specifically 1 John and 2 John—were to combat gnostic, dualistic thinking.

5. Tish Harrison Warren, *Liturgy of the Ordinary* (Downers Grove, IL: InterVarsity Press, 2016), 90.

6. Warren, 94.

7. Warren, 101.

8. Robert Banks and R. Paul Stevens, *The Complete Book of Everyday Christianity* (Downers Grove, IL: InterVarsity Press, 1997), 1128.

9. John Ortberg, from a talk given at Willow Creek Community Church, South Barrington, IL: August 6, 1997.

10. Gabe Lyons, *The Next Christians* (New York: Doubleday Religion, 2010), 39.

11. For more on this, see Charles Taylor's *A Secular Age* (Belknap Press, 2018).

12. Krish Kandiah, *Paradoxology: Why Christianity Was Never Meant to Be Simple* (London: Hodder & Stoughton, 2014), 5.

13. Daniel Van Biema, "Mother Teresa's Crisis of Faith," TIME, August 23, 2007, https://time.com/4126238/mother-teresas-crisis-of-faith/

14. As quoted in Philip Yancey's book *Reaching for the Invisible God* (Grand Rapids, MI: Zondervan, 2002), 13.

15. J.R. Briggs and Bob Hyatt, *Ministry Mantras* (Downers Grove, IL: InterVarsity Press, 2016), 176–177.

16. Robert Browning, *The Complete Poetic and Dramatic Works of Robert Browning* (Boston: Houghton Mifflin, 1887), 105.

17. J. D. Greear, *Gaining by Losing: Why the Future Belongs to Churches that Send* (Grand Rapids, MI: Zondervan, 2015), 95.

18. John V. Taylor, *The Go-Between God: The Holy Spirit and the Christian Mission* (London: SCM Press, 1972), 3.

19. Hugh Halter and Matt Smay, *And: The Gathered and Scattered Church* (Grand Rapids, MI: Zondervan, 2020), 26–27.

20. The Bible Project: "Heaven and Earth": https://www.youtube.com /watch?v=Zy2AQlK6C5k

21. Eugene Peterson, *Practice Resurrection: A Conversation on Growing Up in Christ* (Grand Rapids, MI: Eerdmans, 2013), 11.

22. Peterson, 11–12.

23. Peterson, 28.

Chapter 8: The Prayer of Sacred Overlap: How Jesus Teaches Us to Pray

1. Scot McKnight, *The Jesus Creed: Loving God, Loving Others* (Brewster, MA: Paraclete Press, 2004), 18.

2. Mark also recorded this in Mark 11:25.

3. The Aramaic word for Father is *abba*. According to Kenneth Bailey in *Jesus Through Middle Eastern Eyes*, even today, in at least four countries in the Middle East, *abba* is the first word young children are taught to say.

4. Kenneth E. Bailey, *Jesus Through Middle Eastern Eyes* (Downers Grove, IL: IVP Academic, 2008), 99.

5. Reggie McNeal, *Kingdom Collaborators: Eight Signature Practices of Leaders Who Turn the World Upside Down,* (Downers Grove, IL: InterVarsity Press, 2018), 89.

6. Augustine, *Commentary on the Lord's Sermon on the Mount, with Seventeen Related Sermons,* trans. Denis J. Kavanagh (New York: Fathers of the Church, Inc., 1951), 246.

7. Anne Lamott, *Traveling Mercies: Some Thoughts on Faith* (New York: Anchor, 2001), 134.

8. Bailey, *Jesus Through Middle Eastern Eyes,* 94.

9. Scot McKnight, *Sermon on the Mount: The Story of God Bible Commentary* (Grand Rapids, MI: Zondervan Academic, 2013), 174.

10. McKnight, 175.

11. McKnight, *The Jesus Creed,* 126.

12. Wright, *Surprised by Hope*, 29.
13. Bailey, *Jesus Through Middle Eastern Eyes*,117.
14. Sandra McCracken, "Our Two Spiritual Time Zones," *Christianity Today*, August 18, 2017, https://www.christianitytoday.com/ct/2017/september/our-two-spiritual-time-zones.html.
15. McKnight, *Sermon on the Mount*, 173.
16. McKnight, *Sermon on the Mount*, 180.
17. Gary Moon, *Becoming Dallas Willard: The Formation of a Philosopher, Teacher, and Christ Follower* (Downers Grove, IL: InterVarsity Press, 2018), 206–207.
18. Wright, *Surprised by Hope*, 3.
19. Wright, 250–251.
20. Sweet and Viola, *Jesus: A Theography*, 295.
21. Stan Guthrie, *All that Jesus Asks: How His Questions Can Teach and Transform Us* (Grand Rapids, MI: Baker Books, 2010), 285.
22. Rabbi Gamaliel, *The Babylonian Talmud Tractate Berakot*, trans. Cohen, 182, 67.
23. Anne Lamott, *Bird by Bird: Some Instructions on Writing and Life* (New York: Anchor Books, 1995), 30.
24. See St. Gregory of Nyssa, *The Lord's Prayer, the Beatitudes*, trans. Hilda C. Graef (Nahwah, NJ: Paulist Press, 1978), Sermons 3 and 4.
25. C. S. Lewis, *Mere Christianity* (New York: HarperCollins, 1952), 115.
26. For a greater and deeper treatment of these questions, and of forgiveness, in the Lord's Prayer see chapter 6 ("The Beatitudes 2") in Kenneth E. Bailey's wonderful book *Jesus Through Middle Eastern Eyes*
27. Bailey, *Jesus Through Middle Eastern Eyes*, 125.
28. Joseph Fitzmyer, "Pauline Justification as Presented by Luke in Acts 13," *Transcending Boundaries: Contemporary Readings of the New Testament*, ed. Rehka M. Chennattu and Mary L. Coloe (LAS, 2005), 257–258.
29. Dr. Patrick Krayer, "The Mission of God" (lecture) February 21, 2019, Missio Seminary, Upper Darby, PA. Also see Gary Anderson's book, *Sin: A History*, on debt as the metaphor for sin.

30. Augustine, *Commentary on the Lord's Sermon on the Mount, with Seventeen Related Sermons*, 253.
31. For more on this practice, see http://practicetribe.com/1–28–18 -the-rite-of-forgiveness/
32. Augustine, 124.
33. Dallas Willard, *Eternal Living: Reflections on Dallas Willard's Teaching on Faith and Formation* (Downers Grove, IL: InterVarsity Press, 2015), 236.
34. Paul Miller, *A Praying Life: Connecting with God in a Distracting World* (Colorado Springs, CO: NavPress, 2017), 109.

Chapter 9: Dual Engagement: Evangelism and Discipleship at the Same Time

1. "The Gospel of the Kingdom: An Interview by Keith Giles," Dallas Willard (website), August 2005. Dallas Willard: http://old.dwillard. org/articles/artview.asp?artID=150.
2. My paraphrase.
3. This is the premise of N. T. Wright's book *Surprised by Hope.*
4. This is one of many wonderful aphorisms Dallas Willard would use repeatedly to drive home the point of the centrality of the kingdom of God.
5. Alan Hirsch, *Disciplism: Reimagining Evangelism Through the Lens of Discipleship* (Exponential Resources, 2104), 27.
6. J.R. Briggs and Bob Hyatt, *Ministry Mantras: Language for Cultivating Kingdom Culture* (Downers Grove, IL: InterVarsity Press, 2016), 76–77.
7. Orlando E. Costas, *Christ Outside the Gate: Mission Beyond Christendom* (Maryknoll, NY: Orbis, 1982), 80.
8. Andrew F. Walls, *The Cross-Cultural Process in Christian History* (Maryknoll, NY: Orbis, 2002), 80.
9. Bruxy Cavey teaching, The Ecclesia Network National Gathering, April 11, 2018. The Meeting House–Dillsburg Campus, Dillsburg, PA.
10. *Ministry Mantras*, pp. 173–175.
11. As mentioned in Anne Lamott's book *Bird by Bird: Some*

Instructions on Writing and Life (New York: Anchor Books, 1995), 156.

12. Dallas Willard, *Renovation of the Heart: Putting on the Character of Christ,* Tenth Anniversary Edition (Colorado Springs, CO: NavPress, 2012), 249.

13. Kyle Idleman, *Not a Fan: Becoming a Completely Committed Follower of Jesus,* updated and expanded edition (Grand Rapids, MI: Zondervan, 2016), 134.

14. Neil Cole, *Ordinary Hero: Becoming a Disciple Who Makes A Difference* (Grand Rapids, MI: Baker Books, 2011), 185.

15. Martin B. Copenhaver, *Jesus is the Question: The 307 Questions Jesus Asked and the 3 He Answered* (Nashville, TN: Abingdon Press, 2014), 107–108.

16. Wright, *Surprised by Hope,* 227.

17. John Bright, *The Kingdom of God: The Biblical Concept and Its Meaning for the Church* (New York: Abingdon-Cokesbury, 1953), 223–224.

Chapter 10: Practicing Resurrection Together: Peculiar Practices of the Overlapped Life

1. Steven Pressfield, *Turning Pro: Tap Your Inner Power and Create Your Life's Work* (New York: Black Irish Entertainment LLC, 2012), 108.

2. For more on the overlap of Jesus' humanity and divinity, see Hebrews 2:9–18 and Hebrews 5:1–10.

3. Peterson, *Practice Resurrection,* 3.

4. Peterson, *Practice Resurrection,* 20.

5. Robert Karris, *Luke: Artist and Theologian* (Majwah, NJ: Paulist Press, 1985), 70.

6. For more on this, see Hauerwas and Willimon's book *Resident Aliens* starting on page 71.

7. Leonard Sweet, *From Tablet to Table* (Colorado Springs, CO: NavPress, 2014), 5.

8. Rowan Williams, *Being a Christian: Baptism, Bible, Eucharist, Prayer* (Grand Rapids, MI: Eerdmans, 2014), 53–54.

9. I am indebted to Shane Wood for connecting these dots for me in

his book *Between Two Trees: Our Transformation from Death to Life* (Abilene, TX: ACU Press/Leafwood Publishers, 2019), 23.

10. Here I am writing figuratively. Some of our brothers and sisters in other Christian traditions believe that the receiving of the elements of Communion are the *literal* body and blood of Jesus. My convictions lead me to believe that partaking in the Eucharist and receiving the elements is a *figurative* act, an experiential reminder of the Good News of Jesus.

11. A. J. Swoboda, *Messy: God Likes It That Way* (Grand Rapids, MI: Kregel Publishing, 2012), 170.

12. Adolf Adam, *The Liturgical Year, Its History and Its Meaning After the Reform of the Liturgy*, trans. Matthew J. O'Connell (Collegeville, MN: The Liturgical Press, 1990), 70.

13. Fleming Rutledge, *Advent: The Once and Future Coming of Jesus Christ* (Grand Rapids, MI: Eerdmans, 2018), 7.

14. Karl Barth, *Church Dogmatics IV* 3.1 (Edinburgh: T & T Clark, 1961), 322.

15. Cyril of Jerusalem, Catechetical Lecture 15.1.

16. David Bosch, *Transforming Mission: Paradigm Shifts in Theology of Mission* (Maryknoll, NY: Orbis, 1991), 376.

17. Wright, *Surprised by Hope*, 29.

18. C.S. Lewis, et al. *Bread and Wine: Readings for Lent and Easter* (Walden, NY: Plough Publishing House, 2003), xv.

19. Aaron Damiani, *The Good of Giving Up: Discovering the Freedom of Lent* (Chicago: Moody Publishers, 2017), 35.

20. Joan Chittister, *The Liturgical Year: The Spiraling Adventure of the Spiritual Life* (Nashville: Thomas Nelson, 2009), 113.

21. Damiani, 26.

22. C.S. Lewis, et al., *Bread and Wine: Readings for Lent and Easter* (Walden, NY: Plough Publishing House, 2003), xvii.

23. Jacques-Bénigne Bossuet, *Meditations for Lent* (Manchester, NH: Sophia Institute Press, 2013), x.

24. C.S. Lewis, et. al. *Bread and Wine: Readings for Lent and Easter*, xviii.

25. See Fleming Rutledge's sermon "When God Is Silent" in *Advent:*

The Once and Future Coming of Jesus Christ (Grand Rapids, MI: Eerdmans, 2018), 115-121.

26. Tish Harrison Warren, *Liturgy of the Ordinary*, 107.

27. Wright, *Surprised by Hope*, 293.

28. Wright, 256.

29. John Bright, *The Kingdom of God: The Biblical Concept and Its Meaning for the Church* (New York: Abingdon-Cokesbury, 1953), 193.

30. For a brilliant and succinct explanation of this heaven and earth explanation see the work of The Bible Project at https://thebibleproject.com/explore/heaven-earth/ and https://d1bsmz3sdihplr.cloudfront.net/media/Study%20Notes/heworkbookfinaldigitaldownload.pdf.

31. I know I keep referencing N. T. Wright throughout the book, but the man is legit.

32. See chapter five of N. T. Wright's book *The New Testament and the People of God* (Minneapolis, MN: Fortress Press, 1992).

33. Wright, *Surprised by Hope*, 283.

34. This valuable content and explanation is found in the work of The Bible Project. Read more at: https://thebibleproject.com/explore/heaven-earth/. Also watch their wonderful YouTube video, "Heaven and Earth" at https://www.youtube.com/watch?v=Zy2AQlK6C5k.

35. Wright, *Surprised by Hope*, 5.

36. Wright, *Surprised by Hope*, 5.

Chapter 11: Sacred Celebration: Embracing Joy Amidst a World Riddled with Pain

1. David Brooks, *The Second Mountain: The Quest for a Moral Life* (New York: Random House, 2019), xxii.

2. G. K. Chesterton, *Orthodoxy* (San Francisco: Ignatius Press, 1995), 59.

3. See Acts 8:4–8; 13:49–52; 16:31–34 for a few examples.

4. Robert Farrar Capon, *Between Noon and Three: Romance, Law, and the Outrage of Grace* (Grand Rapids, MI: Eerdmans, 1997), 149.

5. Steve Brown, *A Scandalous Freedom* (West Monroe, Louisiana: Howard Publishing, 2004), 11

6. C. S. Lewis, *Letters to Malcolm: Chiefly on Prayer* (New York: Harcourt, Brace and World, 1964), 93.

7. Josh Noem, "Is This What Heaven Is Really Going to Be Like?" *Grotto*: http://grottonetwork.com/keep-the-faith/belief/what-is -heaven-like/

8. Noem, "Is This What Heaven Is Really Going to Be Like?"

9. For a wonderful article on the necessity of celebration, read W. David O. Taylor, "And God Said to Pastors: Use More Sermon Puns and Plan More Parties," *Christianity Today*, June 6, 2019, https:// www.christianitytoday.com/ct/2019/june-web-only/pastors-worship -and-god-said-more-sermon-puns-more-parties.html.

10. Ben Pitzen, "Joy," The Renew Community, December 16, 2018, Lansdale, PA.

11. This theme runs throughout Steindl-Rast's book, *Gratefulness, the Heart of Prayer: An Approach to Life in Fullness* (Ramsey, NJ: Paulist Press, 1984).

12. Chesterton, *Orthodoxy*, 108.

13. Shane J. Wood, *Between Two Trees: Our Transformation from Death to Life* (Abilene, TX: ACU/Leafwood Publishers, 2019), 119.

Chapter 12: Mandorla Mission: Living Out Fresh Expressions of Church

1. To learn more about what fresh expressions of the Church are and how to start them in your community, see www.freshexpressionsus.org

2. Gerard Manley Hopkins, "As Kingfishers Catch Fire," *Gerard Manley Hopkins: Poems and Prose* (New York: Penguin Classics, 1985), 51

3. For more on this, see Alan Hirsch's book *The Forgotten Ways* (Grand Rapids, MI: Brazos Press, 2006), 182.

4. I first became aware of these seven channels though Q Ideas (www.qideas.org).

5. For more on this, see Alan Hirsch's book *The Forgotten Ways* (Grand Rapids, MI: Brazos Press, 2006), 184.

6. Frost and Hirsch, *The Shaping of Things to Come*, 157–158.

7. If you want to read more about what Fresh Expressions is, read the

short book *Fresh Expressions of Church* by Travis Collins (Franklin, TN: Seedbed Publishing, 2015) for a great introductory exploration.

8. Leonard Sweet, phone conversation, January 10, 2019.

9. Anne Lamott, *Plan B: Further Thoughts on Faith* (Riverhead Books, 2006), 66.

10. Rowan Williams, *Being Christian: Baptism, Bible, Eucharist, Prayer* (Grand Rapids, MI: Eerdmans, 2014), 41.

11. You can watch Andrew explain the pizza-making process and share how he incorporates spiritual discussion and Jesus' parables about yeast at the event I attended: Andrew Jones, "Andrew Jones Pizza Party Explanation," Santa Fe, NM published on February 18, 2008, YouTube video: https://www.youtube.com/watch?v=V88F9mc5daA

12. Alan Hirsch and Michael Frost, *The Shaping of Things to Come* (Peabody, MA: Hendrickson Publishers, 2013), 36.

13. For more on the importance of learning to ask good questions see pp. 90–92 in my book *Ministry Mantras: Language to Cultivate Kingdom Culture.*

14. You can read more about Thomas' experience in his article, "Why I Offer 'Free Prayer' in a Coffee Shop," Faith & Leadership, February 9, 2016, https://www.faithandleadership.com/thomas-rusert-why-i-offer-%E2%80%9Cfree-prayer%E2%80%9D-coffee-shop. Also see "Holy Cow! Pastor Offers Free Prayers at Coffee Houses," Fox News, Feb. 12, 2016, http://www.foxnews.com/opinion/2016/02/12/holy-cow-pastor-offers-free-prayers-at-coffee-houses.html.

15. Preston Yancey, *Out of the House of Bread: Satisfying Your Hunger for God with the Spiritual Disciplines* (Grand Rapids, MI: Zondervan, 2016), 70.

Chapter 13: Faithful Posture: Convicted Civility

1. This phrase caught my attention from the introduction of Richard Mouw's book *Adventures in Evangelical Civility: A Lifelong Quest for Common Ground* (Grand Rapids, MI: Brazos, 2016), xi.

2. Stephen L. Carter, *Civility: Manners, Morals, and the Etiquette of Democracy* (New York: Basic Books, 1998), 15.

3. Norbert Elias, *The Civilizing Process* trans. Edmund Jephcott (New York: Pantheon, 1978), 53.
4. "Woman Dies After Fight Over Grill in Philly Parking Spot," NBC Philadelphia, April 27, 2019, https://www.nbcphiladelphia.com /news/local/woman-dies-after-fight-over-grill-set-up-in-philly -parking-spot/200280/.
5. Stephen L. Carter, *Civility: Manners, Morals, and the Etiquette of Democracy*, 15.
6. Martin E. Marty, *By Way of Response* (Nashville: Abingdon Press, 1981), 81. Also, Richard Mouw picked up on this concept of convicted civility in his book *Uncommon Decency* (Downers Grove, IL: InterVarsity Press, 2010).
7. *Accidental Courtesy: Daryl Davis, Race & America*, directed by Matthew Ornstein (Sound & Vision Productions, 2017), documentary, 1 hour, 40 minutes.
8. Duane Brown, "How One Man Convinced 200 Ku Klux Klan Members to Give Up Their Robes" NPR, August 20, 2017, https:// www.npr.org/2017/08/20/544861933/how-one-man-convinced-200 -ku-klux-klan-members-to-give-up-their-robes.
9. Richard J. Mouw, *Adventures in Evangelical Civility: A Lifelong Quest for Common Ground* (Grand Rapids, MI: Brazos Press, 2016), 86–87.
10. Chuck Colson with Jim Wallis, "Conviction and Civility," *Christianity Today*, January 24, 2011, https://www.christianitytoday .com/ct/2011/januaryweb-only/convictioncivility.html?start=2.
11. C. S. Lewis, *The Weight of Glory* revised ed. (New York: HarperOne, 2001), 46.
12. Ken Burns, "The Secret to Bridging Political Divides," CNN, December 3, 2019, https://lite.cnn.com/en/article/h_683078c6682e 30993ffcfb0487ec4968
13. Ken Wytsma and A.J. Swoboda, *Redeeming How We Talk: Discover How Communication Fuels Our Growth, Shapes Our Relationships and Changes Our Lives* (Chicago: Moody, 2018), 15.
14. Wytsma and Swoboda, 164.

15. William Sloane Coffin, *Credo* (Louisville, KY: Westminster John Knox Press, 2004), 84.

16. Jen Pollock Michel, *Surprised by Paradox: The Promise of And in an Either-Or World* (Downers Grove, IL: InterVarsity Press, 2019), 102.

17. Tim Keller, "How Do Christians Fit into the Two-Party System? They Don't," *New York Times*, September 29, 2018, https://www.nytimes.com/2018/09/29/opinion/sunday/christians-politics-belief.html.

18. Michael Wear, "Rising Above Partisanship," Q Ideas, October 25, 2018, https://www.youtube.com/watch?v=ZnF4mkh3Vmc&feature=youtu.be&t=514.

19. Wear, "Rising Above Partisanship."

20. Tony Evans, "Guest Commentary: Jesus Didn't Come to Take Sides; He Came to Take Over," September 15, 2008, Religion News Service, https://religionnews.com/2008/09/15/guest-commentary-jesus-didnt-come-to-take-sides-he-came-to-take-over1/.

21. Stephen L. Carter, *Civility: Manners, Morals, and the Etiquette of Democracy* (New York: Basic Books, 1998), 229.

22. This was the entire premise of the parable of the Good Samaritan in Luke 10:25–37.

23. To read more on this concept, see the book I cowrote with Bob Hyatt, *Ministry Mantras*, 87–79.

24. For more on this, see *Ministry Mantras*, 223–224.

25. Hugh Whelchel, "What's Wrong with Tolerance?" May 2, 2016, *Institute for Faith, Work and Economics*: https://tifwe.org/whats-wrong-with-tolerance/.

A Final Thought: The Ampersand God

1. Timothy Keller, *Preaching* (New York: Viking, 2015), 62.

2. Keller, *Preaching*, 105.

3. From Krish Kandiah's *Paradoxology* (Downers Grove: IL: InterVarsity Press, 2017), table of contents.